Work-related Violence

Work-related violence has serious negative consequences for individuals and organisations alike, yet there has been little systematic research into the nature and extent of the problem and the full range of its effects. Much of this violence is under-reported and policies, structures and interventions must be established by organisations to investigate and manage both the occurrence and consequences of violence. *Work-related Violence* examines the causes and consequences of violence at work, and offers practical solutions for managers and organisational psychology professionals.

Part I sets the scene both in terms of reviewing the size and scope of the problem and setting out the legal and organisational need for its proactive management. It advocates an integrated and proactive approach, and discusses the intervention and policy implications. Part II illustrates the need for an integrated organisational response to work-related violence in two ways: by examining the nature and extent of violence in specific organisational settings, and by reviewing strategies designed to manage and control such incidents. Four main occupational groups are considered: teachers, health care workers, post office workers, and staff in bars and public houses.

Work-related Violence will be of interest to managers, occupational psychologists and anyone concerned with violence in the workplace.

Phil Leather is Head of the Violence Research Group and Deputy Director of the Centre for Organizational Health and Development at the University of Nottingham. **Carol Brady** is Lead Psychologist for the Mental Health Directorate at Rampton Hospital Authority. **Claire Lawrence** is Lecturer in Psychology and Security Management at the Scarman Centre for Public Order at the University of Leicester. **Diane Beale** is a Research Associate at the Centre for Organizational Health and Development at the University of Nottingham. **Tom Cox** is Professor of Organizational Psychology and Head of the Department of Psychology at the University of Nottingham.

Work-related Violence

Assessment and intervention

**Edited by Phil Leather, Carol Brady,
Claire Lawrence, Diane Beale
and Tom Cox**

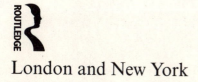

London and New York

First published 1999
by Routledge
11 New Fetter Lane, London EC4P 4EE

Simultaneously published in the USA and Canada
by Routledge
29 West 35th Street, New York, NY 10001

Typeset in Times by Routledge
Printed and bound in Great Britain by Redwood Books,
Trowbridge, Wiltshire

British Library Cataloguing in Publication Data
A catalogue record for this book is available from the British Library

Library of Congress Cataloging in Publication Data
Work-related violence: assessment and intervention/
edited by Phil Leather . . . [et al.].
Includes bibliographical references and index.
1. Violence in the workplace. I. Leather, Philip.
HF5549.5.E43W67   1999
658.4'73–dc21   98–25640

ISBN 0–415–19414–8 (hbk)
ISBN 0–415–19415–6 (pbk)

Contents

Illustrations

Contributors

Editors

Phil Leather BA MA PhD CPsychol AFBPsS is a Lecturer in the Department of Psychology at the University of Nottingham. He heads the Violence Research Group and is Deputy Director of the Centre for Organizational Health and Development. He has worked in the field of work-related violence since 1987.

Carol Brady BA PhD MSc AFBPsS CPsychol is a Chartered Clinical and Forensic Psychologist with many years' experience working with dangerous mentally disordered offenders, and with staff who have suffered trauma in the work setting. She is also an experienced trainer in the management of violence at work.

Claire Lawrence BA PhD is a Lecturer in Psychology and Security Management at the Scarman Centre for Public Order at the University of Leicester. She has researched violence since 1990 and has developed and delivered training aimed at the reduction of work-related violence.

Diane Beale MA MSc is a Research Associate at the Centre for Organizational Health and Development at the University of Nottingham. She has researched the field of work-related violence since 1990. She has established and maintained violent incident reporting systems and designed and delivered violence-related training.

Tom Cox BSc PhD CPsychol FBPsS FRSH FRSA is Professor of Organizational Psychology. He is also Director of the Centre for Organizational Health and Development and is an Expert Adviser on occupational health and stress to the European Commission and World Health Organization.

Authors

Rosie Dickson BA MSc CPsychol is a Chartered Occupational Psychologist and has conducted research into workplace violence. As Programmes

Executive with The Rehab Group (Ireland), she is currently involved in the development and quality assurance of vocational assessment and training programmes for people with disabilities.

Patricia Leighton LLB MPhil AcDipEd FCollP is Professor and Head of the School of Law at the Manchester Metropolitan University. She is an employment lawyer specialising in Health and Safety at Work, in particular, the law relating to stress, violence and harrassment at work.

Gerv Leyden BA DipEdPsych MSc CPsychol AFBPsS is a Local Education Authority Educational Psychologist and is Associate Tutor to the Postgraduate Professional Training Course in Educational Psychology at the University of Nottingham. His research interests include organisational stress, inner-city schools and violence to teachers.

Chris Smewing BA MSc PhD MIPD is a training consultant with Commercial Union Assurance. Previously he has worked as personnel manager, and also a university researcher. His research interests include the evaluation of organisational interventions, particularly in the areas of training, career development, organisational healthiness and employee assistance.

Noreen Tehrani BSc DipCounsellingPsych CPsychol AFPsS MIPM is an Organisational Counselling Psychologist who is an authority on trauma in the workplace, having designed and introduced a number of trauma care programmes within the Post Office. Her research and publications are in assessment, trauma, bullying and counselling.

Preface

Work-related violence has serious negative consequences for individuals and organisations alike, yet there has been little systematic research into the nature and extent of the problem, and the full range of its effects. Much of this violence is under-reported and policies, structures and interventions must be established by organisations to investigate and manage both the occurrence and consequences of violence.

This book directly addresses these issues and provides both a comprehensive review of the area and a guide to effective organisational action. It aims to utilise theory, evidence and practice to manage the problem of work-related violence. For purposes of clarity, it is divided into two related parts.

Part I sets the scene both in terms of reviewing the size and scope of the problem and setting out the legal and organisational need for its proactive management. It advocates an integrated and proactive approach, and discusses the intervention and policy implications.

In Chapter 1, Leather, Beale, Lawrence, Brady and Cox review evidence as to the nature and extent of work-related violence, together with its individual and organisational consequences. They advocate a problem-solving framework to identify the elements of a proactive management strategy which constitutes an integrated organisational approach. In Chapter 2, Leighton explores the ways in which the law has responded to work-related violence, invoking a range of legal sources including the contract of employment, the law of negligence and the statutory framework relating to health and safety at work. She examines the nature and scope of demands upon employers, suggesting effective organisational strategies to protect employees and ensure that employers comply with legal duties. In Chapter 3, Lawrence and Leather examine the social psychology of violence. They outline a social interactionist model of violence arguing that this approach offers most by way of informing intervention and management in the workplace. They stress the importance of examining the context in which aggressive interactions occur, and illustrate the application of theory to practice in the workplace. In Chapter 4, Brady outlines both common and more problematic reactions to assault and argues that the organisation has a vital role to play in supporting assaulted staff. She concludes by detailing appropriate strategies to help both victims and organisations to recover from violent incidents. In Chapter 5, Beale looks at systems for monitoring violence at work. She emphasises the importance of measuring the whole range of violent and aggressive incidents and provides guidance upon setting up effective monitoring systems. The need to preserve information about the process of violent incidents is highlighted, as are the limitations of reporting systems. In Chapter 6, Beale, Lawrence, Smewing and Cox examine organisational and environmental systems which can be used to reduce and manage work-related violence. Using their collective experience across a range of organisational settings, they propose a model which can be used to examine the range of factors which might influence individuals in their interactions within an organisation. They discuss the effects of potentially aggressive triggers, suggest strategies to manage and control work-related violence and present checklists of questions that organisations should consider.

Part II illustrates the need for an integrated organisational response to work-related violence in two ways: by examining the nature and extent of violence in specific organisational settings, and by reviewing strategies designed and intended to manage and control such incidents. Four main occupational groups are considered: Post Office workers, pub staff, teachers and health care workers.

In Chapter 7, Tehrani reviews the work of the UK Post Office in providing an organisational response to provide a safer working environment for its workers by reducing the incidence of trauma and the psychological damage caused to employees by work-related violence. She describes the trauma care programme itself, the issues faced in setting up such a programme and some evidence of its effectiveness. In Chapter 8, Lawrence, Beale, Leather and Dickson detail the full parameters of an integrated approach to violence in the public house setting, based on ten years' experience working with the licensed trade. They outline a range of strategies, aimed at reducing the effect and incidence of violence, employed by a national company, and hence provide a detailed illustration of an integrated organisational approach in practice. In Chapter 9, Leyden examines the problem of violence for the teaching profession. In recent years, schools have become the focus of much media and political attention regarding violence to teachers and pupils from a range of sources. Leyden argues that an effective solution requires a 'systems' analysis of the school and of pupil behaviour, not simply recourse to fortress-like security measures. In Chapter 10, Brady and Dickson review the risks faced by health care professionals and the characteristics of violence in health care settings. They describe possible interventions and emphasise the need for a strategic approach at all levels of the organisation in order to reduce significantly the risk to employees.

In Chapter 11, Leather, Lawrence, Beale, Cox and Brady summarise the principal themes which have been emphasised throughout the book and outline the way forward for the management of work-related violence.

Appendix 1 lists national and international guidance documents on violence at work, and indicates where to access some of these documents via the Internet. Appendix 2 gives an example of a violent incident report form used in the authors' work.

Part I

Work-related violence

Background knowledge and the integrated organisational approach

1 Violence and work

Introduction and overview

Phil Leather, Diane Beale, Claire Lawrence, Carol Brady and Tom Cox

Introduction

Throughout Europe and North America, violence in the workplace is attracting increasing academic attention and growing legal, managerial and governmental concern (Bulatao and VandenBos, 1996; Cox and Leather, 1994; Leather, Lawrence, Beale, Cox and Dickson, 1998; Painter, 1991). On both sides of the Atlantic, for example, government agencies have been active in producing guidelines for the prevention of violence to staff since the mid 1980s. In the UK, the Health and Safety Executive (HSE) and other government agencies have published guidelines covering staff in general (Poyner and Warne, 1986, 1988), in the health services (Health Services Advisory Committee, 1987, 1997), in social services (Department of Health and Social Security, 1988), in education (Education Services Advisory Committee, 1990), in banks and building societies, in the retail sector and in broadcasting (HSE, 1993, 1995, 1996). Similarly, in the US, the Occupational Safety and Health Administration (OSHA) has recently released guidelines for preventing workplace violence for night retail establishments, for health care and social service workers and for community workers (OSHA, 1996a, 1996b, 1996c).

Within both academic and applied contexts, it is now widely accepted that:

- Many more occupational groups are at risk from violence than those originally imagined (Jenkins, 1996; Poyner and Warne, 1986);
- Levels of reported violence grossly understate the size of the problem (Murphy, 1996; Toscano and Weber, 1995);
- Verbal abuse and the threat of violence can be extremely damaging and distressing in their consequences (Wynne and Clarkin, 1995);
- The threat or reality of violence, whatever its form, is a significant source of chronic and/or acute stress for many employees (Duffy and McGoldrick, 1990; Kleber and van der Velden, 1996);
- The consequences of this violence-related stress have a negative impact upon organisational functioning as well as upon individual health and well-being (Barling, 1996; Leather *et al.*, 1998).

The need to manage violence

The nature and extent of the problem

Assessing the true extent of work-related violence is made difficult by the fact that the available research studies and statistical indices often utilise different criteria for (1) what constitutes violence, (2) who is to be involved and (3) where an incident must take place for it to be considered 'work-related'. Some commentators (e.g. Kraus, Blander and McArthur, 1995) focus only upon actual or attempted physical assault, irrespective of the identity and status of the perpetrator, while others (e.g. Folger and Baron, 1996) define it as any form of behaviour that is intended to harm current or previous co-workers, or their organisation.

As a satisfactory definition of work-related violence must include all incidents related to the victim's work, irrespective of the nature of the violence or where it takes place, the definition informing this book is that recently agreed by the European Commission: 'Incidents where persons are abused, threatened or assaulted in circumstances related to their work, involving an explicit or implicit challenge to their safety, well-being or health' (Wynne, Clarkin, Cox and Griffiths, 1997). This definition allows for the full range of circumstances in which a worker might be attacked while in the workplace, while at work or on duty, or in any other circumstances relating to their job. It also gives due weight to psychological as well as physical violence and harm.

A number of types of work-related violence must be distinguished because different work situations lend themselves to different types of violence and the measures that can be taken to manage the problem vary with the type of violence. One widely adopted classification scheme is that proposed by the California Occupational Safety and Health Administration (1995). Here, three broad categories of workplace violence are identified: Type I, planned robberies, where the assailant has no legitimate relationship to the workplace and the main object of the attack is cash or valuable property; Type II, events involving assault by someone who is either the recipient or the object of a service provided by the affected workplace or the victim; and Type III, incidents involving assault by another employee, a supervisor, or an acquaintance of the worker.

Violence can also be defined in terms of who is the perpetrator and who is the victim. These can be workers themselves; clients or customers; those outside the employing organisation but who are related to the worker, i.e. family, friends or acquaintances; or total strangers who have no relationship to the worker or the workplace. This framework offers a rich matrix describing types of violence, some of which are outlined here for illustrative purposes.

Worker-on-worker violence, for example, has attracted much attention and has come to be synonymous with the term 'workplace violence' in the American media (Bulatao and VandenBos, 1996). However, workplace assaults and homicide perpetrated by a co-worker are comparatively uncommon, to the extent that trade unions argue that 'management is hardly credible if it focuses on co-worker incidents and ignores the much larger threat from those who enter the workplace from outside' (King and Alexander, 1996). Worker-on-worker violence encompasses everything from inter-personal animosity, through bullying and harassment (Knorz and Zapf, 1996), to the extreme retaliatory acts of workers who feel that they have been unfairly treated by management or colleagues, as has occurred so dramatically within the US postal service in recent years (Fox and Levin, 1994).

Attacks on workers by their clients generally fall into two main types: (1) attacks by the recipient of a service because that service is somehow perceived to be unsatisfactory, or the expected service has to be withheld, as is sometimes the case for benefit office staff, for example, and (2) protests against workers carrying out a control function, such as the police, security and prison officers. Some workers are open to both these problems, particularly those who fulfil both a caring and a control function, such as social workers, psychiatric nurses and teachers (see Chapter 9). Sometimes such attacks can be displaced onto the family or friends of workers, particularly if they live on the premises.

Trouble between clients or customers, such as assaults or fights, provide dangerous situations for staff to manage. Such situations might be experienced by anyone who has control of premises where clients or customers remain for any length of time, for example by teachers, sports stadium staff, pub or club staff or transport workers, or where there is competition for service, as in retail outlets and bars.

Attacks by strangers, or outsiders, on workers are usually allied to robbery, where the main target of the attack is cash or valuable goods. Less common are terrorist attacks which are politically motivated and targeted at organisations or personnel either for their high public profile and accessibility or for the work they carry out, such as abortion (e.g. LeBourdais, 1995), or experiments on animals. Occasionally, workers' families may be the target of attacks or threat, being used as bargaining tools in demands for money or other purposes.

Attacks by strangers on clients or customers, but also involving workers, include the intruder violence such as that which has recently occurred in British schools in Dunblane and Wolverhampton and the shooting attack in a Tasmanian cafe.

Assaults, or rough handling, by workers on clients, customers, patients, inmates, or members of the public, is obviously undesirable in itself and undoubtedly encourages retaliation against the perpetrators or those associated with them (see Chapter 3). Ill-treatment or abuse of vulnerable clients by a small minority of child-care workers, psychiatric nurses, psychotherapists, police and prison officers, and those running old people's homes has hit the headlines in the UK. Over-zealous control can occur where the dividing line between reasonable and unreasonable force is overstepped by such people as security personnel, police and prison officers, pub staff and teachers.

The value of such classification schemes is that they highlight the fact that work-related violence is not a single, unitary phenomenon, but rather is multi-dimensional. As is continually emphasised throughout this book, accuracy in identifying and monitoring incidents is the first step in their successful management (Chapter 5), since it is this accuracy which facilitates an understanding of how and why such incidents occur. This, in turn, informs both targeted intervention strategies (Chapters 6, 8 and 9) and helps efforts at recovery and rehabilitation (Chapters 4 and 7).

Whatever the criteria by which work-related violence is defined and classified, the picture remains alarming. In the US, for example, homicide causes around twenty workplace deaths each week (Jenkins, 1996), with the total number of victims in the workplace being around one million annually (US Department of Justice, 1994), of whom almost 160,000 sustain physical injury.

While fewer statistics are available about violence at work in Britain, those that do exist show a similarly disturbing picture. The 1992 British Crime Survey (Mayhew, Aye Maung and Mirrlees-Black, 1993), for example, noted that assaults at work had more than doubled from 1981 to reach around 360,000 in 1991. Regarding violence in general, for the year ending June 1996, the overall number of recorded offences of violence against the person showed an increase of 10% over the previous year (Povey, Taylor and Watson, 1996).

While homicide and severe physical assault represent the extreme forms which work-related violence might take – and those which attract the greatest amount of media attention – they are not the most typical. Bulatao and VandenBos (1996), for example, estimate on the basis of US government data that only 1 in 650 workplace crimes of violence (i.e. 0.2%) involved homicide. Greenberg and Barling (1995) report that, while only 1.5% of their sample of 136 men reported using physical violence, around 75% admitted to some form of psychological violence against co-workers, subordinates and supervisors.

Official figures undoubtedly understate the real size of the problem for there is a gross lack of reporting of violence at both the national and organisational level (Painter, 1987). Estimates in the US and the UK suggest that between 30% and 80% of physical assaults go unreported (Murphy, 1996), while the level of under-reporting of verbal abuse and threats of assault is thought to be even higher (Toscano and Weber, 1995). In short, while 'the overwhelming magnitude of this trend toward workplace violence cannot be overstated' (Barling, 1996), the problem, although a massive one, remains largely unrecognised by employers and government alike (Randall, 1997).

Who is at risk?

The problem of work-related violence is not confined to those occupations that traditionally were expected to encounter violence, such as the police, prison officers, psychiatric nurses and those handling cash and valuable goods (Jenkins, 1996; Poyner and Warne, 1986, 1988). The reality or threat of violence has, in fact, become a major concern for a variety of occupations.

Nigro and Waugh (1996) noted the higher than average risks to a range of public sector employees and challenged public employers to assume leadership in challenging the problem. Teachers, for example, are not only open to assault themselves, but are expected to deal effectively with violence between students in an increasingly violent environment (Everett and Price, 1995). There is a detailed discussion of violence in schools in Chapter 9.

A great deal of published research has concerned health care workers. In the US, 106 health care workers were the victims of workplace-related homicide between 1980 and 1990 (Goodman, Jenkins and Mercy, 1994). Much of the literature deals with staff in psychiatric hospitals, particularly those involved with in-patient care; for example Poster and Ryan (1994) found that 76% of nurses in psychiatric hospitals in the US had been physically assaulted at least once. However, a wide range of health care staff have been found to be at high risk of violent assault (see, for example, Whittington, Shuttleworth and Hill, 1996). Violence within health care work is considered in more detail in Chapter 10.

Social workers are another group whose vulnerability to violence has been increasingly researched. Grimwood and La Valle (1993), for example, found that 32% of survey respondents had been victims of physical violence, 68% had encountered threats of physical violence and 92% had been verbally abused. Rey (1996) stated that 'client violence perpetrated against social workers has increased during the past decade as violence in society and the media has increased, social service resources decreased, and clients have become increasingly powerless', but stressed that 'violence education efforts must reject the notion that risk "comes with the territory" in the social work profession'.

A range of other occupations, particularly those in service industries, are known to be subject to work-related violence. Table 1.1 shows that those workers who suffer the highest rates of workplace homicide in the US are concentrated in the retail and transport industries and law enforcement. 38% of occupational homicides occurred in retail establishments (Erickson, 1996; Jenkins, 1996). The depth of concern for retail staff within both the UK and the US has been shown by the publishing of guidelines for them in dealing with violence (HSE, 1995; OSHA, 1996a). The risks associated with working in the bars and other licensed premises (see Table 1.1) have been studied extensively by Leather, Lawrence, Beale, Cox and colleagues at the University of Nottingham and is considered in detail in Chapter 8.

Within the transport industry, violence has become a disturbing problem. Taxicab drivers run by far the highest risk from homicide of all workers in the US, as seen in Table 1.1. In the UK, the threat or reality of violence has been shown to be a significant source of stress for bus drivers (Duffy and McGoldrick, 1990; Leather, Goggin and Lawrence, 1997).

As Table 1.1 shows, law enforcement personnel also suffer high rates of workplace homicide. Research has included studies on the police (e.g. Brandl, 1996), trial court judges (Little and Fong, 1995) and bailiffs (Psychological Services, n.d.).

Whose responsibility?

In the past, violence in any way related to the workplace has been regarded as the province of security professionals, the police and the criminal justice system. More recently, however, it is also being seen as a hazard that should be assessed and managed by organisations in order to provide a safe workplace for their employees (Cox and Leather, 1994; Nigro and Waugh, 1996; Simonowitz, 1995) as required under legislation such as the Occupational Safety and Health Act (1970) in the US and European Community legislation, embodied in the UK in the Management of Health and Safety at Work Regulations (HSE, 1992) and the Reporting of Injuries, Diseases and Dangerous Occurrences Regulations (1995).

The management of violence at work is an issue for those concerned with the psychological health of workers for five important reasons: first, workers directly involved in, or witnessing, violent incidents at their place of work may suffer post-trauma reaction, whether or not there has been any physical injury (Flannery, 1996; Stockdale and Phillips, 1989); second, vulnerable workers may be adversely affected by the fear that they could be victims of

Table 1.1 Frequency and rate of workplace homicide in highest-risk occupations, i.e. more than three times the average rate, US 1990–1992.

Occupation	Workplace homicides 1990–1992 (excluding New York City and Connecticut for 1992)	
	Number	*Rate per 100,000 workers*
Taxicab driver/chauffeur	140	22.7
Sheriffs/bailiffs	36	10.7
Police and detectives	86	6.1
Gas station/garage	37	5.9
Security guards	115	5.5
Stock handlers/baggers	95	3.5
Supervisors/proprietors-sales	372	3.3
Sales counter clerk	18	3.1
Bartenders	20	2.3
Logging occupations	6	2.3

Source: Adapted from Jenkins (1996)

attack in the course of their work (Lawrence, Dickson, Leather and Beale, 1996; Rey, 1996); third, stress at work may contribute to employees becoming violent, as discussed by Jones and Boye (1992), Fox and Levin (1994) and Pastor (1995); fourth, employee stress may lead to a deterioration in service delivery, stimulating dissatisfaction and thus an increased likelihood of violence from clients (Stockdale and Phillips, 1989); fifth, the behaviour of staff handling a problem situation may calm that situation or may lead to it escalating into violence.

Managing violence: an integrated organisational approach

Following Cox and Cox (1993), this book takes the view that the problem of work-related violence, like all psychosocial hazards at work, can be most effectively managed within the framework of practice that has proven successful in managing the more tangible hazards found in the workplace, such as toxic chemicals or dangerous machinery. Fundamentally, this practice utilises a problem-solving approach to hazard control and risk management (Cox and Tait, 1991). In the UK, this approach is made explicit in the Regulations for the Control of Substances Hazardous to Health 1988 (COSHH) and the subsequent Amendment (1990), although it derives from the early impetus of the Health and Safety at Work Act 1974 and the requirement for assessments set out in the EC Framework Directive 89/391/EEC, implemented in the UK through the Management of Health and Safety at Work Regulations (HSE, 1992: Regulation 3).

As with the US Occupational Safety and Health Act of 1970, such legislation mandates that, in addition to hazard-specific standards, employers have a general duty to provide employees with a workplace free from recognised hazards likely to cause death, injury or harm. With respect to work-related violence, this means that employers can be cited for violating this general duty of care if a recognised hazard of violence is ignored and nothing done to prevent or diminish it.

These various regulations impose an obligation upon employers to undertake an assessment of the health risk associated with any particular hazard and, in parallel, to assess the effectiveness of existing systems for both minimising exposure to it and limiting any harm that might result from such exposure. Work-related violence should be managed in exactly the same proactive way, that is, through the six basic steps of the so-called 'control cycle' (Cox and Cox, 1993), a systematic method of problem-solving and organisational learning. These steps are:

1   Problem or hazard identification, analysis and assessment of risk
2   Design of intervention strategies
3   Planning and implementation of strategies
4   Implementation

5   Evaluation and monitoring
6   Feedback to earlier stages

(Dickson, Leather, Beale and Cox, 1994)

The steps of the control cycle can be conceptualised as a series of recursive stages in a cycle of activities which ensure that the process of developing safe work environments is continuous (Cox and Leather, 1994). Five particular requirements are central to the success of the control cycle as a management strategy; these are:

- acceptance by all members of the organisation of both the reality of the problem and their part in addressing it;
- rigorous and complete hazard identification and analysis;
- an integrated approach to the design and targeting of intervention strategies;
- evaluation and feedback;
- a written policy to give both substance and direction to the entire prevention programme.

Acceptance of the problem: management commitment and employee involvement

Crucial to the formulation and success of any violence-prevention programme is the acceptance that there is a problem to be managed and controlled. Such acceptance demands both management commitment and employee involvement. Management commitment means more than a simple statement or pronouncement of intent; rather, it includes such things as:

- a demonstrated and visible concern for employees' emotional and physical health and safety;
- the active involvement of senior and line managers in the programme;
- an appropriate allocation of authority to those responsible for establishing and maintaining the programme;
- an appropriate allocation of resources to establish and maintain all of the various elements of the programme;
- a comprehensive programme of aftercare for those experiencing or witnessing violent incidents;
- a commitment to evaluating the programme, both in part and in whole.

Employee involvement should be demonstrated by, amongst other things, the prompt and accurate reporting of incidents, compliance with safety and security measures, and a willingness to take part in training programmes designed to foster appropriate responses to escalating aggression.

Hazard identification and analysis

Hazard identification and analysis involves the assessment and analysis of hazardous situations, that is those situations where violence is more likely or where a pattern of violence can be detected, and measuring the harm that results. In the case of work-related violence, however, the hazard is not as easily identifiable as a toxic chemical or faulty piece of machinery. People become aggressive and violent for many reasons, for example in response to a grievance, as a means of 'saving face', or in an attempt to gain money or status (Tedeschi and Nesler, 1993; Berkowitz, 1993). Any individual encountered in the workplace or through the conduct of one's job can, therefore, be regarded as the potential hazard, with the hazardous situation being any difficult, problematic or volatile interaction with this person which makes violence more likely.

The system established to identify, measure and monitor work-related violence therefore constitutes the backbone of any violence-prevention programme. The goal of such a system is not only to identify the nature and scale of the problem, but, more importantly, to identify the patterns of assault which can be targeted in subsequent interventions. As Poyner and Warne (1988) put it: 'Without information about incidents of violence it is not possible to develop a methodological analysis, nor is it likely that effective strategies for prevention can be found.'

Incident analysis of this kind includes the on-going recording and analysis of incident report data, the use of designated surveys or violence audits, and the evaluation of workplace security measures. Incident analysis attempts to identify and analyse any apparent trends in injuries or incidents, with particular attention being paid to pinpointing those situations and occasions where employees are most at risk. Periodic surveys and audits seek to strengthen the monitoring data by identifying new or previously unnoticed risk factors and enabling further study and deeper analysis of known problem areas. The evaluation of workplace security measures looks more broadly at the context of incidents and hazardous situations and notes the work processes and procedures together with the physical factors of the worksite which put employees at greater risk of assault.

As well as focusing upon the nature of actual assaults, be they physical or verbal, any system for managing work-related violence must address both the full circumstances in which incidents occur and the fact that intimidation and the threat of violence can be equally serious in their consequences. This is difficult, not least because psychosocial hazards may not be so visible as physical hazards and are often subjective. A verbal assault, for instance, may be perceived as a violent incident by some but not by others. It will depend upon who is doing the threatening, as well as the context and history of the incident, for example whether the perpetrator has a 'track record' of violence and whether the threat is part of a wider problem of intimidation.

The subjective nature of much actual and perceived violence makes the adoption of a thorough analysis of the various forms that violence might take, and the harm that might result, all the more critical.

Intervention strategies

Three types of intervention or control are available to organisations in dealing with work-related violence (Cox and Leather, 1994).

- *Preventative strategies* are often geared towards the reduction of identified 'triggers' of violence within the workplace, particularly concerning work procedures or social interactions. Implementations can be focused upon employee training, work design and environmental change;
- *Timely reactive strategies* depend upon the procedures in place to enable management and staff to cope with a violent or potentially violent incident as it arises, in order to prevent its development or reduce its impact;
- *Rehabilitative strategies* aim to offer support to employees to help them cope with the aftermath of their direct or indirect involvement in a violent incident.

In this way, interventions are not focused simply upon the violent incident itself. Attention is also paid to what can be done before an incident occurs, by means of prevention and preparation, and after an incident has happened, by means of after-care, rehabilitation and both organisational and personal learning. In addition, each of these kinds of intervention must be addressed and adapted for each level of the organisational structure. Some preventative strategies, for instance, are geared towards the individual employee or work-group in the form of training in awareness and conflict resolution. Other preventative strategies are implemented at the organisational level, however, as they may involve a reorganisation of the way in which work is structured or carried out, the resourcing of security measures and equipment, and changes to the physical design of the worksite.

Examples of timely reaction include practising conflict resolution (at the individual level), adopting an emergency action plan (for the work-group or team) and implementing a code of practice (for the organisation as a whole), particularly regarding the availability and direction of line manager support. Rehabilitative, or post-incident, measures should provide comprehensive treatment for both victimised employees and those who may be traumatised by witnessing an incident of violence. Again requisite actions can be identified at all levels within the organisation, from the necessity of prompt first aid and empathy at the worksite to the provision of effective longer-term trauma-crisis counselling and critical incident stress debriefing. Such an holistic response can be termed an 'integrated organisational approach' to the management and control of violence and is illustrated in more detail in Table 1.2.

Table 1.2 An integrated organisational approach to the problem of work-related violence.

Organisational level	Type of intervention		
	Prevention	Timely reaction	Rehabilitation
Organisation	Work practices Environmental planning Safety in design Clear guidelines and policies Support	Relationship with support organisations	Security and Health and Safety reports Support Follow-up Counselling Compensation Learning
Team	Communication Vigilance Support Emergency action plan Training	Effective back-up Support	Support Dealing with other work issues Learning Vigilance
Individual	Awareness Empathy Social skills Relaxation	Calming Negotiating Closing Safe practices	Safety Comfort First aid Support

Evaluation and feedback

The provision of information on the effectiveness of intervention strategies is an essential part of the control cycle. Where information about the nature and character of violent incidents feeds forward to inform the design of intervention strategies, feedback on the effectiveness of these interventions aids in their continual refinement and improvement. In part, such feedback comes from the recording system established to monitor the incidents of violence which occur. There is no substitute, however, for rigorously designed evaluation studies which, as a minimum, should include both pre- and post-intervention measures and the use of a control or comparison group.

Written policy

As Cox and Cox (1993) point out, the whole range of possible actions for managing and controlling a hazard needs to be integrated into a coherent programme. A policy or code of practice on violence is a good starting point for this coherence, especially if it specifies the arrangements, resources and organisation available to support efforts at prevention, timely reaction and rehabilitation. Strategy, in effect, should be translated into policy. Policy, in turn, finds expression in practice, which consists of a variety of procedures. The policy therefore sets the basic standards against which the development of effective control strategies can be monitored and evaluated. 'Such standards and targets should represent what is tolerable, what is desirable and what is reasonably practicable' (Cox and Cox, 1993: 204).

At a minimum, the policy or code of practice should:

- communicate a clear statement of zero tolerance for work-related violence, whatever its form;
- encourage employees to report incidents swiftly and fully;
- inform employees of the structures and arrangements established to combat violence, including:

  - what training is on offer to help them deal with violent incidents;
  - what they can expect from their line manager and other support functions in the event of an incident;
  - how, and to whom, they are to report incidents;
  - what rehabilitation or aftercare facilities are available;

- state unequivocally that no reprisals will be taken against an employee who reports or experiences work-related violence; and
- assign resources and authority to those responsible for the various elements in the programme.

Organisations which are likely to be successful in managing work-related violence are those which measure and evaluate their performance and that of their control strategies against pre-determined plans and standards. The assessment which underpins this evaluation does not focus solely upon outcomes, for example in terms of the number of incidents reported, but also looks at the processes involved in the implementation of the plans set in compliance with the standards agreed.

Conclusion

This brief review of the problem of work-related violence has shown that:

- there has been little systematic research investigating the nature and extent of violence at work and the full range of its effects;
- levels of violence of all types are grossly under-reported;
- work-related violence is a problem of 'overwhelming magnitude' (Barling, 1996) with serious negative consequences for individuals and organisations alike; and
- policies, structures and interventions must be established to manage both the occurrence and consequences of violence.

It is imperative that the problem of work-related violence is tackled using an integrated organisational approach if it is to be effective. Such an approach addresses prevention, timely reaction and rehabilitation at all levels within the organisation (individual, work-group, overall policy and practice). The way is now open for policy makers, management, academics and employees to work towards the implementation of proactive strategies to provide safer work environments and a healthier workforce.

References

Barling, J. (1996) 'The prediction, experience and consequences of workplace violence', in G. R. VandenBos and E. Q. Bulatao (eds) *Violence on the Job*, Washington, DC: American Psychological Association.

Berkowitz, L. (1993) *Aggression: Its Causes, Consequences and Control*, New York: McGraw-Hill.

Brandl, S. G. (1996) 'In the line of duty – a descriptive analysis of police assaults and accidents', *Journal of Criminal Justice*, 24, 255–264.

Bulatao, E. Q. and VandenBos, G. R. (1996) 'Workplace violence: its scope and the issues', in G. R. VandenBos and E. Q. Bulatao (eds) *Violence on the Job*, Washington, DC: American Psychological Association.

California Occupational Safety and Health Administration (Cal/OSHA) (1995) *Cal/OSHA Guidelines for Workplace Security*, San Francisco, CA: State of California, Department of Industrial Relations, Division of Occupational Safety and Health.

Control of Substances Hazardous to Health Regulations (1988) London: HMSO.

Control of Substances Hazardous to Health (Amendment) Regulations, Statutory instrument No: 2026, London: HMSO.

Cox, S. J. and Tait, N. R. S. (1991) *Reliability, Safety and Risk Management*, London: Butterworth-Heinemann.

Cox, T. and Cox, S. (1993) *Psychosocial and Organizational Hazards at Work: Control and Monitoring*, European Occupational Health Series No. 5. Copenhagen: WHO Regional Office for Europe.

Cox. T. and Leather, P. J. (1994) 'The prevention of violence at work', in C. L. Cooper and I. T. Robertson (eds) *International Review of Industrial and Organizational Psychology*, Vol. 9, pp. 213–245. Chichester: Wiley and Sons.

Department of Health and Social Security (1988) *Violence to Staff. Report of the DHSS Advisory Committee on Violence to Staff*, London: HMSO.

Dickson, R., Leather, P., Beale, D. and Cox, T. (1994) 'Intervention strategies to manage workplace violence', *Occupational Health Review*, 50, 15–18.

Duffy, C. A. and McGoldrick, A. E. (1990) 'Stress and the bus driver in the UK transport industry', *Work and Stress*, 4, 17–27.

Education Services Advisory Committee (1990) *Violence to Staff in the Education Sector*, Health and Safety Commission, Sudbury, Suffolk: HSE Books.

Erickson, R. J. (1996) 'Retail employees as a group at risk for violence', *Occupational Medicine–State of the Art Reviews*, 11, 269–276.

Everett, S. A. and Price, J. H. (1995) 'Students' perceptions of violence in the public-schools – the Metlife survey', *Journal of Adolescent Health*, 17, 345–352.

Flannery, R. B. (1996) 'Violence in the workplace, 1970–1995: a review of the literature', *Aggression and Violent Behaviour*, 1, 57–68.

Folger, R. and Baron, R. A. (1996) 'Violence and hostility at work: a model of reactions to perceived injustice', in G. R. VandenBos and E. Q. Bulatao (eds) *Violence on the Job*, Washington, DC: American Psychological Association.

Fox, J. A. and Levin, J. (1994) 'Firing back: the growing threat of workplace homicide', *Annals of the American Academy of Political and Social Science*, 536, 16–30.

Goerth, C.R. (1988) 'Violence in the workplace emerges as growing health and safety problem', *Occupational Health and Safety*, 57 (5), 53.

Goodman, R. A., Jenkins, E. L. and Mercy, J. A. (1994) 'Workplace-related homicide among health-care workers in the United-States, 1980 through 1990', *JAMA – Journal of the American Medical Association*, 272, 1,686–1,688.

Greenberg, L. and Barling, J. (1995) 'Predicting employee aggression: roles of person behaviours and workplace factors', Manuscript in preparation cited by Barling (1996) 'The prediction, experience and consequences of workplace violence', in G. R. VandenBos and E. Q. Bulatao (eds) *Violence on the Job*, Washington, DC: American Psychological Association.

Grimwood, C. and La Valle, I. (1993) 'Beware of the client', *Community Care*, 12.8.93, 15.

Health and Safety Executive (1992) *The Management of Health and Safety Regulations*, Sudbury, Suffolk: HSE Books.

—— (1993) *Prevention of Violence to Staff in Banks and Building Societies*, Sudbury, Suffolk: HSE Books.

—— (1995) *Preventing Violence to Retail Staff*, Sudbury, Suffolk: HSE Books.

—— (1996) *Violence to Workers in Broadcasting*, HSE Information Sheet, Entertainment Sheet No. 2.

Health Services Advisory Committee (1987) *Violence to Staff in the Health Services*, Health and Safety Commission, Sudbury, Suffolk: HSE Books.

Health Services Advisory Committee (1997) *Violence and Aggression to Staff in Health Services*, Health and Safety Commission, Sudbury, Suffolk: HSE Books.

Jenkins, E. L. (1996) 'Workplace homicide – industries and occupations at high-risk', *Occupational Medicine – State of the Art Reviews*, 11, 219–225.

Jones, J. W. and Boye, M. W. (1992) 'Job stress and employee counterproductivity', in J. C. Quick, L. R. Murphy and J. J. Hurrell (eds) *Stress and Well-Being at Work*, Washington DC: American Psychological Association.

King, J. L. and Alexander, D. G. (1996) 'Unions respond to violence on the job', in G. R. VandenBos and E. Q. Bulatao (eds) *Violence on the Job*, Washington, DC: American Psychological Association.

Kleber, R. J. and van der Velden, P. G. (1996) 'Acute stress at work', in M. J. Schabraq, J. A. M. Winnubst and C. L. Cooper (eds) *Handbook of Work and Health Psychology*, Chichester: Wiley.

Knorz, C. and Zapf, C. (1996) 'Mobbing – a severe form of social stressor at work', *Zeitschrift für Arbeits- und Organisationspsychologie*, 40, 12–21.

Kraus, J. F., Blander, B. and McArthur, D. L. (1995) 'Incidence, risk-factors and prevention strategies for work-related assault injuries – a review of what is known, what needs to be known, and countermeasures for intervention', *Annual Review of Public Health*, 16, 355–379.

Lawrence, C., Dickson, R., Leather, P. J. and Beale, D. (1996) 'The mediation of support from the first line manager in the relationship between fear of violence and well-being and job outcome measures: a case study', *Proceedings of the British Psychological Society Occupational Psychology Conference*, January, 285–289.

Leather, P., Goggin, K. and Lawrence, C. (1997) 'On the buses: the effects of violence on public transport staff', in The British Psychological Society, *Occupational Psychology Conference Book of Proceedings*, Leicester, United Kingdom: The British Psychological Society.

Leather, P., Lawrence, C., Beale, D., Cox, T. and Dickson, R. (1998). 'Exposure to occupational violence and the buffering effects of intra-organizational support', *Work and Stress* 12(2).

LeBourdais, E. (1995) 'Potential for violence causing fear among Canadian doctors who perform abortions', *Canadian Medical Association Journal*, 152, 927–932.

Little, R. E. and Fong, R. S. (1995) 'Occupational-related victimization of trial court judges', *Sociological Spectrum*, 15, 463–471.

Mayhew, P., Aye Maung, N. and Mirrlees-Black, C. (1993) *The 1992 British Crime Survey*. Home Office Research Study 132, London: Home Office Research and Statistics Department.

Murphy, S. (1996) 'Managing the risk', *Health and Safety at Work*, July, 18–20.

Nigro, L. G. and Waugh, W. I. (1996) 'Violence in the American workplace – challenges to the public employer', *Public Administration Review*, 56, 326–333.

Occupational Safety and Health Administration (1996a) *Guidelines for Preventing Workplace Violence for Health Care and Social Service Workers*, OSHA 3148–1996. Washington, DC: US Department of Labor, Occupational Safety and Health Administration.

—— (1996b) *Guidelines for Workplace Violence Prevention Programs for Night Retail Establishments*, Draft. Washington, DC: US Department of Labor, Occupational Safety and Health Administration.

—— (1996c) *Protecting Community Workers against Violence*, Fact sheet No. OSHA 96–53. Washington, DC: US Department of Labor, Occupational Safety and Health Administration.

Painter, K. (1987) 'It's part of the job', *Employee Relations*, 9 (5), 30–40.

—— (1991) 'Violence and vulnerability in the workplace: psychosocial and legal implications', in M. J. Davidson and J. Earnshaw (eds) *Vulnerable Workers: Psychosocial and Legal Issues*, Chichester: Wiley.

Pastor, L. H. (1995) 'Initial assessment and intervention strategies to reduce workplace violence', *American Family Physician*, 52, 1,169–1,174.

Poster, E. C. and Ryan, J. (1994) 'A multiregional study of nurses' beliefs and attitudes about work safety and patient assault', *Hospital and Community Psychiatry*, 45, 1,104–1,108.

Povey, D., Taylor, P. and Watson, L. (1996) 'Notifiable offences: England and Wales, July 1995 to June 1996', *Home Office Statistical Bulletin*, 18/96.

Poyner, B. and Warne, C. (1986) *Violence to Staff. A Basis for Assessment and Prevention*. Health and Safety Executive. London: HMSO.

—— (1988) *Preventing Violence to Staff*. Health and Safety Executive. London: HMSO.

Psychological Services (n.d.) *Dealing with Aggressive People: Course Evaluation for the Lord Chancellor's Department*. Farningham, Kent: Psychological Services.

Randall, P. (1997) *Adult Bullying: Perpetrators and Victims*, London: Routledge.

Rey, L. D. (1996) 'What social-workers need to know about client violence', *Families in Society – the Journal of Contemporary Human Services*, 77, 33–39.

Simonowitz, J. A. (1995) 'Violence in health care: a strategic approach', *Nurse Practitioner Forum*, 6 (2), 120–129.

Stockdale, J. and Phillips, C. (1989) 'Physical attack and threatening behaviour – new survey findings', *Occupational Health*, 41, 212–216.

Tedeschi, J. T. and Nesler, M. S. (1993) 'Grievances: development and reactions', in R. B. Felson and J. T. Tedeschi (eds) *Aggression and Violence: Social Interactionists Perspectives*, pp. 13–47, Washington DC: American Psychological Association.

Toscano, G. and Weber, W. (1995) *Violence in the Workplace: Compensation and Working Conditions*, Washington DC: US Department of Labor, Bureau of Labor Statistics.

US Department of Justice (1994) *Violence and Theft in the Workplace.* (NJC-148199), Annapolis Junction, MD: Bureau of Justice Statistics.

Whittington, R., Shuttleworth, S. and Hill, L. (1996) 'Violence to staff in a general hospital setting', *Journal of Advanced Nursing*, 24, 326–333.

Wynne, R. and Clarkin, N. (1995) 'Workplace violence in Europe – it is time to act', *Work and Stress*, 9, 377–379.

Wynne, R., Clarkin, N., Cox, T. and Griffiths, A. (1997) *Guidance on the Prevention of Violence at Work.* Luxembourg: European Commission, DG-V.

2 Violence at work

The legal framework

Patricia Leighton

Introduction and objectives

This chapter has four major aims:

1 To set out the legal framework and legal rules which have relevance to violence at work.
2 To identify clearly the nature and practical impact of the law's demands on employers and managers.
3 To illustrate the application of this legal framework to the workplace through case law and examples.
4 To reflect on the role of law more generally in responding to violence at work.

The perspective of this chapter is predominantly a UK one, although many areas of law have resonance in other legal jurisdictions. There are, however, some significant and basic differences in legal approach as between the common law jurisdictions, typified by the UK, US, Canada and Australia, and the civil law one which dominates continental Europe.

Different legal traditions have an important and growing impact on the way in which violence at work is responded to and analysed. There are also differences, say, in the role of legislation, courts, employment contracts and case law. Hence, although an increasing number of jurisdictions are recognising the problem of violence at work, the different legal traditions and structures will materially affect the way law itself responds. The common law tradition (insofar as it treats violence as a major legal issue at all) stresses organisational responsibilities, but also individual rights.

However, at the outset, it should be noted that, in most legal systems, violence at work is rarely, or never, defined explicitly by law nor is it the subject of discrete legal regulation. In essence, such violence has to have applied to it basic legal rules, probably developed to deal with entirely different work-related or non-work-related problems or issues. It is, therefore, a question of adapting or evolving legal rules to the phenomenon of violence.

There are also preliminary questions which need to be posed. These are whether law should have a role in, especially, the less dramatic forms of violence such as bullying and harassment; and, if so, whether law can have a significant impact on curbing it. The UK Conservative government from 1979 onwards, and especially in the 1990s, was committed to 'deregulation' at the workplace, using the argument that law adds unnecessary burdens on business (UK Government, 1992). This position has altered following the election of a Labour government in May 1997, bringing with it a rejection of simplistic arguments that law inevitably makes business less competitive, and also the acceptance that law is needed to provide basic worker protections.

Despite these conflicting views, UK law has, indeed, developed remedies for victims, can punish wrongdoers and can thereby send out clear signals; but it does much more. Law establishes the standards expected of employers and employees in the 1990s, both in general terms and in the detailed response it expects of an employer in any given situation. It will specify, for example, whether 'bleepers', protective clothing, barriers, etc. should have been provided to protect staff. In making these demands it will, of course, draw on research findings and professional advice, as well as established and appropriate case law. Most importantly, law is now requiring employing organisations to have an effective strategy to deal with all forms of violence.

For the purposes of this chapter, 'violence' will be considered to include not only physical violence, but also threats of violence, bullying, harassment and intimidatory behaviour more generally.

The incidence of violence appears to be growing, affecting wide sections of the workforce, although violence in some occupations has been much highlighted and researched (Education Services Advisory Committee, 1990). Hostages may be taken to force employees to hand over keys, disclose sensitive information or, perhaps, give access to a computer system. Similarly, employees may be physically attacked or threatened. However, it is not always for cash. Transport and hospital staff, receptionists, social workers and the many and varied staff who deal with the public and who often have to reject claims for cash or relay bad news are in the forefront. They may be verbally or physically abused. Threats or abuse may come over the telephone or in person; it may be a regular occurrence or rare. The source of the violence or threat may be a client, a customer, a complete outsider or a colleague in the office. The problem may even arise at a social occasion such as an office party.

It is established that violence, or the threat of it, is a prime work stressor for many employees who are, perhaps, often told, 'It's part of the job!' and that they will not therefore be able to obtain compensation when they suffer an injury or stress. Such assumptions are now increasingly challenged by law.

A case study

A recent example concerned an employee described as a 'chauffeur' but who, in reality, provided a protective role for a wealthy businessman and his family in London. One afternoon, when he was at his employer's house, along with his employer's wife and children, the employee was attacked by thugs as he went to open the front door. He was pushed aside, hit on the head with the barrel of a gun and hospitalised. There was no 'panic button' in the house; he had had no training in security, no equipment, etc. and he alleged that he tackled the thugs to protect his employer's family. A few days after the incident his employer sacked him for 'incapability' and he was unable to bring an unfair dismissal claim under UK legislation as he had not been continuously employed for two years.

He was off work for two years; his marriage ran into difficulties because of a consequent depressive illness. His claim from the Criminal Injuries Compensation Board took several years and his claim for compensation for negligence against his ex-employer was highly problematic. The basis of the legal action was that the employer had failed to take reasonable care for his safety.

The employee's difficulty was that the employer argued, first, that he could not have been reasonably expected to foresee the risk of violence; second, even if he had, there was little he could have done to take care of his employee and, third, that the 'have a go' response of the chauffeur had actually caused the injuries. Yet, many would argue that the risk of a violent attack on an employee of someone with conspicuous wealth, living in an area with high crime levels, was exactly the sort of thing that could have been anticipated and should have been responded to. It was, perhaps, far more likely than his being injured falling down stairs, suffering a back injury or even being injured in a road crash! Despite this, his legal claim is still continuing, some five years on from the incident.

The practical and legal contexts

In applying legal rules to given workplace situations, it is important to establish two contexts. The first is the way in which violence might manifest itself in terms of the perpetrators of violence. The second is the legal framework itself.

The practical context

An employee can be injured:

- by another *employee*: this could be through fighting, bullying, threats or harassment; the injury could be inflicted intentionally or carelessly, though more likely the former;
- by a *non-employee* who is a part of the working environment: this could include a patient, client, customer, traveller, pupil at school, taxpayer, benefit seeker, etc.;
- by a *complete outsider*: this could include a burglar or other type of apparent criminal using violent and threatening behaviour, as in the case study above.

An employee may also commit an act of violence to a third party as well as to a fellow employee.

The legal context

Relevant legal rules are taken from a variety of sources, and are set out below. However, it is important to note that there is no discrete body of legal rules labelled 'violence at work'. Rather, as considered above, the approach of law is to respond to an identified problem by harnessing and applying established legal rules. The law moves in an incremental and pragmatic way and seeks the most appropriate response. The legal rules are therefore taken from a variety of sources, each set of legal rules having a particular approach, and offering, generally, a different type of remedy for victims. However, in any given workplace situation, each of the different sets of legal rules may well have a role to play. Employers must, therefore, be prepared for legal claims to be presented in a variety of ways. Some claimants will want compensation for physical injuries, or for stress; others will want improvements in security arrangements at the workplace to prevent an incident. Yet others, perhaps dismissed following an incident or for raising complaints, will want their job back, or compensation for losing it.

It should also be borne in mind that violence, threats and harassment are also, potentially, the concern of the police and the criminal justice system. The crimes involved might range from attempted murder, manslaughter, grievous bodily harm, through to common assault and threatening behaviour or similar. Conduct which might be categorised as sexual harassment in a workplace context could also contravene the Sexual Offences Act, 1869 and subsequent legislation in the UK.

Relevant legal rules governing violence at work are primarily taken from the following sources:

- The law of *contract* relating to the employment relationship and the statutory protections applicable to it, including protection from unfair dismissal (Employment Rights Act, 1996, sections 94–132; see also Leighton, 1997).
- The law relating to sexual and racial *discrimination*, insofar as it provides protection from some forms of harassment and threats (Race Relations Act, 1976; Sex Discrimination Act, 1975).
- *European* employment law rules, especially the 1991 European Recommendation on Dignity at Work, dealing primarily with harassment but with a wider potential; the Recommendation's Preface clearly anticipates that protection should be provided for other groups typically subjected to abuse and bullying at work such as new recruits, young workers, gay workers, those with disabilities and ethnic minority groups.
- The common law of *negligence* which can provide compensation for those who suffer physical or psychological injury.

- The *criminal law* relating to violence and threats.
- The *statutory legal framework* relating to health and safety at work, especially the Management of Health and Safety at Work Regulations, (Health and Safety Executive, 1992) which implements European directives in the UK, and comparable provisions in other EU member states. Most developed countries have a statutory health and safety framework which may cover violence.

The role of law: the traditional approach

Law has not always seen violence as a serious issue. Sometimes it has condoned violence. Case law dating from the nineteenth century, but with recent instances, has allowed employees to attack either other employees or third parties if their employer's property was at risk. In such cases the employer was held vicariously liable to compensate victims for the attack, providing the employee in question was genuinely protecting property, as opposed to pursuing a personal vendetta against the victim (see, for example, Pollard Bros *v*. Parr and Sons, 1927; Warren *v*. Henleys Ltd, 1948). The force also has to be 'reasonable', i.e. proportionate to the danger or threat of danger or injury involved. Anxieties about threats to individuals or to the employer's property is never allowed by law to be the pretext for a vicious attack or a personal vendetta.

On the other hand, the law relating to employment contracts has long allowed employers to curb violence through disciplinary codes, especially with respect to fighting between staff. Such fighting is typically grounds for summary dismissal, ranking alongside theft and gross disobedience as serious workplace issues. Where employees have challenged the dismissal, that dismissal has usually been upheld, unless the employer failed to pursue disciplinary procedures correctly or fairly.

The employer is entitled by law to adopt a strong stance on violence. It is seen by judges and industrial tribunals as a serious matter. Many disciplinary codes specify 'fighting' as grounds for instant dismissal or suspension. Indeed, even where a code does not specifically mention fighting, an employer may be entitled to dismiss. Such decisions were made in the cases of Parsons *v*. McLoughlin (1978) and Barley *v*. BP Oil (Kent Refinery) Ltd (1980).

In Parsons *v*. McLoughlin (1978) a shop steward was dismissed for fighting. Fighting was not, as such, specified as gross misconduct in the company's disciplinary code. None the less the dismissal was held to be fair. The judges commented:

> It ought not to be necessary for anybody, let alone a shop steward, to have in black and white, in the form of a rule, that a fight is going to be something that is to be regarded as grave by management.

There is no doubt that an attack on a customer or client would be viewed similarly by judges. However, it is important to remember that, however serious the incident, disciplinary procedures should be followed. Even if procedures have not been set down, the law would normally expect an employer, after a violent incident, to comply with the following rules (see Advisory, Conciliation and Arbitration Service, 1987):

- To investigate fully the circumstances by talking to the parties and to witnesses, and exploring whether there was provocation or any other factor which might explain the violent response.
- To interview the parties, explaining the seriousness of the situation and the possible consequences for the employee.
- To allow the employee to state his or her case and to be represented by another, such as a trades union official, a colleague or a lawyer.
- To avoid bias or prior knowledge of the alleged facts by those investigating and interviewing. (The importance of this rule was illustrated in Slater *v*. Leicestershire Health Authority, 1989), in which bias was found where a manager who had carried out the investigation into alleged misconduct also conducted the disciplinary hearing.)

After the investigation, even where it is reasonable to consider that an employee has been violent towards a colleague or third party, consideration should be given to the previous record of the employee, the likelihood that it was a 'one off' incident and the possibility of re-deployment, etc. to remove the opportunity for recurrence.

Finally, it is essential that the employer adopts a consistent response to violent incidents. In The Post Office *v*. Fennell (1981) an employee was instantly dismissed following an assault on a fellow employee in the canteen. The dismissal was held to be unfair because there had been a number of previous and similar violent incidents where the alleged perpetrators had *not* been dismissed.

Disciplinary hearings are not subject to the rules of a law court; cases do not have to be proved 'beyond reasonable doubt'. It is simply necessary that the employer had reasonable grounds for belief, as well as that the dismissal or suspension was a reasonable response to the facts. Even a technically 'innocent' employee can be fairly dismissed.

The law in the UK appears, therefore, to provide clear rules for employers regarding their response to employee violence either towards other staff or towards third parties. It suggests that an appropriate response be as follows:

1   That violence should ideally be specified as a disciplinary matter, be clearly set out in disciplinary rules and provide grounds for instant dismissal, where the incident is a serious one.
2   That violence be defined carefully so as to include not only fighting and

assaults but also threatening behaviour, bullying and harassment of all sorts.

3   That all incidents of violence be responded to and carefully investigated and, if appropriate, the disciplinary procedures be invoked. These might include giving a warning or suspension as well as dismissal.

4   That disciplinary hearings be handled carefully so as to allow for explanations and any mitigating factors personal to the alleged perpetrator, or the work environment, to be considered.

5   That disciplinary decisions be fairly arrived at and carefully communicated.

6   That any wider implications of the violent incident be considered. This might include ineffective management, the presence of disruptive staff, undue work pressure, availability of alcohol etc.

The last point is vital to ensure that a violent incident is not merely seen as particular to the individuals concerned but might indicate wider problems. These, too, will probably need to be addressed to avoid other incidents.

The conclusion must be drawn that employment law has been supportive of employers wishing to establish a non-violent culture by applying rigorous disciplinary standards and procedures. Where, therefore, the perpetrator is a fellow employee there is no reason to see the issue as in any way problematic, but law does emphasise appropriate handling of violence, or allegations of violence, as vital.

What are the legal duties to prevent violence?

In principle, the legal duties for employers to prevent violence are clear cut. The contract of employment contains two important implied obligations, which apply regardless of the type of contract, the work being done or the function of the organisation. The first of these is the obligation to provide a workplace with minimal exposure to risks. These have clearly been taken to include the risk, or reality, of violence. The other obligation on employers, and one of considerably increased importance, is that often described as one of 'mutual trust and confidence'; other commentators call it one of 'trust and support' (Leighton and O'Donnell, 1995).

There have been several instances where employers have been found to be in breach by failing to provide an adequate response to fears of violence by employees. The leading, and now well-established, case on the matter is that of Keys v. Shoe Fayre Ltd (1978). Here, a relatively young and inexperienced female employee expressed concerns regarding 'mugging' when she took cash to the bank. There had, indeed, been some reported incidents of mugging in the neighbourhood. When she refused to go the bank she was dismissed. It was held that the employer had broken this implied obligation of trust and support. He had failed to take her concerns about violence seriously, failed to explore alternative ways of getting cash to the bank and had been generally unsupportive.

Breaking the implied obligation to provide support for employees concerned about violence, bullying or harassment is a breach of contract. It will usually entitle the employee to allege that they have been constructively dismissed, that is, the lack of support from their employer makes it impossible for them to continue to work for the organisation such that, even though they resign, they are treated as having been dismissed. They can then claim for unfair dismissal and it will be difficult for the employer to defend the case other than by disputing the facts.

It is important to note that a more attractive option for employees may be to make a claim for breach of contract in the County Court. This is because there is not the upper 'cap' of around £11,000 for compensation which normally applies in industrial tribunals. However, a breach of contract claim can also be made in an industrial tribunal, 'piggy backing' on an unfair dismissal claim. Where the injuries are relatively slight this is a sensible approach by victims.

The law is therefore clear. The employer who either fails to respond to the reality of violence, or to be supportive to those who fear it, is, in principle, breaking the employment contract. The practical implications are that the law requires employers to take seriously risks relating to violence and to develop a coherent and appropriate response. This would include:

- Establishing a culture whereby concerns about threats and violence can be raised by employees openly and without prejudice, in confidence if necessary.
- Providing an effective mechanism to investigate problems and explore possible options to remove or alleviate problems.
- Applying disciplinary procedures carefully and rigorously.
- Reviewing regularly the overall incidence and nature of violent incidents and issues.

It is possible to compare this approach to violence with that of legislation and case law in the US. The UK approach stresses organisational and managerial responsibilities through the employment contract to prevent violence. In the US there is no similar broadly based obligation, although, in some states, courts will infer obligations from company handbooks and the like and, in California, the Labour Code requires employers to implement an injury and illness prevention programme. This itself can then provide the basis of implied obligations to provide for safety in individual employment contracts (Mathiason and Schuyler, 1996).

What is the law's response to harassment, bullying, etc?

The UK legal rules applicable to non-physically violent situations are currently evolving, with the law beginning to focus as much on threats, bullying and harassment as on attacks in the more traditional sense. Law generally finds it easier to respond to situations where the evidence is clear and where the perpetrator is the person before the law court. Situations where harassment, bullying and threats take place are more problematic, but the law aims to make the employing organisation responsible, alternatively or jointly, with the individual perpetrator. The argument is that employers should have prevented a problem by managing their staff more effectively. The law's approach is typified by recent case law on harassment, where the harmful acts can range from use of offensive or threatening language through to assaults causing physical injury.

Since the early 1980s the failure of an employer to prevent harassment has entitled some victims to claim that they have been sexually or racially discriminated against. The essence of the law is that harassment took place because of the victim's sex or race. In other words, their vulnerability to such behaviour puts an obligation on the employer to prevent it and the failure to do so constitutes discrimination against the victim. For a claim to succeed, the claimant has, technically, to show that, had they been of the other sex or another race, they would have been treated better. Case law provides clear examples ranging from touching and stroking though to violent sexual assaults. The fact that the perpetrator(s) considered it 'playful', 'harmless fun', 'part of an initiation process' etc., has been held to be irrelevant. Similarly, the fact that the incident occurred during a social event and/or off work premises has not prevented the employer being held responsible for the conduct of relevant staff.

A useful case to illustrate some of the problems faced by both individual employees and their managers, and one that provides clear guidelines on how not to deal with these issues, is the case of Van den Berghen *v*. Nabarro Nathanson (1994).

The facts arose from a Christmas lunch, at a restaurant, for the staff of a section of a firm of solicitors. Six female secretaries attended. Unknown to the claimant the other five secretaries presented chocolate penises to the male solicitors. At the end of the lunch the claimant alleged that one of the trainee solicitors in his late 40s put his arm round her, squeezed her breasts and repeated this even when she moved away from him.

She complained to a senior partner the following day; he said the matter could go no further as there had been no witnesses. The trainee solicitor was advised not to put his arms round people. The claimant was then 'sent to Coventry' by colleagues. Three months later she was made redundant. Her claim for sex discrimination was successful; her employers were ordered to pay £4,500 and the trainee solicitor £200. Without knowledge of all the workplace facts it can only be speculated upon that the case represents a typical clash of expectations and standards. A Christmas party is traditionally a time for being relaxed and was clearly thought by the majority of those attending to be an appropriate setting for jokes of a sexual nature. One employee did not share these views. She was ostracised. She 'ought' to have followed the stream. However, the industrial tribunal reaction was severe;

£4,500 is high for current compensation levels at industrial tribunals. The claimant had a right to her stance and was entitled to protection. It was not relevant that it was a party – 'it was still an office occasion'.

A glance through some recent sexual harassment cases before industrial tribunals reveals some interesting pointers to how sexual harassment is currently viewed by tribunals. Comments or conduct made in a jokey way, such as strip-o-grams, can be unlawful harassment. Even one-off remarks (e.g. 'Hiya, big tits' – a remark by a young manager at a departmental meeting to a 43-year-old married woman supervisor) can be discriminatory. Sexual comments and constant pressure of a homosexual nature by an older man to a young trainee was also seen as discriminatory, but here the law required questions to be asked as to whether, had the trainee been female, the outcome would have been different! This curious approach merely highlights the fact that treating harassment as a dimension of anti-discrimination legislation is not only highly inappropriate and complicated but prevents the problem being located in a correct legal framework. Health and safety legislation is clearly the better framework.

However, anti-discrimination law is evolving and EU law has adopted a broader and more relevant approach. This is the European Recommendation on Dignity at Work (1991) which, as well as defining types of conduct indicative of failure to provide employees with dignity, and focusing on groups especially at risk (women, young workers, people with disabilities, gay people, etc.), establishes a model Code to be developed by employing organisations. The model Code requires employers to identify which employees are at risk, in what way and from whom. It requires effective management procedures to educate, to consult, to establish policies and otherwise to respond to violence, threats and harassment. It sees a key role for trade unions and/or employee representatives to develop, support and communicate a policy.

The importance of the Recommendation is that it not only establishes standards for workplaces but, by developing a strategy which sees freedom from threats and violence as a 'right', puts the responsibility to provide this firmly on management. The Recommendation is also important in that it explicitly challenges some widely held views, for example, that violence or threats are acceptable as part of the job, that harassment is merely 'high spirits', that it is the responsibility of employees themselves to diffuse or otherwise cope with problems, or that it is legitimate in some way for managers or supervisors to harass or undermine new or different types of staff in order to preserve their pre-eminence. If violence, bullying or harassment are 'unacceptable' to the victim (even if others might tolerate the same conduct or find it amusing) a claim can be made to appropriate courts or tribunals across the EU, using the Code in the Recommendation as the 'benchmark' of employer conduct.

The law of negligence

This is potentially an effective legal response to violence, regardless of whether the violence is caused by a fellow employee, the employer or an outsider. It ought not to matter whether the violence takes place on or off the premises so long as the violence is in some way associated with work. Most legal systems have rules which broadly equate with those in the UK, although it is likely that UK rules are more developed than most.

The victim of a serious act of violence at work who is, as a consequence, disabled and has reduced or no opportunities to work will probably seek substantial compensation from their employer if the employer has failed to adequately protect them. They could, of course, sue the perpetrator, but this is not usually pursued as employees who have arguably committed the harm rarely have adequate personal insurance cover. In assessing compensation, the law has a formula based on loss of future earnings, pain and suffering, and reduced opportunities to enjoy life. It is possible to estimate the size of a claim, although it clearly depends on age and earnings at the time of the incident. Sums in excess of £200,000 are becoming less uncommon and mirror the sorts of sums awarded following an accident at work or a work-related stress illness (e.g. Walker *v.* Northumberland County Council, 1994).

The law of negligence in the UK poses the following questions. First, whether the employer should have reasonably foreseen that there was a risk of violence occurring. The answer will depend on a range of factors, such as any evidence of previous incidents, the nature of the work itself (i.e. whether it is dealing with potentially violent people) and, most crucially since 1993, whether workplace risk assessments under the health and safety statutory framework have identified violence as a 'significant' risk, as considered below.

If the employer should have reasonably foreseen the risk, then the second question the law asks is whether the employer had taken reasonable care to protect staff, and possibly others as well, such as pupils, patients, hotel guests, etc. The standard of reasonable care expected will be established with reference to what the reasonably competent hypothetical employer would have done by way of protective measures (e.g. training, security equipment, safer procedures, etc.) in the same situation. If the law determines they would have done more, then the employer will be held liable.

Today, with the incidence of violence at work increasingly well documented and well understood, it is more difficult to allege that you were unaware of problems or unsure what to do. Management literature and conference presentations are full of ideas of good advice and good practice in responding effectively to violence.

Interestingly, whereas case law in the UK has emphasised the responsibility of an employer to protect their employees from violence, case law in the USA has tended to concentrate on the possible negligence of an employer who employs a violent employee. Negligent hiring is a popular cause of action against employers in many states by victims who have, say, been shot or molested by an employee (Underwriter Ins. Co. *v.* Purdie, 1983). The emphasis in the US is very much on public protection rather than on ensuring that there are policies and practices at the workplace itself to prevent violence between staff or protect staff from outsiders.

The statutory framework of health and safety law

The interesting issue in the UK is that, despite data showing the growing impact of violence at work, the Health and Safety Executive (HSE) has only recently required employers to record or report violence and its aftermath as an 'accident', under the Reporting of Injuries, Diseases and Dangerous Occurrences Regulations 1995 (RIDDOR 95). This brings the UK in line with most other European legal frameworks. The Annual Reports of the Health and Safety Commission (HSC) considered workplace violence in 1990–1 (HSC, 1991) along with other concerns such as sick-building syndrome, stress, smoking, etc., but the most recent report, for 1995–6 (HSC, 1996) still makes little reference to violence.

Under The Management of Health and Safety at Work Regulations (HSE, 1992), Regulation 3 requires all employers to undertake and respond to risk assessments for their workplaces. The risk of violence is clearly covered and, for many employment sectors, that particular risk will be considerable. The strategy of law requires 'preventative measures' at the workplace and eschews any idea that violence is a different type of risk or is one which is tolerable.

It is generally thought that the most important piece of UK legislation dealing with safety at work is the Health and Safety at Work (HSW) Act 1974. This established the regulatory framework, refined the existing inspection and enforcement procedures, and defined the legal duties to all at, or affected by, work. However, the approach of this law was geared to the manufacturing sector and to accidents typical of industry, mining and the like.

The HSW Act also sets the standard of care required to comply with the legal duties as one of 'reasonable practicability'. This somewhat imprecise legal standard has now, broadly, been overtaken by a standard of 'strict' liability (i.e. you must do all the necessary things to comply with law, not just take 'reasonable' steps) derived from the European health and safety framework. The European directives, which now cover a wide range of workplace issues (e.g. noise, chemicals, display screen work, manual handling, etc.) have a consistent approach to risks and their prevention.

European law has not adopted a specific directive on violence for the good reason that, in the context of European law's approach to workplace issues generally, there is no reason to treat violence separately. The law imposes a general duty on employers to seek out and analyse all workplace risks and deal with them. The law therefore places three key health and safety duties on the employer which are established, in the UK, by the

Management of Health and Safety at Work Regulations (HSE, 1992). They are to:

- efficiently assess all significant workplace risks (Regulation 3),
- respond to risk assessments by introducing preventative measures (Regulation 4), and
- monitor and regularly review workplace safety (Regulation 4).

The most common workplace risks tend to relate to work equipment, materials and premises. However, for many workers the risk of violent attack, or threat of attack, is a major one. The risk arises regularly and, because of the type of workplace or work activity, the consequences could be serious, even fatal, and the employer *must* introduce effective preventative measures.

The nature of these measures will clearly depend on the work but will often include:

- training of staff to counteract or diffuse violence,
- use of physical barriers, screens etc.,
- warning devices and means of summoning assistance.

Chapter 6 outlines such measures in more detail. However, it will often be important to review work practices and procedures. Solo working should be avoided, for example, and interview or discussion situations should be carefully prepared for and managed. Teams or shifts will probably need to balance inexperienced with experienced staff on duty.

There will also be the need to plan for and manage any incidents that do occur and to investigate them fully. In all of this the law is merely expecting good practice to be applied and experience learnt from.

The Management of Health and Safety at Work Regulations also introduced a requirement for all employers to establish effective procedures to deal with 'serious and imminent danger' so as to enable employees at risk to leave work and 'proceed to a place of safety' (Regulation 7). Clearly, the law has in mind fire, gas leaks, bomb scares and the like. However, in principle, the 'serious and imminent danger' from a violent patient, client, pupil, etc. could be covered. If an employee leaves the workplace but is subsequently disciplined or dismissed, they can complain to an industrial tribunal (Employment Rights Act, 1996, Section 100). In practical terms, employers will have difficulty in defending such claims unless the employees in question responded to danger inappropriately, given the information and training they were provided with by their employers.

The law also imposes duties on employees. Employees must not endanger the health and safety of others, must comply fully with health and safety instructions and must bring to the attention of their employer any shortcomings or problems regarding health and safety arrangements. This clearly includes arrangements to ensure personal safety and security in a context of the risk of violence. This duty is not an 'optional extra' for staff but is seen by law as an effective way of ensuring that standards are both maintained and raised. However, the responsibility of establishing, communicating and ensuring compliance with procedures to prevent all forms of violence rests primarily with the employer.

Conclusion

The law in the UK provides a varied yet effective legal framework which requires responses to workplace violence. It is clearly not seen as a work risk different from others or one to be treated less seriously. The law is placing responsibilities on employers to respond to violence, or the threat of violence, even if no actual incidents have occurred. It cannot be assumed that any given work situation is free from violence, bullying or harassment. Overall, any review of the law's response to violence will identify the following features. First, that law is recognising the problem. Second, that the response varies from jurisdiction to jurisdiction, largely dependent on legal traditions and the extent to which wider social and psychological workplace issues find support from law. It is no coincidence that those legal systems which have found a response to, say, stress, musculo-skeletal problems, smoking and alcohol abuse at work (the Nordic countries, UK, Australia, for example) have also developed the most coherent and positive response to violence. Such responses are more easily developed where legal rules have a generic base through developing concepts such as 'support' and 'risk management' for employees and others. These concepts generate rules requiring organisational policy and practice, as contrasted with ad hoc responses to individual problems.

The UK's approach is instructive. Initially it struggled to find appropriate legal approaches and, arguably, errors were made. In my view it has been unhelpful to place harassment and bullying in the anti-discrimination 'box'. Indeed, early UK case law from the 1970s had (properly) seen violence as a workplace risk which required a response through the employment contract, the law of negligence and then the standard health and safety framework. EU health and safety legislation has, similarly, seen violence as merely one of a wide range of workplace risks requiring managerial responses (although the extent to which EU legislation has been translated into effective law in member states is unclear.) Against this background, the 'diversion' into anti-discrimination law has been unfortunate.

It cannot be argued yet that law is providing adequate support for victims of work-related violence. Case law moves slowly and legislation is not always enforced. However, a complex patchwork of legal remedies is potentially available to victims and, with the 'softer' issues of employment law evolving more strongly, the expectation must be that employing organisations either develop effective preventative strategies or risk successful claims from victims.

References

Advisory, Conciliation and Arbitration Service (1987) *Discipline at Work, The ACAS Advisory Handbook*, London: ACAS.

Barley *v.* BP Oil (Kent Refinery) Ltd (1980) ICR 642.

Education Services Advisory Committee (1990) *Violence to Staff in the Education Sector*, Health and Safety Commission. London: HMSO. Reissued by HSE Books, Sudbury, Suffolk, August 1996.

European Recommendation on Dignity at Work (1991) Recommendation 92/C 27/04.

Health and Safety Commission (1991) *Annual Report of the Health and Safety Commission 1990/91*, London: HMSO.

—— (1996) *Annual Report of the Health and Safety Commission 1995/96*, London: HMSO.

Health and Safety Executive (1992) *Management of Health and Safety at Work Regulations*, London: HMSO.

Keys *v.* Shoe Fayre Ltd (1978) IRLR 476.

Leighton P. (1997) *The Work Environment: The Law of Health, Safety and Welfare*, 2nd Edition, London: NB Publications.

Leighton P. and O'Donnell, A. (1995) *The New Employment Contract*, London: NB Publications.

Mathiason, G. G. and Schuyler, M. (1996) 'The law of workplace violence', *Occupational Medicine: State of the Art Reviews*, 11(2), 315–334.

Parsons *v.* McLoughlin (1978) IRLR 65.

Pollard Bros *v.* Parr and Sons (1927) 1 KB 236.

Post Office *v.* Fennell (1981) IRLR 221.

Reporting of Injuries, Diseases and Dangerous Occurrences Regulations 1995 (RIDDOR 95) SI 1995 No. 3163, London: HMSO.

Slater *v.* Leicestershire Health Authority (1989) IRLR 16.

UK Government (1992) *People, Jobs and Opportunities*, UK Government White Paper, London: HMSO.

Underwriter Ins. Co. *v.* Purdie (1983) 145 Cal. App. 3d 57, 69.

Van den Berghen *v.* Nabarro Nathanson (1994) IRLR 340.

Walker *v.* Northumberland CC (1994) IRLR 35.

Warren *v.* Henleys Ltd (1948) 2 All ER 935.

3   The social psychology of violence and aggression

Claire Lawrence and Phil Leather

Aggression does not occur in a social vacuum…[it] stems from aspects of the social environment that instigate its occurrence and influence both its form and its direction.

(Baron, 1977: 122)

This chapter will examine theories which attempt to explain why people become aggressive and violent, focusing particularly on social interactionist views of aggression (Felson and Tedeschi, 1993; Leather and Lawrence, 1995). Such views typically emphasise the importance of a variety of influences during conflict situations, but pay particular attention to the social interchange or interaction between individuals. Following this approach, the chapter will examine those interactions and *situations* which increase or decrease the likelihood of aggressive incidents taking place. It is envisaged that this emphasis will more readily inform the development of policies and intervention strategies to manage violent and aggressive behaviour at work. In addition, this chapter will examine complementary ideas, models and views which provide additional perspectives to promote further understanding of aggressive incidents. It will discuss the contributory roles of social development, the environment, arousal, anger and alcohol, in the exhibition of violence and aggression. The role of biological factors (including genetic, hormonal and neural influences) will not be considered here, but readers are directed towards other sources (Moir and Jessel, 1995; Monahan and Steadman, 1994; Renfrew, 1997).

Early views treated aggression either as an inevitable part of a person's biology (e.g. Lorenz, 1966), or simply as a behavioural act. Buss (1961) offered the classic behavioural definition, seeing aggression as the delivery of harm by one organism to another. Within this model, neither the way those involved in the aggressive event view the interaction, nor the setting in which it takes place, are considered. Rather, the perceptions of those involved in the aggressive or violent incident are predominantly ignored. It is these perceptions, however, which are central to the social interactionist account of aggression – in particular, the intentions, expectations and judgements of those involved, together with the influence of the prevailing social and environmental standards (Cox and Leather, 1994).

Siann (1985) offers a definition suggesting that four conditions must apply for a behaviour to be described as aggressive:

1 The person intends to carry out the behaviour.
2 The behaviour takes place within an interpersonal situation characterised by conflict or competition.
3 The behaviour is performed intentionally to gain a greater advantage than the person being aggressed against.
4 The person carrying out the behaviour has either provoked the conflict or moved it on to a higher degree of intensity.

From the above definition, it is clear that aggression does not necessarily involve physical assault or injury. Indeed, according to Siann, it is the additional use of force or physical intensity which characterises the term 'violence' (Siann, 1985).

Following these definitions, the present chapter outlines a particular model which emphasises the role of aggression within social interaction. It is not the purpose here to provide a complete review of all the possible explanatory models, rather to outline the elements of models deemed to have the most relevance to practice. Readers interested in a more detailed examination of the various competing models are referred to Siann (1985), Geen (1990) and Berkowitz (1993).

Aggression in social interaction

Set within its social context, aggression usually occurs as a result of interpersonal interactions in a range of settings. Typically, aggressive behaviour becomes more likely as each individual involved responds to the other's actions, words or posture in such a way as to escalate the interaction to a point where the options to respond peacefully become more and more limited. However aggressive situations begin, the pattern of escalation is usually the result of one, or often both, protagonists attempting to establish credibility or save face at the expense of the other in a confrontational way, i.e. to 'win' as the other 'loses' (Goffman, 1959).

Within the social interactionist perspective, it is the participants' perceptions and understanding of both the social interaction and the setting in which it takes place which are of particular importance (Gibbs, 1986). The following example (Example 3.1) will be referred to again later in this chapter to illustrate how seemingly straightforward incidents of aggression can be examined within a social interactionist framework.

Example 3.1

Jack goes into a department store. It is very busy and many people are waiting in a queue to be served. Two men in front of Jack are whispering to each other and laughing. They keep looking round towards Jack. One of the men (Peter) then picks up his bag and swings it over his shoulder. As he does so, the bag swings against Jack's head, knocking Jack slightly sideways. Peter offers no apology.

Depending on how Jack interprets Peter's actions and lack of apology, he may decide to react in very different ways. It is these interpretative processes and the factors which influence them which are now examined in greater detail.

The role of interpretation and cognitive factors

In examining aggression, the emphasis of psychological theory has moved from a simple cause-and-effect model towards an interpretative one, with issues of intention and motive being central. The interpretation and labelling of a behavioural episode as 'aggressive', therefore, entails complex social judgements about the participants' intentions and motives, set within the norms and expectations relevant to the particular social situation (Siann, 1985).

In order to develop strategies for the reduction of violence and aggressive behaviour in the workplace, we must first seek to understand the conditions in which we describe a person's behaviour as 'aggressive' and the processes by which individuals behave aggressively. By doing this, we are able to manage our workplaces using practices which reduce the likelihood of aggressive behaviour being chosen as an appropriate action, and which promote an environment where other options for dispute resolution are offered. Furthermore, Zillman (1978) has shown that, when people have sufficient information to enable them to label an attacker's intentions as malicious, they are more likely to retaliate. In this way, understanding the processes by which we label behaviour as aggressive is crucial in developing strategies to reduce misinterpretation and retaliatory aggression.

According to Novaco (Novaco 1978; Novaco and Welsh, 1989), in understanding whether or not a behaviour is aggressive towards us, we must consider the 'aggressor's' possible intentions and motives, and whether his or her actions can be justified or mitigated. If actions are judged to be harmless or justified, then the accompanying emotions we are likely to experience will be benign. If, however, we judge the actions to be malevolent and intended to harm us, our emotions may be more intense, as we feel upset, angry, frightened and so on. We must therefore decide how we are going to respond. Aggression escalates, according to Cox and Leather (1994), when the response is viewed, in turn, as being excessively aggressive by the other person (see Figure 3.1 and Example 3.2). The way in which people make judgements of aggression are influenced by a range of factors including the personalities of the people involved, the social and physical environment they are in, the act itself, the relationship between those involved, the presence of alcohol or drugs and the presence of observers. These factors will be examined later in the chapter.

A trigger can be viewed as the action (or in some cases, the lack of action) which can spark off an aggressive escalation. Here, the trigger for

---

Example 3.2

Jack goes into a department store. It is very busy and many people are waiting in a queue to be served. Two men in front of Jack are whispering to each other and laughing. They keep looking round towards Jack. Jack interprets their actions as evidence that they are poking fun at him. One of the men (Peter) then picks up his bag and swings it over his shoulder. As he does so, the bag swings against Jacks head, knocking Jack slightly sideways (trigger). Jack immediately thinks that Peter has knocked him purposefully. Peter offers no apology, which makes Jack still more convinced of his malevolent intentions (thoughts). Jack feels angry and humiliated (feelings). He pushes Peter roughly saying 'What are you playing at?' (behaviour/new trigger).

Peter is surprised by Jack's outburst, as he had not intended to knock Jack with his bag and had not realised that he had done so. He considers that Jack has not given him chance to apologise before becoming hostile (thoughts). As a result, Peter quickly becomes angered (feelings), and shouts at Jack, telling him to get lost (behaviour).

Jack was the bag hitting his head. Jack could have dismissed this as accidental and shrugged it off. However, Jack had also interpreted the men's earlier laughter as poking fun at him. This influenced his judgement and he thought the action was deliberate and malevolent. He might have felt frightened or upset, and therefore have chosen to remain silent or to leave the queue. As it was, Jack felt angry and humiliated. He therefore rejected the options of ignoring the men, of leaving the queue or of politely asking Peter to be careful; instead, he chose to react in a more hostile manner. Jack's response then acted as a trigger for Peter, and so the cycle began again, with the options for peaceful resolution becoming less available.

Placing the aggressive incident in its setting

According to the social interactionist standpoint, aggression is understood within the context of the entire social episode. Supporters of this view identify aggressive behaviour as a *natural* product of certain types of encounters,

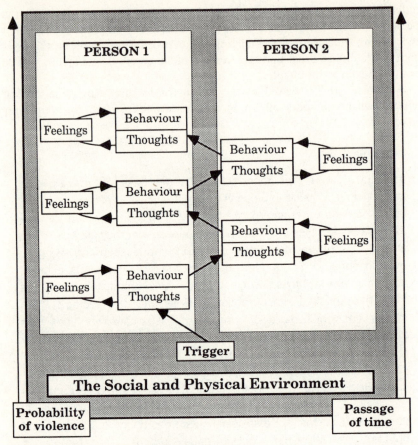

Figure 3.1 Escalation of aggressive incidents
Source: Adapted from Cox and Leather, 1994

particularly those in which there is conflict or competition between individuals. There is, as a result, a movement away from the premise that aggressive interchanges are naturally dysfunctional, and towards the view that such exchanges are merely one possible strategy individuals may choose as a normal consequence of the tensions and conflict which exists in human relations (see Novaco and Welsh, 1989).

Some theorists distinguish between instrumental aggression and emotional or angry aggression. Instrumental aggression is traditionally viewed as a relatively planned action, employed with the primary purpose of achieving some goal. A frequently used example of instrumental aggression would be the bank robber who uses force or threat of violence to achieve his or her goal of financial gain. Emotional aggression, alternatively, usually describes aggressive behaviour which is not perceived as having been planned as such, but which is, rather, a spontaneous response to some unpleasant or stressful situation or encounter (e.g. Berkowitz, 1993). An example of this emotional aggression would be the public house customer who 'lashes out' at another customer during a heated argument. The behaviour is described as having no goal other than inflicting harm on the other person. The reason for choosing violent means to end the dispute is said to be a result of the negative emotions which build up within the 'aggressor'.

This 'split' view of aggressive behaviour does not explain situations under which aggressive behaviour is not chosen *above other possible actions*, e.g. apologising, walking away or arguing verbally in a non-threatening manner. Working within the social interactionist framework, we must consider that the beliefs, expectations and norms of individuals acting within the aggressive exchange are of paramount importance in the process of understanding why specifically aggressive or violent behaviour is chosen. Effective preventative action might crucially depend on whether the behaviour is driven instrumentally or emotionally, or some combination of the two. It is important to recognise that actions which, on the surface, appear to be primarily emotionally driven do, in fact, contain instrumental elements.

Taking the example of the two customers in the pub mentioned earlier it is possible to view this action in the light of social interactionist view, as being *instrumental* to achieving a specific goal. Possible goals in this instance could be, amongst other possible reasons:

1   the individual wants to end the interchange quickly and so uses violence in order to bring the argument to a close;
2   the individual is losing face in the verbal argument and perceives the use of violence as a way of regaining face in the eyes of any onlookers and of maintaining a positive self-image; or
3   the individual senses that his 'opponent' will strike first and so is attempting to 'gain the upper hand'.

There is at least one goal to be achieved by behaving aggressively in this situation, either the termination of an unpleasant encounter, or the restoration of self-image (Felson and Tedeschi, 1993).

Despite this change in the way aggression is viewed, the question remains: Why is aggression or violent behaviour used to achieve the desired goal on some occasions, but not on others? In attempting to answer this question, supporters of the social interactionist perspective emphasise the significance of the situational and interpersonal factors at work in any episode. Significantly, in recent years many psychologists have turned their attention towards emphasising the role of the social environment which 'frames' or sets the scene in which behaviour and social interactions take place. This shift in emphasis, they maintain, is crucial in understanding the extent to which norms may exist for aggressive behaviour as a method of conflict resolution (Leather and Lawrence, 1995).

Norms are the established rules of conduct for any specific situation or encounter. For example, the norms governing the way one greets a friend may be quite different from those governing the way one would greet a client. Norms can also be inferred from cues in the environment. For instance, one may behave differently in a fast-food outlet than in an expensive 'high-class' restaurant, although the function of the two establishments is primarily to provide ready-cooked meals. In the same way, there are norms governing social interactions which develop over time and as a result of the changing relationships between people and the places they occupy.

Knowledge of the norms or rule system of any particular interaction or setting is vital in evaluating whether a rule has been broken or a norm violated and, if this is the case, in identifying the 'injured' parties. This identification of perceived 'wrongdoing' may be an important component in the development of an aggressive encounter (Tedeschi and Nesler, 1993). Indeed, Felson (1984) examined the roles of both perceived norm violations and punishments. He proposed that when norm violations are punished, the way in which the punishment is viewed (i.e. as an expected or fair response to the incident or as an aggressive act in itself), may determine the likelihood of retaliation. Thus, a cycle of escalating aggressive behaviour can develop, as each individual involved retaliates in the light of what they perceive to be unfair treatment.

Norm violations may not always lead to aggression. Instead, aggression is more likely in situations where a person views the violation to be unfair or unjust (Folger and Baron, 1996). In particular, individuals who perceive themselves to have been treated unfairly are motivated to look for an explanation for the unfairness. In addition, the availability of an opportunity to apologise for mistakes and correct errors can reduce the likelihood of negative reactions to seemingly unfair actions or decisions.

Individuals perceiving some injustice may have a range of options open to them. To illustrate the situational and interpersonal 'framing' of possible aggressive behaviour, we will briefly examine the options open to the 'victim' of perceived injustice in a simple interpersonal exchange (following Tedeschi and Nesler, 1993).

1   If the victim does not believe that any action taken by him or herself will redress the injustice experienced, or if he or she believes that undesired retaliatory acts may ensue, either from the individual violating the norm or from others, then no action may be taken.

2   In certain situations, the violating behaviour may be reappraised and deemed to have been justified or acceptable given external demands, e.g. if the action was demanded by a higher authority, of if the good achieved from the action outweighed the negative effects.

3   Alternatively, the offending person may simply be forgiven. This then allows the victim to reject other forms of more confrontational redress which may not be advisable or appropriate in the situation.

4   The victim may decide, however, to demand some redressing action from the wrongdoer. A refusal to comply may intensify the conflict resulting in a further escalation of the incident into an aggressive encounter.
5   Lastly, the victim may decide to punish, or seek punishment for, the 'harm doer'. The aim of punishment is usually to deter the wrongdoer from similar actions in the future and/or to redress the power relationship between the individuals. Problems arise, however, when one party perceives the punishment to be arbitrary or excessive, particularly if this occurs at an early stage in the interaction. In these cases, there is a threat of retaliatory action of a higher intensity.

Finally, it would be wrong to assume that the social interactionist perspective totally rejects any role of individual characteristics in the search for an understanding of aggressive behaviour. Indeed, Tedeschi (1983) maintains that individuals who lack the confidence or ability to resolve conflict using non-aggressive methods are more likely to use violence. More recently, work by Dodge, Price, Bachorowski and Newman (1990), has revealed evidence for a 'hostility attributional bias'. This bias is the tendency to assume that provocative actions (and even some ambiguous actions) from others were intentional and malevolent. People who have a hostility attributional bias, therefore, are quick to become aggressive in response to such provocation.

To summarise, the social interactionist viewpoint maintains that aggressive behaviour is motivated by complex subjective factors. The way in which incidents are perceived and classified, and the setting in which they take place, are crucial in determining the stream of events in any human encounter, of which violent or aggressive interchanges are simply an example.

This chapter will now consider other accounts which are intended to explain aggressive and violent interactions. These views complement the social interactionist approach and provide a richer understanding of aggressive and violent behaviour.

Social learning position: the role of social development

> A complete theory of aggression must explain how aggressive patterns are developed, what provokes people to behave aggressively, and what maintains their aggressive actions.
>
> (Bandura, 1978: 31)

Whilst the social interactionist perspective emphasises the importance of the 'rules' of social interaction between people in providing 'guidelines' for dealing with conflict and grievances, the social learning position considers the role of learning in social development.

The social learning school of thought developed as a movement which argued that aggression was generally used to achieve a desired end. This, proponents claim, occurs by a child or adult learning that aggression is not only acceptable in some situations but is also rewarded, that is, in some situations, violence pays off. This revelation can take place either by the individual directly observing someone else using aggression successfully to achieve some desired goal, or through mass-media representations of violent behaviour (Bandura, 1978).

This learning process involves the assimilation of complex skills in the art of aggression through imitation (modelling) followed by reward for the aggressive behaviour (reinforcement). Bandura, the most well-known proponent of this school, accepts that certain aversive experiences or emotional states, e.g. pain or humiliation, may lead to aggressive behaviour, but points out that such states may just as easily lead to other forms of behaviour such as withdrawal, dependent behaviour or drug and alcohol use. He also goes on to argue that rewards received by the aggressor may be sufficient to encourage them to use that method to achieve their goals in the future. Reward may take the form of a direct reinforcement of their behaviour, as when an individual receives money by mugging another person, or by indirect reinforcement, as when that individual receives respect and admiration from peers after mugging someone. Furthermore, an individual may learn that behaving aggressively can prevent negative experiences from occurring, as when, confronted with a bully, the individual decides to strike out first, thus deterring the bully from further action.

As a result of the increasing emphasis placed upon the significance of an individual's interpretative processes, Bandura has more recently adapted his theory to argue that, in the presence of a learned rejection of aggressive behaviour, the likelihood of an individual acting in an aggressive manner will be greatly reduced. This is due to a 'self-regulatory mechanism', that is a set of standards learned through direct teaching or from the individual's own experiences (Bandura, 1983). The individual will experience a disapproval of their own behaviour. This implicit 'self-punishment' will result in the individual being less likely to act in the same way in the future. Individuals may still act in an aggressive manner on occasion, however, if this self-regulatory mechanism is not supported, or is challenged. For example, when confronted with significant pressure from others to behave aggressively, then aggressive behaviour may be more likely.

Anonymity and deindividuation: accountability and group influence

We have already discussed the importance of 'norms' in providing a code of conduct for a given situation or environment. In most societies, these norms generally inhibit the use of intentional and malevolent behaviour towards another person. Norms are upheld by individuals for many reasons, but particularly for fear of social disapproval and/or punishment. It follows, then, that in situations where an individual's identity is unknown, the norms which demand socially acceptable behaviour may not apply so great a restraining influence.

Zimbardo (1970) described this phenomenon as 'deindividuation'; it comprises a reduction in the extent to which a person monitors their own behaviour and a reduction in concern about the way in which others perceive them. Consequently, the person has less inhibitions about acting in a way which is counter to the norm system of the situation.

This deindividuation may occur in a number of ways:

1 by an individual being anonymous, that is, unknown to others present, which can result in a reduction in the likelihood of blame and disapproval;
2 by an individual being a member of a group, which increases anonymity and reduces individual blame, guilt or responsibility;
3 by the situation being characterised by a lack of clear rules for behaviour, as this can reduce the strength of the norms operating;
4 by an individual being under the influence of alcohol or drugs, which allows the person to later disassociate themselves from their intoxicated behaviour.

Zimbardo's approach presupposes that the individual has some kind of latent drive to behave aggressively in some situations and that this drive is normally constrained by the social mores of the culture or group the person acts within. In contrast, Diener (1980) suggests that when an individual is in a group, and becomes deindividuated, aggressive behaviour may follow because the individual becomes less self-reflective. Instead, their attention is shifted to the external situation. As a result, the individual may be influenced by the information available in the environment when determining the most appropriate type of behaviour. For example, at a football match, one supporter in a group of fans may behave aggressively to rival fans if others behave aggressively and the environment supports conflict. Other researchers argue that a combination of deindividuation and a heightened attendance to external cues from other group members may underlie inner-city youth gang violence.

Evidence for deindividuation in driving situations has also been observed by Ellison, Govern, Petri and Figler (1995) who measured the frequency and duration of horn-honking in a controlled field study. They found that subjects who were driving a convertible car with the roof up (and were therefore less identifiable) honked at a stationary, confederate driver for longer and more often than subjects who were driving a convertible car with the top down (more identifiable).

The effect of arousal on aggression

The frustration–aggression hypothesis, which claimed that frustration is always at the root of aggressive behaviour (see Dollard, Doob, Miller,

Mowrer and Sears, 1939), was criticised by theorists who rejected this simplistic approach. One group in particular argued that frustration may be just one of a number of stimuli which may increase a person's state of 'arousal' or readiness for activity. In this aroused state, an individual may be more activated to respond to a situation in an aggressive manner.

The experience of arousal, and the ways in which an individual labels or identifies this experience, will be affected by both the internal state of the particular individual, and the situation within which that individual is acting. This is particularly the case if there are no immediate or obvious explanations for the arousal experienced (Schachter, 1964). If a person feels aroused and uptight, but there are no obvious reasons for this arousal, it is likely that they will interpret their state in terms of the most salient information available; for example, they could attribute their arousal to the temperature of the room, or the level of noise, or their general health etc. If, under such circumstances, another person provokes them in some way, the aroused person will often view their arousal as their reaction to the other's behaviour (Schachter and Singer, 1962). This can result in 'scape-goating' another individual, who 'happens to be in the wrong place at the wrong time', for a relatively trivial offence.

Adding on to this idea that aggression can be the result of a 'cognitive labelling' of a generalised aroused state, Zillman (1971) examined the effect of more than one arousing event occurring in sequence. In short, he argued that some of the arousal from one event may be carried over to add to the arousal experienced as a result of a second event. Zillman showed two types of arousing film to a group of individuals after they had been provoked. One of the films depicted violence, whilst the other was sexual. The group who watched the erotic film behaved more aggressively than those who watched the violent film. The erotic film had been more arousing than the violent film and it appears that, following provocation, the general arousal was labelled as anger which was, in turn, exhibited as aggression. The timing of arousing events is important; if the time span between the arousing events is too long, then the arousal experienced in the first event will be diminished. There are problems with this approach, however, as arousing, but happy and joyous feelings are more likely to inhibit aggressive behaviour (Bandura 1973). It appears that the affective nature and degree of the arousal is important in determining its connection with subsequent aggressive action.

When aggression is the chosen response

In this section, we will examine the kind of situations in which an aggressive response is more likely.

According to Ferguson and Rule (1983), a person may provoke an aggressive response in another individual when certain conditions are met. It is not enough to say that a frustrating event always results in an aggressive encounter.

Indeed, there are many occasions when one is frustrated in the achievement of some goal, but aggressive behaviour does not normally occur, for instance, when a footballer is successfully tackled yards away from the goal.

Ferguson and Rule developed a scheme of conditions to be considered about any behaviour in order to ascertain whether provocation is sufficient to warrant an aggressive attack. A person, they argue, is more likely to judge an action to be sufficiently provocative to justify them retaliating if:

1 The behaviour was intended. Intention is usually attributed to a person if:

i   there were other behaviours they could have used in the same situation;
ii the individual would reap some benefit by behaving in that manner;
iii the individual had to overcome difficulties to behave in that manner;
iv the individual had behaved in a similar way in the past.

2 The behaviour was performed as a result of malice or malevolence. An action is usually considered to be malevolent if:

i   that action has some beneficial end result for persons other than the victim;
ii that action is a retaliation for some previous aggressive behaviour.

3 The outcome of the behaviour (i.e. some degree of harm) was foreseen by the protagonist. An action is perceived as being foreseeable when:

i   negligence to perform some action results in an obvious harm to another person, e.g. failure to remove an obstacle from a public stairway, resulting in somebody falling;
ii in performing some action, scant or no regard is paid to the harmful by-products of the action on others, e.g. driving too fast, so being unable to avoid knocking down a pedestrian.

If the behaviour is *not* deemed to have been intended, then we must examine whether the person still knew the harmful consequences of their actions. If a behaviour is deemed to be unintentional *and* unforeseeable, then it will probably be judged to be an accident. Acts which are judged to have been intended and malevolent, however, are usually perceived to be more provoking, and more blameworthy. In this situation, any anger experienced as a result of the harmful behaviour may be directed at the harm-doer.

Furthermore, according to Shaver (1985), the process of attributing blame begins with an action for which there is a single and personal cause, e.g. a person hitting someone. If the person did not intend the final consequences of their actions, but should have been able to foresee them, then they will be found to be negligent. If, however, the person *did* intend the consequences, but did not realise how bad the consequences would be (e.g. the actor meant to hit someone in order to cause them a small degree of pain, but did not realise that the victim would fall as a result, and break their arm), or if they were coerced into carrying out the action, then they will be judged to be responsible. Blame, according to Shaver, can only be attributed under conditions where the action was voluntary, intentional and without acceptable justification.

The effect of the physical environment

We have seen that whether or not aggressive behaviour occurs may depend on the individual's evaluation of the other person(s) involved and the environment in which the behaviour is set. So far we have discussed 'environment' predominantly in terms of the norm system or prescriptions for behaviour it offers. In this section we will turn to examine some of the more direct ways in which the environment may increase the likelihood of that individual behaving in an aggressive or violent manner. The means by which the physical environment affects behaviour in this way is still a subject for debate. The most generally accepted view is that the degree to which stress is experienced, and the coping strategies available to deal with this stress, are crucial (Cox and Leather, 1994). Although many aspects of the physical environment have been linked with aggressive behaviour, in this section, we shall concentrate on the effects of heat and crowding.

Heat

Evidence for the relationship between high temperatures and high levels of aggression is far from clear-cut. Data obtained from archival and field studies, largely from examination of natural temperature in periods of social unrest, suggest that, as temperature rises, so too does aggressive behaviour (see Geen, 1990 for a review). Evidence from laboratory studies does not support this. Laboratory studies tend to suggest that, at low temperatures, aggressive behaviour is negligible; as temperatures begin to rise, so too does the incidence of aggressive behaviour; but as temperatures rise still further, the incidence of aggressive behaviour diminishes (Bell, 1992). However, in most experimental conditions, participants were free to leave the study at any point. At high temperatures, many participants did choose to do this, resulting in fewer remaining participants available to act in an aggressive manner. Thus, participants had the choice whether to act aggressively or to escape – a luxury not available in many in real-life situations.

Crowding and personal space

Although the link between territoriality and aggressive behaviour has been demonstrated within many species in the animal kingdom, there is very little support for the same link in humans. However, significant work has been carried out examining aggressive behaviour and violations of people's 'personal space'. Personal space can be described as the area surrounding a person which acts as an imaginary buffer, and into which other people are not welcome to enter. Evidence suggests that an invasion of this personal space can produce aggressive responses (Worchel and Teddlie, 1976).

This area of designated personal space has been termed the 'personal space bubble'. It is usually represented as an egg-shape around a person, with a boundary quite close to the person at the front, but larger at their back. Not surprisingly, different people have larger or smaller personal space bubbles, and each person may allow some people to enter that space, whilst avoiding such close proximity with others. Indeed, violent offenders serving prison sentences have a larger personal space bubble than do non-violent offenders.

It is difficult to find any direct link between density of population and aggressive behaviour, especially as the situation and perceptions of the individuals involved may be different in every case (Geen, 1990). More stable links have been demonstrated, however, between aggressive behaviour and the more subjective experience of crowding. It is likely that this experience of crowding is connected to issues of personal space and competition for resources.

The role of alcohol

The idea of a simple link between alcohol and aggression is frequently used to explain national violent crime statistics, specific violent events and domestic violence. Indeed, many seemingly motiveless murders are connected with alcohol use. Such events all connect alcohol with violent crime.

There is little evidence to suggest that individuals become spontaneously aggressive after consuming alcohol. However, when provoked, intoxicated individuals have been shown to respond more aggressively than sober control individuals. Indeed, studies have found such increased aggression at levels of intoxication as low as around 30 mg/100 ml (e.g. Kelley, Cherek and Steinberg, 1989). Despite these findings, when non-aggressive alternatives are available, intoxicated individuals do not react any more aggressively than their sober controls (Gustafson, 1993). It must be noted, however, that due to the ways in which alcohol can reduce cognitive functioning, intoxicated people may be less able to appreciate the existence of other alternatives, particularly if these alternatives are less obvious.

There is also some evidence to suggest that intoxicated individuals may simply be complying with the stereotyped view that society has of 'the drunk'. On some occasions, this stereotype may be the cheerful person who talks a little too loudly, or indeed, the aggressive person who seems suddenly ready to 'pick a fight'. However, research in this area is very divided, with findings not repeated after replication. It is likely, therefore, that a range of other factors play a more important role. Such factors include: the situation in which the alcohol is drunk; the personality of the drinker; and the availability of alternative, peaceful courses of action in the face of conflict.

Conclusions

This chapter has outlined the social interactionist perspective regarding aggressive behaviour. It has emphasised the importance of processes of perception, interpretation and judgement of intention, responsibility and blame. It has also examined the significance of social norms and their influence over the appropriateness of certain behaviours and interactions in specific situations.

For any workplace to become less at risk from violence and aggression, employers must ensure that the way in which work is designed does not serve to generate an environment which promotes rather than reduces aggressive and violent methods of conflict resolution. As a result, this chapter has aimed to provide background information about the processes involved in aggressive interactions in order to assist in the construction of safer work practices and social interactions which reduce the likelihood of aggressive behaviour. In particular, this chapter has pointed clear ways forward in the development of procedures and practices aimed at reducing work-related violence and these are identified below. A more detailed outline of many of these principles can be found in Chapter 6.

- Organisations should be aware of the basic psychological mechanisms which underpin aggressive escalation.
- Organisations must be aware of points of conflict and grievance, i.e. those situations where aggression and violence are more likely to occur.
- Employees should carefully consider the ways in which their own behaviour may be interpreted by others.
- Organisational standards, norms and rules regarding conflict situations should be communicated to staff and clients implicitly and/or explicitly.
- Individuals who may have to deal with conflict situations should ensure that their own behaviour reduces the likelihood of aggression, and is not perceived as malevolent or intentionally obstructive.
- A positive atmosphere and culture should be nurtured in order to promote benign or benevolent emotions amongst both the clients, or customers, of the organisation and its employees.
- Interactions at, and between, all levels within the organisation should be perceived to be fair and consistent to avoid grievances developing.
- Organisations should provide alternative, non-physical, means of settling grievances in order to reduce the likelihood of retaliation.
- Aggressive and violent behaviour should not be rewarded, especially if the aggressive behaviour is witnessed publicly.
- Physical environments, queuing procedures and organisational procedures should be managed to:

i   reduce the degree to which they incite conflict and arousal;
ii provide adequate services and physical resources (e.g. the need for privacy or for relevant information).

• Employees should be aware of the effects of their own and others' use of alcohol or drugs, whether prescribed or illegal.

References

Bandura, A. (1973) *Violence: A Social Learning Analysis*, New Jersey: Prentice-Hall.
——— (1978) 'Learning and behavioural theories of aggression', in I. L. Kutash, S. B. Kutash, L. B. Schlesinger and associates *Violence: Perspectives on Murder and Aggression*, San Francisco: Jossey-Bass.
——— (1983) 'Psychological mechanisms in aggression', in R. G. Geen and E. I. Donnerstein (eds) *Aggression: Theoretical and Empirical Issues*, New York: Academic Press.
Baron, R. A. (1977) *Human Aggression*, New York: Plenum.
Bell, P. A. (1992) 'In defense of the negative affect escape model of heat and aggression', *Psychological Bulletin*, 112(2), 342–346.
Berkowitz, L. (1993) *Aggression: Its Causes, Consequences and Control*, New York: McGraw-Hill.
——— (1983) 'The experience of anger as a parallel process in the display of impulsive "angry" aggression', in R. G. Geen and E. Donnerstein (eds) *Aggression: Theoretical and Empirical Reviews*, Vol. I: Theoretical and Methodological Issues, pp. 103–133, New York: Academic Press.
Buss, A. H. (1961) *The Psychology of Aggression*, New York: Wiley.
Cherek, D. R., Steinberg, J. L. and Vines, R. V. (1984) 'Low doses of alcohol affect human aggressive responses', *Biological Psychiatry*, 19, 263–267.
Cox, T. and Leather, P. J. (1994) 'The prevention of violence at work', in C. L. Cooper and I. T. Robertson (eds) *International Review of Industrial and Organizational Psychology*, Vol. 9, pp 213–245. Chichester: Wiley and Sons.
Diener, E. (1980) 'Deindividuation: the absence of self-awareness and self-regulation in group members', in P. Paulus (ed.) *The Psychology of Group Influence*, Hillsdale, NJ: Erlbaum.
Dodge, K. A., Price, J. M., Bachorowski, J. A. and Newman, J. P. (1990) 'Hostile attributional biases in severely aggressive adolescents', *Journal of Abnormal Psychology*, 99, 385–392.
Dollard, J., Doob, L. W., Miller, N. E., Mowrer, O. H. and Sears, R. R. (1939) *Frustration and Aggression*, New Haven, CT: Yale University Press.
Ellison, P. A., Govern, J. M., Petri, H. L. and Figler, M. H. (1995) 'Anonymity and aggressive driving behaviour: a field study', *Journal of Social Behaviour*, 10(1), 265–272.
Felson, R. B. (1984) 'Patterns of aggressive interaction', in A. Mummendey (ed.) *Social Psychology of Aggression: From Individual Behaviour to Social Interaction*, pp. 107–126, Berlin: Springer-Verlag.
Felson, R.B. and Tedeschi, J.T. (eds) *Aggression and Violence: Social Interactionists' Perspectives*, Washington, DC: American Psychological Association.
Ferguson, T. J. and Rule, B. G. (1983) 'An attributional perspective on anger and aggression', in R. G. Geen and E. Donnerstein (eds) *Aggression: Theoretical and*

Empirical Reviews, Vol. I: Theoretical and Methodological Issues, pp. 41–74, New York: Academic Press.

Folger, R. and Baron, R. A. (1996) 'Violence and hostility at work: a model of reactions to perceived injustice', in G. R. VandenBos and E. Q. Bulatao (eds) *Violence on the Job*, Washington, DC: American Psychological Association.

Geen, R. G. (1990) *Human Aggression*, Milton Keynes: Open University Press.

Gibbs, J. J. (1986) 'Alcohol consumption, cognition and context: examining tavern violence', in A. Campbell and J. J. Gibbs (eds) *Violent Transaction*, Oxford: Blackwell.

Goffman, E. (1959) *The Presentation of Self in Everyday Life*, Garden City, NY: Anchor.

Gustafson, R. (1993) 'What do experimental paradigms tell us about alcohol-related aggression?' *Journal of Studies on Alcohol*, Supplement 11, 20–29.

Kelley, T. H., Cherek, D. R. and Steinberg, J. L. (1989) 'Congruent reinforcement and alcohol: interactive effects on human aggressive behaviour', *Journal of Studies on Alcohol*, 50, 399–405.

Leather, P. and Lawrence, C. (1995) 'Perceiving pub violence: the symbolic influence of social and environmental factors', *British Journal of Social Psychology*, 34, 395–407.

Leventhal, H. (1980) 'Toward a comprehensive theory of emotion', in L. Berkowitz (ed.) *Advances in Experimental Social Psychology*, Vol.13, pp. 139–207, New York: Academic Press.

Lorenz, K. (1966) *On Aggression*, New York: Harcourt Brace Jovanovich.

Moir, A. and Jessel, D. (1995) *A Mind to Crime*, London: Michael Joseph.

Monahan, J. and Steadman, H. J. (1994) *Violence and Mental Disorder: Developments in Risk Assessments*, Chicago: University of Chicago Press.

Novaco, R. W. and Welsh, W. N. (1989) 'Anger disturbances: cognitive mediation and clinical prescriptions', in K. Howells and C. R. Hollins (eds) *Clinical Approaches to Violence*, Chichester: John Wiley and Sons Ltd.

Renfrew, J. W. (1997) *Aggression and its Causes: A Biopsychosocial Approach*, New York: Oxford University Press.

Rule, B. G. and Nesdale, A. R. (1976) 'Emotion, arousal and aggressive behaviour', *Psychological Bulletin*, 83, 851–863.

Schachter, S. (1964) 'The interaction of cognitive and physiological determinants of emotional state', in L. Berkowitz (ed.) *Advances in Experimental Social Psychology*, Vol. 1, pp. 49–80, New York: Academic Press.

Schachter, S. and Singer, J. (1962) 'Cognitive, social, and physiological determinants of emotional state', *Psychological Review*, 69, 379–399.

Shaver, K. G. (1985) *The Attribution of Blame: Causality, Responsibility and Blameworthiness*, New York: Springer-Verlag.

Siann, G. (1985) *Accounting for Human Aggression: Perspectives on Aggression and Violence*, Boston: Allen and Unwin.

Tedeschi, J. T. (1983) 'Social influence theory and aggression', in R. G. Geen (ed.) *Aggression: Theoretical and Empirical Reviews*, pp. 135–162, New York: Academic Press.

Tedeschi, J. T. and Nesler, M. S. (1993) 'Grievances: development and reactions', in R. B. Felson and J. T. Tedeschi (eds) *Aggression and Violence: Social Interactionists' Perspectives*, pp. 13–47, Washington, DC: American Psychological Association.

Welch, S. and Booth, A. (1975) 'The effect of crowding on aggression', *Sociological Symposium*, 14, 105–127.

Worchel, S. and Teddlie, C. (1976) 'The experience of crowding: a two-factor theory', *Journal of Personality and Social Psychology*, 34, 30–40.

Zillman, D. (1971) 'Excitation transfer in communication-mediated aggressive behaviour', *Journal of Experimental and Social Psychology*, 7, 419–434.

—— (1978) 'Attribution and misattribution of excitatory reactions', in J. H. Harvey, W. J. Ickes and R. F. Kidd (eds) *New Directions in Attribution Research*, Vol. 2, Hillsdale, NJ: Erlbaum.

Zimbardo, P. G. (1970) 'The human choice: individuation, reason and order versus deindividuation, impulse and chaos', in W. J. Arnold and D. Levine (eds) *Nebraska Symposium on Motivation*, Lincoln, NE: University of Nebraska Press.

4   Surviving the incident

Carol Brady

Introduction

The effects of violence can be devastating. When an incident has ended, it may be just the beginning for the victim. Most people recover within days or weeks but, for some, the rest of their lives is blighted. Apart from the effect on the individual, violence disrupts the functioning of organisations, impairs organisational effectiveness and can be costly both in terms of staff morale and efficiency, and in lost time through sickness absence (Mackay, 1994).

Understanding the nature and range of reactions possible in response to such incidents enables organisations to help staff in coping with the aftermath of work-related violence. Recovery from the trauma depends not only on the individual and characteristics of the incident, but on how the organisation responds. A case illustration of one organisation's response can be found in Chapter 7 of this volume.

This chapter describes the reactions which might be expected in staff who have been assaulted, and less common, but more severe, reactions which can occur. Consideration is given to how best an organisation can support staff who have been verbally or physically assaulted.

Reactions which might be expected

Typical responses to assault are shown in Table 4.1. Immediately following the incident, individuals may be injured or in pain. They may be confused and are likely to be shocked, upset, tearful and shaking; they may, perhaps, be embarrassed at what has taken place, and at being the centre of attention. The opposite can also occur due to the production of adrenalin during the incident. Individuals may experience an immediate elation, feel energetic and competent to return to work. However, when the adrenalin subsides, exhaustion sets in, and the true impact of the incident becomes apparent. Someone who appears to have suffered minimal impact may lose control later.

In the days and weeks that follow, victims experience a range of symptoms (see Table 4.1). Often these diminish with time. Reactions to violence tend to follow a pattern which has been identified with a bereavement reaction

Table 4.1 Reactions that might be experienced by individuals following assault

Possible reactions following assault		
Immediately following assault	In the days following assault	In the long term
Physical pain	Fear	Lack of confidence
Shaking	Anger, resentment	Situation specific anxiety
Crying	Exhaustion	Feeling 'burnt out'
Fear	Denial of effects	Depression
Shock	Feeling of loss	Post-traumatic stress
Disbelief	Guilt, shame, humiliation	disorder
Confusion	Poor concentration	
Embarrassment	Lack of confidence	
Anger	Anxiety in similar situations	
Feeling 'energised'	Sleep difficulties	
Feeling 'ready to work'	Depression	
	Attempts to make sense of what happened	

(Ochberg, 1988). Initially, individuals are in a state of shock and disbelief about what has taken place. They may go through a period in which they even deny that it has happened, or deny its significance for them. Anger and resentment may follow, then a struggle to resolve the question of why this should happen to them. They may become depressed before moving on to adjust to a new life situation. There is no set time course for this, and people may not go through each stage in a linear fashion.

However they move through their response, victims are likely to experience a range of emotions soon after the assault, including fear and anger about what happened. A loss of confidence in the ability to cope with work is common, particularly in relation to situations or clients similar to those involved with the assault. Victims who are anxious about a recurrence tend to overestimate the likelihood of it happening again, and to avoid situations where they believe this is possible. Work may also become difficult due to impaired concentration, further reducing their confidence in their ability to cope with the job.

This loss of confidence can come to be associated with a more general loss of self-esteem, deepening into depression, with associated poor sleep patterns, lack of appetite and feelings of hopelessness.

Fear

The victim is likely to react with fear during the incident and at some point afterwards. Immediately following the trauma, relief may predominate, and fear only develop later, particularly on returning to the scene of the incident. I, myself, was subject to assault and held captive in my office by a patient. The incident lasted only minutes, but resulted in a minor physical injury. I experienced relief and exhaustion for the rest of the day at home, but felt some fear and trepidation on returning to work the next day.

The fear may be focused solely upon the perpetrator, but can generalise to any potential aggressor. This can be exacerbated by the individual avoiding situations in which they perceive risk, thus 'incubating' the fear (Eysenck, 1976).

Anger

It is natural for the victim to feel angry towards someone who has harmed them. If the anger is not expressed in some way, the victim can become increasingly resentful and may develop a hatred of the assailant in particular, or of people whom the victim perceives as similar. Victims often feel angry towards others involved in the incident, who might have contributed to its occurrence, perhaps by failing to prevent it. Those who fail to respond appropriately after the incident are also targets for anger. Feelings of irritation and shortness of temper are common and the expression of angry feelings may be often misdirected at spouses and children, making family life difficult.

Guilt

Survivors of major incidents, where lives have been lost, often experience guilt at still being alive. Staff can also feel guilty that an incident has occurred at all. This is particularly the case for those in the 'helping professions', where the assailant may be someone the staff member has known for some time, or at least is someone they should be helping. Staff also tend to believe that they have failed professionally by not being able to defuse the situation successfully, and blame themselves more if attacked more than once. If the incident exposes existing negative or aggressive feelings the staff member has towards the client, or produces feelings of aggression and wishes for revenge which are difficult to acknowledge, feelings of guilt may result.

Such staff are trained to cope with other people's problems and to understand and accept their often difficult clients, so it is not surprising that they look to their understanding of the client to explain the violent incident. Often workers are less understanding of themselves, however, and some expect that they should be able to cope with anything. This can lead to risk taking, e.g. paying a home visit alone to a client with a history of violence. Staff can find it hard to admit to each other, let alone to their managers, that they are afraid of assault, or that they have been assaulted.

Colleagues may inadvertently scapegoat the victim to protect themselves from the fear that such attacks arouse in work groups. Explaining the assault as the victim's fault defends against the fearful thought: 'It could happen to me.' Paradoxically, victims can also defend against anxiety about future assaults by blaming themselves for causing the incident. This denies their own helplessness by implying that there was some choice or control inherent in the situation. However, blaming the victim is maladaptive in the longer term, as it leaves the victim feeling guilty and doubting their ability; it also leaves possible procedural faults unscrutinised.

Loss

The assault victim may suffer loss in a variety of forms. A colleague may have lost their life in the incident, or there may be loss through injury or ill-health following the assault. There may also be significant psychological loss. Janoff-Bulman and Frieze (1983) suggest that people manage their lives comfortably when they believe in (1) a personal invulnerability, (2) a fair and predictable world, and (3) their ability to cope with challenges presented to them. When they become a victim, the person can lose their sense of the 'just world', that is the belief that if one behaves a certain way (e.g. are a 'good' person) then the world will respond certain way (i.e. 'bad' things will not happen). The assault may make them face the actuality that bad things can happen to anyone. The loss of this innocence can be painful.

In addition, if they held rigid views about the world being fair, they may make the leap from 'bad things only happen to bad people' to 'therefore I must be a bad person', rather than evaluating the original construct. In an attempt to answer the almost universal question 'Why me?', the answer 'because you deserved it', leads to a loss of self-esteem, and the possible development of depression.

Challenging basic assumptions about safety leads individuals to recognise their true vulnerability and experience an associated loss of confidence. My own experience of assault led me to appraise the risks inherent in the design and location of my office and to conclude that I was at appreciable risk. In the days following assault, this led me to keep the office door locked from the inside when alone. This stopped as the fear wore off and confidence returned.

A temporary loss of confidence in the workplace is common, but if the incident has been particularly traumatic, then the individual may feel changed in a fundamental way. Here, the loss can take on the proportion of a loss of sense of self, and the individual struggles to re-evaluate who they are, in relation to what has happened. Traumatic incidents can force people to experience emotions they have never felt before, and they may be unsure of what this means in terms of how the experience has changed them.

Withdrawal

Victims of assault may feel that others do not understand the profound emotions produced in them, and the significance of the event. They may be correct in this assumption, and this lack of understanding can be problematic. Family members may suggest that it is best for the victim to put what happened behind them, at a time when they still feel the need to talk. Faced with this, and with feelings they may prefer not to expose, victims can with-draw into themselves, creating distance between the victim and family members, who may misinterpret this as aloofness. In the work setting, the victim may become suspicious of others who wish to help, particularly if responsibility for the incident is in question. Bamber (1992) points out that, without the opportunity for debriefing, staff tend to isolate themselves and deny any effect. As the victim becomes withdrawn and rejects help, interven-tion can become difficult. The difficulties victims might have in trusting others should be taken into account in the planning of support services within organisations.

These are all normal reactions to what has been an abnormal situation. In the majority of cases symptoms will improve within weeks, but longer-term disturbance can occur, as indicated in Table 4.1. In addition, delayed reactions complicate the picture. In organisational terms, lack of confidence and anxiety about the work situation become problematic if unresolved, resulting in staff staying away from work and, in extreme cases, resigning because they feel unable to cope.

Post-traumatic stress disorder

Post-traumatic stress disorder (PTSD) has become a well known, but some-what overused, term following the disasters of recent years. PTSD in fact refers to a very specific syndrome. To be diagnosed as suffering from PTSD, using the DSM-IV criteria (American Psychiatric Association, 1994), the individual must have experienced, witnessed, or have been confronted by an event, or events, that involved actual or threatened death or serious injury, or a threat to the physical integrity of self and others. The person's response to this should have involved fear, helplessness or horror.

In addition to experiencing such an event, individuals must meet a set of criteria for symptoms. First, there is *persistent re-experience* of the traumatic event in at least one of the following ways:

1 Recurrent and intrusive distressing recollections of the event;
2 Recurrent distressing dreams of the event;
3 Acting or feeling as if the event were recurring in the sense of reliving the episode;
4 Intense distress when exposed to events that symbolise or resemble an aspect of the original event;
5 Physiological reactivity on exposure to internal or external cues that symbolise or resemble an aspect of the event.

Second, there is *persistent avoidance* of stimuli associated with the trauma and *numbing of responsiveness* as indicated by at least three of the following:

1 Efforts to avoid thoughts or feelings associated with the trauma;

2   Efforts to avoid activities, people or situations that arouse recollections of the trauma;
3   Inability to recall an important aspect of the trauma;
4   Markedly decreased interest or participation in significant activities;
5   Feelings of detachment or estrangement from others;
6   Restricted range of affect, for example, an inability to have loving feelings;
7   Sense of foreshortened future.

Third, there are *persistent feelings of increased arousal*, which were not previously present, as indicated by at least two from:

1   Difficulty in falling or staying asleep;
2   Irritability or outbursts of anger;
3   Difficulty in concentrating;
4   Hypervigilance;
5   Exaggerated startle response.

These symptoms must have lasted for *at least one month*, and the disturbance must cause clinically significant distress, or impairment in daily functioning.

DSM-IV differentiates between acute and chronic PTSD. Symptoms of acute PTSD are resolved within three months of their onset. When symptoms last longer than three months, chronic PTSD is diagnosed. Onset of symptoms later than 6 months after the traumatic incident is described as a delayed onset reaction. This can occur years after the incident.

The following is an example of an individual who developed chronic PTSD after a violent incident at work:

John is a leisure centre manager, of ten years' experience. Six months ago he was locking up, when he was attacked by a group of youths. He was badly beaten and had eight weeks off work. Since the incident he has had a recurring dream about it, and suffers anxiety symptoms whenever he goes into the part of the building where it took place (re-experiencing).

He avoids thinking or talking about the incident, and has lost interest in his job. He also feels that he no longer enjoys life as he used to (avoidance/numbing).

John is much more jumpy than he was before, and is easily startled. He has difficulty concentrating for long on any task. He loses his temper frequently at home. He finds he shouts at his children for small things which previously did not bother him (increased arousal).

Diagnosing PTSD can be difficult, particularly as it is commonly associated with concurrent depression, anxiety or substance abuse, and there is the possibility of delayed reactions. The following example illustrates the cost of failing to recognise this.

Martin and his wife Sara managed a successful restaurant. One night, after closing time, they were attacked by two intruders who tied them up, beating Martin badly and threatening to harm Sara if he did not hand over all the cash on the premises.

After the incident, Sara suffered badly, becoming too anxious to work in the restaurant at night, for several weeks. She also had difficulty staying at home alone at night and needed a friend with her when Martin was at work. He responded 'wonderfully', returning to work immediately he was physically able, managing on his own until Sara was able to return. He supported her through a difficult time, and gradually she recovered.

Some months after the incident, Martin began to drink more than usual, at first 'just to get him off to sleep'. Gradually his drinking increased. His relationship with Sara deteriorated; he grew moody and withdrawn. The restaurant began to decline, and there were complaints from customers. Sara left and the situation worsened. Eventually, his employers suggested Martin move on.

A couple of years later, one of Martin's employers attended a workshop on dealing with violence in the workplace, and was shocked to find that Martin might have been suffering from the effects of the violence to which he had been subject.

Severity of reaction

The degree of the reaction suffered depends to some extent on characteristics of the person who has been assaulted. However, it would be a mistake to assume that a physically strong 'macho' man who has been the victim of assault will necessarily cope better than someone small and physically weaker. Such an attack may change his view of himself so much that he might find it harder to cope afterwards. Factors which are important in determining the severity of reaction to trauma include:

- Level of stress or exposure
- Pre-existing personality or psychological disorder
- Family history
- Coping style
- Support.

Correlation between the stress inherent in the situation and the resultant pathology tends to be low. However, in order for PTSD to develop, it seems that the stress has to be of a sufficient intensity to force people to consider fundamental questions about themselves and the world (Scott and Stradling, 1992).

Particular characteristics of the incident are important. For example, being accidentally injured in an incident is likely to be less psychologically threatening than being sought out deliberately by an assailant to be threatened and attacked. Incidents also vary in predictability, time course, frequency and degree of physical harm inflicted. Kilpatrick Saunders, Amick-McMullan *et al.* (1989) found that physical injury and a life threatening situation increased the risk of the development of 'crime related PTSD'. Fullilove, Fullilove, Smith and Winkler (1993) found that the likelihood of PTSD, in a sample of women who used drugs, was strongly associated with the number of violent traumas reported.

However, the experience of actual violence is not necessary for a severe reaction to set in. Wykes (1994) rightly emphasises the role of appraisal in determining the outcome. If a victim believes they are in a life-threatening situation, even if objectively they are not, then a severe reaction may occur.

It would seem somewhat obvious that a pre-existing psychological disorder would make an individual vulnerable to the effects of stress. A community survey (Helzer, Robins and McEvoy, 1987) found that behavioural problems before the age of 15 years predicted PTSD in the event of trauma. The indices used in the scoring overlap with DSM-IV diagnosis for antisocial personality disorder. It is interesting to note that the indices cited are also commonly seen in young people who suffer trauma as children, often in the form of physical and sexual abuse: e.g. running away from home, early sexual experience and academic underachievement. It may be that the survey has tapped the effect of early experience of trauma predicting future vulnerability to trauma.

Family history of psychiatric disorder has been implicated in the development of PTSD by two studies. Davidson, Swartz and Storck (1985), and McFarlane (1988) both found that over half of their samples of PTSD victims had a family history of psychiatric problems.

It is likely that the way these factors operate is through their effect on the coping or cognitive style of the individual. In dealing with problems, active coping has been identified as more adaptive than passive coping and avoidance. Passive copers and avoiders have been found to suffer higher levels of distress in response to traumatic events (see McFarlane, 1988).

Social support, in particular from someone in the role of confidant and from a spouse, has been found to exert a buffering effect in relation to stress and a direct effect on psychological well-being (Brown and Harris, 1978; Turnbull, 1988). Additionally, the importance of organisational personnel has been demonstrated by Lawrence, Dickson, Leather and Beale (1996) in relation to workplace violence. Isolated individuals are more vulnerable to the effects of stressful situations, particularly violent incidents which threaten personal security, and where the person is fearful of being alone. Support can take many forms, from informal contacts through to counselling and therapy. Whatever the source and nature of support, the role of appraisal (i.e. whether or not they perceive support as available or useful) is important if there is to be a protective effect.

Thus the degree of reaction experienced is largely determined by individuals' own perceptions of the situation. This will be influenced by their previous history and by their current cognitive style and coping mechanisms. It may be difficult to help the victim; however, in times of crisis constructs can become more fluid and amenable to change. When individuals are forced to re-evaluate their views, colleagues and employers may be in the best position to help the person make life changes to overcome the trauma they have faced.

Helping the victim become a survivor

The process of helping people recover from trauma should involve all levels of organisations, through an integrated organisational approach to the problem of violence. The importance of appraisal is important. If the individual perceives the organisation as taking the issue of violence seriously, through policies and procedures, they are likely to feel more supported than if no such policy is in place. However, policies must be backed up with action and with the development of a culture which demonstrates to staff that their safety is important and that anyone who is assaulted is cared for.

The process of helping the victim through the incident should have begun long before it happened, by preparing staff for the possibility of being assaulted. Staff training should include information, supported by leaflets, outlining possible reactions to violence and sources of appropriate help. If staff do not understand what is happening to them, they may perceive their reactions as unusual, and be afraid to reveal their symptoms at an early stage. Normalisation of their responses to an extreme situation can do much to reassure them.

Self-help

If you have been the victim of an assault, there are a number of things you can do to help yourself. The key to recovery is communication about what happened, how you feel and what help you want. The first step is to tell someone what has happened, particularly if it was not witnessed. Accept the help your colleagues offer, and take time out, even if you feel 'high' and want to go on working. If you need medical attention, get it. If a trusted colleague offers to take you home, allow them to do so; you may not be fit to drive yourself. If this has not been offered, and you would like it, then *ask*. Other people may be unsure what help you would like; so tell them. Allow yourself to be upset, if that is how you feel. Perhaps it is embarrassing to do so at work, but make sure someone knows how you feel inside. Talking will help you to make sense of it. Treat yourself gently. It is important to get the right balance between having the rest you need and returning to your normal routine.

The return to work can trigger memories of what happened and you may feel anxious. It is helpful to try to go on as usual, but be aware of how you feel and if it is too difficult, then tell someone. The memories may stay for some time. You are the only one who really knows how this has affected you. Other people may guess about how you feel, but they are not mind readers. Some people need extra support, and if your symptoms become very difficult to cope with, there are people who can help. If your organisation does not provide counselling services, you can ask your GP to refer you to your local clinical psychology department.

You may also wish to seek advice about prosecuting your assailant. Your employer may help with this, or your union or staff organisation can offer advice.

Helping a colleague

Colleagues are often at a loss to know what to do for the best, and staff can be aided in this by having pre-incident information.

If a colleague has been assaulted, there are a number of things that you can do to help. If you are the first on the scene, you may need to alert your manager, and perhaps the emergency services. Assuming they have had any necessary medical attention, it is helpful for someone to take them home, and perhaps stay with them until a family member arrives. They need to feel safe and comfortable, and to be able to relax. Even at this early stage, they can be assisted to regain a normal pattern of behaviour. If they are physically able, make a cup of tea together, for example. This is more helpful than you doing everything for them.

Your colleague needs to accept and understand what has happened. Recovery may take some time, but encouraging them to talk about it, and listening to them, will be an important contribution. They may be embarrassed to talk, but if you gently encourage them, by not being embarrassed to ask, you can help them to discuss it. Reassuring your colleague that it is normal to feel scared, angry, embarrassed or tearful after such an event can help them understand that they are not abnormal.

As time goes on, you can play an important role in keeping an eye on your colleague. They may take some time to recover from what happened, or they may appear to do so very quickly, but get worse some time later. If you are alert to how they are getting on at work, you are in a good position to suggest they ask for help, if things are not going well.

You also have a role to help your colleague explore the way forward for the future. There may be changes that you think could prevent such an incident happening again, which you could tell your manager about. Thinking about how to go forward from the incident is helpful, not just for your colleague, but also for you and your co-workers.

While you are helping your colleague, be aware of your own feelings. You may feel frightened about the possibility of being in a similar situation. It may have been a shock for you to have this happen at work. Be gentle with yourself too, and seek further help for yourself if you need it.

The role of the organisation

The response of the organisation to an assault on an employee is vital. Managers may be in a difficult position with regard to such events if they have an investigatory role which confounds their attempts to support staff. However, some of the complaints of feeling 'let down', which staff frequently make after assault, could be remedied. The following two examples illustrate this graphically:

Harry was a middle-aged man working as an inspector for a public utility. He was called to a house to investigate a complaint. The female householder accompanied him upstairs to inspect an appliance. He could find little wrong, but she insisted that he repair it. He explained that he was not allowed to do so and she became abusive, refusing to let him leave until a repair had been completed. Harry's only escape was to physically manoeuvre the woman out of his way. Meanwhile she hurled abuse at him and physically tried to prevent him from leaving. Badly shaken, he managed to reach his van and called the office, only to be told no-one was available. Eventually a manager came out to the house and went to see the householder. When he came out, he told Harry that he could not understand what the fuss was about, as the woman had been pleasant to him.

Such a response would not encourage staff members to report future incidents. Additionally, Harry was not helped by the reaction of his male colleagues who thought it a great joke that a woman had taken him prisoner.

Jane and her sister both worked for a local authority. Jane was sexually assaulted in the workplace, by a male colleague, and was sent home. No-one informed her sister about the assault. Jane travelled home alone – on the same bus as her assailant!

The mistakes inherent in these examples might seem obvious, but both situations did actually occur. Failing to meet the needs of staff who have been assaulted can lead to lowering of morale amongst the whole work group. Yet training and support are still lacking in many vulnerable work situations.

Lyons, La Valle and Grimwood (1995) report a study of 791 social workers; 92% had suffered verbal abuse from clients and 32% had suffered physical violence. Although they reported receiving support from colleagues, 41% of those verbally or physically assaulted said they had not received any support from their manager. A significant association was found between lack of management support and the decision or intention to change job or leave social work altogether. Just 10% of social workers supported by their manager after violent attack said that they had seriously considered leaving social work, whereas more than double that percentage (23%) of those receiving no management support intended to leave.

Where organisations do provide support, retention of staff is likely to be less of a problem. Lawrence *et al.* (1996) found that high levels of perceived support from area managers resulted in an increase in job satisfaction and organisational commitment in a sample of licensees.

Making the right moves

Organisations can do much to combat the negative effect of violent incidents by using them as opportunities to show how much staff are valued, through giving good and appropriate support. In addition, lessons learned from incidents should inform future practice and procedures to reduce the risk of violence occurring again.

As part of the integrated organisational approach to the problem of violence, the organisation should have procedures in place whereby assaulted individuals are cared for in the immediate and the longer-term aftermath. These procedures should include:

1   Immediate comfort and support. The immediate concern should be the safety and physical well-being of the victim. The manager should ensure that the assailant is no longer in the workplace and that no staff are at further risk. If necessary, the emergency services should be called and medical attention should be sought, if required.

Peers can do much in the immediate aftermath to provide comfort and support, but there should be an expression of management support and understanding as soon as possible. In Harry's case this was not apparent. Apparent lack of interest on the part of managers can result in the victim feeling more angry with the management than with the assailant.

Victims' families should be prepared to receive them home or, if the victim lives alone, some support should be contacted. It is helpful if a work colleague is permitted to take the victim home, and wait there until other support arrives.

2   Routine and sympathetic debriefing should take place once the victim has got over the initial shock of what has happened. This does not mean psychological debriefing, which will be described later, but simply spending time hearing from the victim what happened. Where a disciplinary investigation is necessary, this should be carried out by a different manager, if possible.

3   Information should be given to victims about the reactions they might expect in themselves after an assault, and about how they can access appropriate help. Providing this information again at the time of an incident reassures staff by normalising experiences and by giving guidelines on how to care for themselves and how to seek further help.

4   Access to specialist help from a trained counsellor should be facilitated by the organisation. Larger organisations can set up their own counselling service, while smaller organisations may be able to purchase counselling services jointly. Where this is not possible, staff should be given information on local NHS provision, and be made aware of how to access clinical psychological and psychiatric help through their general practitioner.

5   Psychological debriefing can be particularly relevant where a group of staff has been involved or affected by an incident. This usually requires an external facilitator as the necessary skills are unlikely to exist within most organisations.

Psychological debriefing

Psychological debriefing is a specific form of crisis intervention employed with groups of people who have experienced a traumatic event together. It is useful when such a group is involved in a major incident or when a group of staff have witnessed the severe assault of another staff member. The process has specific aims and should not be seen as a form of counselling or group therapy. It takes the form of a single session which is usually held around seventy-two hours after the incident has taken place. The main objective is to reduce the likely psychological impact on the people who attend the session by helping them understand their own responses. Dyregrov (1989) has shown that debriefing can prevent the development of adverse reactions through increasing the individual's sense of control. The debrief can be useful as a way of identifying those who might need to access further help (Mitchell and Everly, 1993). It must not be seen as an operational debrief or part of an inquiry.

There are various models of debriefing which all follow a structured format. The following illustrates Mitchell's (1983) approach. For others see Dyregrov (1989) and Raphael (1986). Debriefing involves seven clear phases:

1   *Introductory phase* which sets up the process by which the debriefing will work, including complete confidentiality.

2   *Fact phase* in which each person at the meeting briefly describes what happened for them during the incident so that a clear picture of events can be pieced together.
3   *Thought phase* during which people describe their thoughts as the event unfolded, and the decisions they made at the time.
4   *Reaction phase* in which the leader asks participants about their feelings; sharing these helps establish the normality of reactions.
5   *Symptom phase* in which participants describe in detail the symptoms they experienced at the time and afterwards.
6   *Preparation phase* during which the facilitator draws together the reactions of the group and outlines some of the experiences they may face in the coming weeks.
7   *Re-entry phase* which focuses on future planning and coping, in terms of peer and family support. One of the aims here is to encourage support between members of the group.

Specialist counselling services

The provision of specialist counselling services to employees forms an important part of the organisational response to the problems engendered by violence at work. However, setting up such a service must be handled with the greatest of care and the sensitivities of the workforce must be taken into account. Staff may resist using the service due to the stigma attached to the experience of symptoms. The provision of counselling services must be seen as part of an organisational culture in which staff are not expected to tolerate violence as 'part of the job', and in which anyone suffering the effects of aggression is respected. Utilising the service must be seen as a positive way of moving on after incidents, not as something which one is ashamed to admit.

Hodgkinson and Stewart (1991) suggest a range of characteristics which should be present in services provided for the victims of major disasters. Most are relevant to the individual suffering from violence at work.

1   *Credibility*: Those providing the service should be credible, in terms both of their training and qualifications to practise and of their knowledge of the organisation and the problem of violence within it. The purpose and process of counselling must be clearly explained, so that the victim understands that the service offered will be of help to them.
2   *Acceptability*: The service should be offered in a way that reinforces the culture of respecting the individual. The physical environment in which it takes place should be suitable, and choices should be offered to the victim, for example, regarding the gender of counsellor they see; this is particularly important in the case of sexual assault.
3   *Accessibility*: The service should be accessible to staff in terms of both geography and time off work to attend. It must be easy for staff to make

contact with the service in a confidential manner, if they wish, without having to go through a third party, particularly not line management.

4   *Proactivity*: The service should be well advertised and should seek out any potential clients, who have been reported as being involved in an incident, in a gentle and appropriate manner.

5   *Continuity*: The service should provide access to the same counsellor until the client has been discharged.

6   *Terminability*: The counselling sessions should be seen as having an end point at some time in the future, to emphasise to the client that they will recover and move on. Clients should also be made aware that they can choose to end the relationship at any time.

7   *Confidentiality*: This is vital in any counselling relationship, but it becomes even more significant within this type of service. Ensuring total confidentiality for staff has implications for accessibility and for the acceptability of the counselling setting. Staff may prefer to be seen away from the worksite so that colleagues are not aware that they are being seen. As far as possible this should be respected in the commissioning plan. It takes time to build a culture where accessing such a service holds no stigma.

Those who exhibit symptoms of PTSD require specialised psychological intervention. If the organisation does not provide such interventions as part of the counselling service, referral to local mental health services will be necessary. The cognitive behavioural therapy approach has been found to be particularly useful (Saigh, 1992). Where concurrent substance abuse or depression occurs, referral to appropriate services is vital.

Conclusion

The experience of violence at work can have damaging and lasting effects for individuals, work groups and organisations. However, if the aftermath of violent incidents is handled well, the individual and the organisation both benefit. Appropriate responses by the organisation in the days and weeks after the incident and the provision of appropriate specialist services are both vital. However, it is important for managers to be sensitive to the development of a culture in which staff feel able both to make use of such services and to admit to having a need for them. This begins with creating a culture where they can admit to an incident having occurred in the first place. To create such a culture, organisations require policies incorporating safety-conscious procedures, backed up by the resources required to employ them. Violence must be seen as a common problem to be tackled at all levels of the organisation, as must the scapegoating of staff who may be unlucky enough to suffer its consequences.

References

American Psychiatric Association (1994) *Diagnostic and Statistical Manual of Mental Disorders: DSM-IV*, Revised 4th Edition, Washington DC: American Psychological Association.

Bamber, M. (1992) 'Debriefing victims of violence', *Occupational Health*, April, 115–117.

Brown, G. W. and Harris, T. O. (1978) *The Social Origins of Depression: A Study of Psychiatric Disorder in Women*, London: Tavistock.

Davidson, J., Swartz, M. and Storck, M. (1985) 'A diagnostic and family study of post-traumatic stress disorder', *American Journal of Psychiatry*, 142, 90–93.

Dyregrov, A. (1989) 'Caring for helpers in disaster situations: psychological debriefing', *Disaster Management*, 2, 25–30.

Eysenck, H. J. (1976) 'The learning theory model of neurosis – a new approach', *Behaviour Research and Therapy*, 14, 251–267.

Fullilove, M. T., Fullilove, R. E., Smith, M. and Winkler, K. (1993) 'Violence, trauma and post-traumatic stress disorder among women drug users', *Journal of Traumatic Stress*, 6, 533–543.

Helzer, J. E., Robins, L. N. and McEnvoy, L. (1987) 'Post-traumatic stress disorder in the general population: findings of the Epidemiological Catchment Area Survey New England', *Journal of Medicine*, 317, 1,630–1,634.

Hodgkinson, P. E. and Stewart, M. (1991) *Coping with Catastrophe: A Handbook of Disaster Management*, London: Routledge.

Janoff-Bulman, R. and Frieze, R. (1983) 'A theoretical perspective for understanding reactions to victimisation', *Journal of Social Issues*, 39, 1–17.

Kilpatrick, D., Saunders, B., Amick-McMullan, A., *et al.* (1989) 'Victim and crime factors associated with the development of crime-related post-traumatic stress disorder', *Behaviour Therapy*, 20, 199–214.

Lawrence, C., Dickson, R., Leather, P. and Beale, D. (1996) 'The mediation of support from the first line manager in the relationship between fear and violence and well-being and job outcome measures: a case study', *Proceedings from British Psychological Society Occupational Psychology Conference*, Eastbourne, 3–5 Jan.

Lyons, K., La Valle, I. and Grimwood, C. (1995) 'Career patterns of qualified social workers: discussion of a recent survey', *British Journal of Social Work*, 25(2), 173–190.

Mackay, C. (1994) 'Violence to health care professionals: a health and safety perspective', in T. Wykes (ed.) *Violence and Health Care Professionals*, London: Chapman and Hall.

McFarlane, A. C. (1988) 'The aetiology of post-traumatic stress disorders following a natural disaster', *British Journal of Psychiatry*, 152, 116–121.

Mitchell, J. T. (1983) 'When disaster strikes: the critical incident stress debriefing process' *Journal of Emergency Medical Services*, 8, 36–39.

Mitchell, J. T. and Everly, G. S. (1993) *Critical Incident Stress Debriefing: An Operations Manual for the Prevention of Traumatic Stress among Emergency Service and Disaster Workers*, Ellicot City, US: Chevron Publishing Corporation.

Ochberg, F. (1988) *Post-Traumatic Therapy and the Victims of Violence*, New York: Brunner Mazel.

Raphael, B. (1986) *When Disaster Strikes: A Handbook for the Caring Professions*, London: Unwin Hyman.

Saigh, P. A. (ed.) (1992) *Post Traumatic Stress Disorder: A Behavioural Approach to Assessment and Treatment*, New York: Macmillan.

Scott, M. J. and Stradling, S. C. (1992) *Counselling for Post-Traumatic Stress Disorder*, London: Sage Publications.

Shepherd, J. P., Levers, B. G. H., Preston, M., *et al.* (1990) 'Psychological distress after assaults and accidents', *British Medical Journal*, 310, 849–850.

Turnbull, C. A. (1988) 'Stress and social support: the well-being of non-working mothers from a disadvantaged area', unpublished PhD thesis, University of Nottingham.

Wykes, T. (ed.) (1994) *Violence and Health Care Professionals*, London: Chapman and Hall.

5 Monitoring violent incidents

Diane Beale

Introduction

Guidelines for organisations in dealing with violence to staff invariably recommend the recording of all incidents of violence. This would appear to be a simple process, but, in practice, it requires careful design and planning to create and sustain an effective system. Further, it must not be seen as an independent system but as an integral part of an overall organisational strategy for monitoring and tackling violence. This chapter describes the benefits of an efficient system of monitoring violent incidents and suggests points to consider in setting up and running such a system. It is illustrated by reference to the Keeping Pubs Peaceful Incident Reporting System which has run within Allied Domecq Retailing (ADR), and in collaboration with the Centre for Organizational Health and Development at the University of Nottingham, since 1987, to monitor incidents of violence within its public houses. Experience in co-ordinating this system has indicated successful strategies, limitations, problem areas and pitfalls. How the reporting system fits into the overall strategy for tackling violence is outlined in Chapter 8.

In the past it has been unclear whether there was a legal duty to report violent incidents at work to the Health and Safety Executive, or local authorities, under the Reporting of Injuries, Diseases and Dangerous Occurrences Regulations 1985, as there was debate as to whether 'accidents' included violent incidents. Consequently, there is a lack of statistical information, at national level, regarding violence at work. Even under the revised Reporting of Injuries, Diseases and Dangerous Occurrences Regulations 1995 (RIDDOR 95), violent incidents involving people at work have to be reported only if they (1) cause death or certain types of major injury to people at work, (2) result in them staying in hospital for more than twenty-four hours or being absent from work for more than three consecutive days or (3) cause other people to be taken from the scene to hospital. In these regulations a violent incident is not specified as one of the categories of dangerous occurrence that requires to be reported whether or not injury resulted. In other words, the revised regulations have confirmed violence as a health and safety issue but the duty to report is dependent on the outcome of the incident rather than its nature.

While the introduction of the revised regulations has acted as a spur to organisations to establish systems for reporting and recording violent incidents, it would be a wasted opportunity if they only reported and recorded internally those incidents that were required to be reported externally, as discussed by Beale, Cox and Leather (1996). Most compellingly, reporting systems in organisations provide the means by which staff summon emergency and longer-term help from the management to deal with difficult situations. Such situations will not necessarily be reportable under RIDDOR 95; however, records of all such incidents are valuable as learning tools for organisations and as evidence of action taken by management. Further, it must be incumbent upon an employer to record all violent, or potentially violent, incidents in order to fulfil the requirements under the Management of Health and Safety Regulations (Health and Safety Executive, 1992) to 'make a suitable and sufficient assessment of the risks to the health and safety of his employees to which they are exposed whilst they are at work'. Work-related violence is increasingly being regarded as a vital concern for management as the costs, both personal and commercial, become more evident (Bulatao and VandenBos, 1996; Health and Safety Executive, 1993b). Consequently, the introduction or remodelling of a reporting system must be accompanied by a determination on the part of management at all levels to tackle the sources of violence and to give support to those who experience it.

The guidance documents for dealing with violence to staff, listed in Appendix 1, overwhelmingly recommend the recording of incidents of violence, but few give useful information about running an effective system. Those which do give more detailed consideration of reporting systems include the Health Services Advisory Committee (1997) *Violence and Aggression to Staff in Health Services*; Health and Safety Executive (1995) *Preventing Violence to Retail Staff*; Education Services Advisory Committee (1990) *Violence to Staff in the Education Sector*; Department of Health and Social Security (1988) *Violence to Staff*. Poyner and Warne (1988) include case studies which have some details of the recording systems and analyses used. The Health Services Advisory Committee (1986) *Guidance on the Recording of Accidents and Incidents in the Health Services* gives useful information about accident-reporting systems which is equally applicable to the reporting of violent incidents.

The monitoring of violence

In order to monitor the violence experienced within an organisation, and therefore assist in evaluating the extent of the risk involved, it is necessary to obtain both quantitative measures of the frequency of incidents and qualitative information about the types of incidents, the circumstances in which the incidents occurred and how the incidents progressed.

Complete monitoring of violence requires:

1   initial measures of the nature, severity and extent of the problem, employees' attitudes to violence, how much they feel at risk and how much support they feel they receive,

2   an on-going means of collecting more detailed information about individual incidents, i.e. a reporting and recording system, to learn more of the nature of incidents and to identify common factors, and

3   periodic studies to update the initial findings, identify trends and changes, to validate the results from the reporting system and to provide a measure of under-reporting.

These ingredients are interdependent, each providing information for the others to optimise their effectiveness and to build up a more complete picture of the problem so that intervention strategies can be designed, implemented and evaluated. Of course, the activities of initial problem identification, the establishment of a reporting system and follow-up studies are themselves all interventions. Such activities raise awareness of the issue of violence among both employees and management; further, they indicate to employees that management is sufficiently concerned to investigate and monitor the problem. It is important that the methods and the manner in which these operations are carried out help employees to see the interventions as positive and encouraging, rather than threatening. This will also depend largely on the underlying organisational culture.

Useful information from reporting systems

The strength of reporting systems is that they can highlight particular features of incidents which occur frequently and should be investigated further with a view to reducing the associated risks. Moreover, particular occurrences which happen infrequently but have very serious consequences can be brought to the attention of management and employees in general. The introduction of a reporting system which records only the outcome of incidents and little about the incident as a process wastes a valuable learning resource.

A few examples of the types of result that the ADR reporting system provides are illustrated here in Figures 5.1 to 5.3, which are based on a summary report to the Company (Beale, Lawrence, Leather and Cox, 1995).

Features of the general setting can be examined, such as the type of premises, the location and degree of crowding when incidents occurred. Profiles of aggressors can be built up in terms of, for example, sex, age and type of customer or staff and correlated with type of incident. Simple frequency information, concerning days of the week and times of the day, can indicate, or confirm, times of highest risk. For example, Figure 5.1 shows that, in this case, one-third of incidents occurring around closing time.

Not only common events but also events of low frequency can be identified. These can be important to indicate the types of event which, although

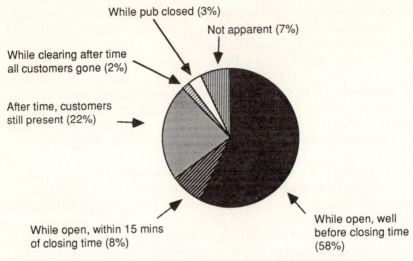

While pub closed (3%)

Not apparent (7%)

While clearing after time
all customers gone (2%)

After time, customers
still present (22%)

While open, within 15 mins
of closing time (8%)

While open, well
before closing time
(58%)

Figure 5.1 The timing of incidents in relation to closing time

they may attract considerable media attention, are not a major problem or
are declining in frequency. Conversely, they can be a warning of events that
may not be common but may be very serious when they do occur.

Every violent incident is a *process* which has many possible contributing
factors and which develops over time. It is impossible through a reporting
system to ascertain every detail for every incident. However, simply 'pigeon
holing' cases into 'types' gives oversimplified, and possibly misleading,
results which are of very limited use. Each reporting system has to find a
compromise on detail. Content analysis of the early incidents reported in
the ADR system produced a simple classification of incidents which was
soon found to be inadequate as the number and range of incidents grew.
A large amount of information was being lost. The present approach taken
is to note down as many details as possible from the description of the incident and then to group them into initiation, development, culmination and
ending. In this way the recording system mirrors the view of an incident as a
dynamic and unfolding process.

Detailed information on each stage is given in the summary reports to
emphasise the fact that so many different factors may be involved. It is
necessary to alert management and licensees to the very wide range of
behaviours and events that have led to incidents, to the different ways that
incidents have been handled and to some of the consequences. These are
given to enable licensees to be trained in methods to reduce the risk of
violence occurring, to know methods of resolving conflict and to handle the
aftermath of any incidents.

The events that initiated the reported violent incidents are summarised in
Figure 5.2. An important finding, for example, is the comparatively small
proportion of reported incidents that were obviously pre-planned, such as

armed robberies. Most incidents started as the type of customer misbehaviour or argument that is encountered by pub staff on a regular basis. This should be used to alert licensees and management to the fact that there is much more risk of injury to staff from customer behaviour than from planned criminal activity (Beale, Dickson, Leather and Cox, 1992).

Looking at common events that happened at the climax of incidents provides information vital for senior and line management to (1) appreciate the type of incidents and dangers that their staff are facing, for instance that over half of the reported incidents involved a physical attack on members of staff, and (2) provide appropriate support. Further, it provides input for staff training by indicating particular danger points in a situation, such as the ejection of troublemakers, staff going outside, and the possibility of continued action after the incident appeared to be over, for example, the assailant returned later or there was an attack on the outside of the pub.

Another approach which views the incident as a process utilises the techniques of sequence analysis. Logical pathway modelling analyses sequences in reported incidents in terms of (1) the problem situations, (2) the ensuing behaviours and (3) the resultant harm (Beale, Cox, Clarke, Lawrence and Leather, 1998). Such modelling reveals high probability pathways through incidents which link common initiating problems, staff interventions, physical attacks, injury to both staff and customers and damage to property. It also identifies the stages in the development of incidents at which most such injuries and damage occur. For the ADR incidents, these are shown in Figure 5.3.

Such results can be used to alert and train staff about the danger points in incidents and to design and prioritise strategies to reduce the risks from future violence. For example, in the ADR pubs, the most common type of incident consisted of customers misbehaving in some way (such as being rowdy or stealing from the bar), a member of staff intervening then being physically attacked and sustaining physical injury. This finding provides the

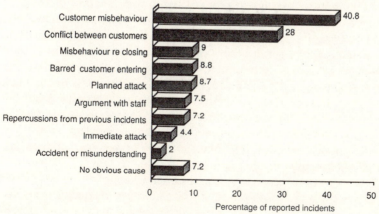

Figure 5.2 Initiation of reported incidents

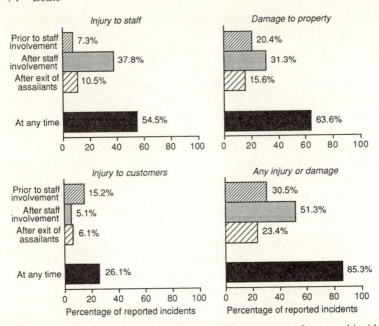

Figure 5.3 Injury and damage incurred at different stages of reported incidents

impetus for exploring in more detail (1) strategies that reduce the likelihood of customers misbehaving in the pub, (2) effective methods of staff intervention in problem situations which reduce the likelihood of them being physically attacked, (3) measures which can protect staff if they are physically attacked and (4) emergency procedures to minimise the adverse effects on staff should they be physically injured (Leather, Lawrence, Beale and Maxwell, 1996). Such detailed methods of analysis give a more useful picture of the types of incident that are occurring within an organisation.

It is possible to correlate outcome measures, such as the number and severity of injuries or damage to property, with other features of the incidents, such as the number of assailants or whether weapons were involved. In the ADR system a simple measure was introduced to enable reporting licensees to indicate how serious they rated the incident to be. Licensees took a large number of factors into account. As expected, the outcome in terms of injury was seen to have a significant effect on the seriousness rating, but a variety of other factors were also significant and yet more were evident from licensees' comments. This indicates that all management personnel need to be aware that employees may consider a particular incident to be very serious, even though there was little physical injury or damage, and that staff may be psychologically affected and may need more sympathetic support than at first sight seems necessary, as discussed in Chapter 4.

Requests for management action, from employees reporting incidents, can be used to provide evidence for modifying the behaviour of both employees and management, for example, in drawing up a check list of actions for line managers and security staff to take after an incident, and indicating actions or attitudes that are not helpful.

Limitations of reporting systems

It has to be recognised that a detailed reporting system can take years to establish with any reliability. Results taken over a short time period are likely to be unrepresentative, giving undue importance to some features or types of incidents while missing other important details. Reporting systems also suffer from a range of other limitations which demand that they should not be used alone in determining the extent or nature of violence or the assessment of risk.

Amount of detail

There will always be a conflict between the amount of information that is required for proper assessment of incidents by analysts and the amount of time that employees can afford to spend completing reports. A form that takes too long to complete will militate against less serious incidents being reported. A compromise has to be reached. Additionally, it has to be acknowledged that reports of incidents may contain only the employee's version of events and therefore they are not completely objective. However, other methods of gathering information, such as security videos and police records, have different drawbacks, particularly for gaining information on large numbers of incidents (Beale *et al.*, 1998).

Information on psychological harm

The normal time scale for the reporting of incidents does not allow for a valid assessment of the consequent psychological harm. While physical injury is normally obvious within a short time, psychological harm, in the form of post-trauma reactions and, more particularly, post-traumatic stress disorder (Choy and de Bosset, 1992), may not be evident until some considerable time later. This time delay undoubtedly results in the loss of information about this type of outcome in reporting systems. It is also likely that a 'macho' organisational culture could make people reluctant to admit to psychological problems.

In addition, it is becoming increasingly recognised that repeated exposure to abuse, threats and minor acts of aggression can have a cumulative effect and may lead to prolonged duress stress disorder (Scott and Stradling, 1994). However, the individual acts of violence may be considered too minor to report and the threat to the psychological well-being of the employees goes unrecognised. Particular reporting strategies may be required for jobs where such exposure occurs, as discussed later.

Under-reporting

It is well established in the literature that reporting of both accidents and violent incidents at work suffers from substantial under-reporting, (e.g. Painter, 1987). Both the initial study for ADR (Hillas, Cox and Higgins, 1988) and the follow-up study (Dickson, Leather, Beale and Cox, 1994) bore this out; in the 1994 study, around 61% of licensees said they had not reported incidents which had occurred. In general, the most common reasons cited were that incidents were not considered serious enough, that no injuries occurred, that there was nothing the employing organisation could (or would) do or that it was too time consuming to report. This last reason would be particularly applicable to occupations where there is a high frequency of 'low level' violence.

Employees have to see a 'pay-off' in order to take the time and trouble to report an incident; this pay-off is obvious for incidents where there has been injury or damage requiring repairs or time off work or where the police are involved and legal action may follow. Other incidents may have been equally upsetting for employees or customers but have had little physical outcome and require less obvious management action. Reporting of such incidents may elicit little in the way of immediate action or support from management. Further, the organisational culture may be such as to cause employees to expect that reporting will produce a negative reaction, for example, in questioning their professional competence.

Painter (1987) noted that employees within public services exercise a high level of tolerance towards those who abuse them at work, citing such factors as unemployment, ill-health, poverty, cuts in services, staff shortages and long queues as mitigating factors. Similarly, there is evidence from the ADR incident reports that pub staff make allowance for the effects of alcohol, for special occasions, family circumstance or known character. Additionally, in service industries, employees might feel that taking further action would lose customers, particularly in areas with close-knit communities and strong family ties. In other words, they may accept a certain amount of violence as 'part of the job'.

Perceptions of violence

People's ideas about, and tolerance of, violent behaviour vary widely. Some regard abuse and shouting as violence while, at the other extreme, some don't regard fighting as violence unless it involves a weapon or more than two people (Dickson *et al.*, 1994). Such differences of opinion inevitably affect employees' decisions about whether to report a particular situation. Similarly, what they think their managers will regard as violence will also affect their decision to report.

Reporting phenomena

Many apparent trends seen in reporting of incidents may not reflect trends in the actual occurrence. Factors which were seen to affect the number of incidents reported within ADR included awareness campaigns, widespread training about violence, changes in organisational structure, changes of personnel and changes of policy. Other factors which might affect reporting are increased media coverage of similar problems, civil and criminal court proceedings and changes in legislation.

Information on successful strategies

Reporting systems only obtain information on situations where there has been a breakdown in acceptable behaviour and violence has resulted. They fail, in general, to gather information about situations which were potentially dangerous but were handled successfully and defused without violent outcome. Information of this type is essential in the design of organisational intervention strategies. Similar considerations apply in the reporting of accidents where the reporting of 'near misses' gives insight into how accidents might occur and how they might successfully be avoided (Van der Schaaf, Lucas and Hale, 1991).

Within the ADR system reporting of the successful handling of situations has been encouraged through information leaflets sent to licensees and through training, but few cases have actually come through the reporting system. This type of information is much more likely to be obtained in discussion with licensees, particularly during violence related training courses.

Introducing reporting systems

The establishment of a reporting system requires careful planning along the lines of the control cycle shown in Figure 5.4 (adapted from Cox and Cox, 1993).

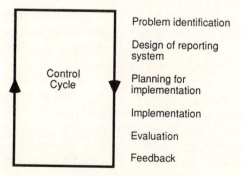

Control Cycle

Problem identification

Design of reporting system

Planning for implementation

Implementation

Evaluation

Feedback

Figure 5.4 Control cycle for a reporting system

Problem identification: initial research

It is essential that as accurate a picture as possible of the nature of the problem, the work context and the organisational structure and culture is obtained before embarking upon the design of a reporting system. Assumptions from a few case studies or hearsay may lead to the setting up of a system that is ineffective in its operation or which misses important information. Time needs to be spent at this stage in examining previous records and relevant literature, in carrying out in-depth interviews with relevant personnel and in conducting large-scale surveys of employees, as outlined in Chapter 8.

Design of a reporting system

It is important throughout the design of a system to ensure that it is acceptable both to those employees who will have to report and to those who will have to operate the system, to management and to unions. Consultation, negotiation and dissemination of information at all stages is essential, otherwise the system may founder through lack of co-operation. Employees need to be reassured that the reports of incidents will be used positively to help solve their problems, not negatively as evidence about their ability to do their job. As one security manager remarked 'We need to let them know it's safe to report incidents.' It is also important that people can be confident that details of incidents are held securely and confidentially. Organisations must not be so concerned with covering themselves legally that they don't provide a user-friendly reporting service which actually benefits their workers.

The detailed objectives of reporting systems will vary across organisations and between different working groups; they must be determined from the outset so that they can be incorporated into the design. Most reporting systems have to fulfil two basic functions. First, they must be the means by which staff summon emergency help from their employing organisation. Second, they must provide records of the incidents for the organisation both to retain and to submit to the relevant body to fulfil legal requirements, i.e. the HSE or the local authority, in the UK. One of the pitfalls in setting up systems is that these two functions are dealt with separately by different departments and the systems set up by each detract from the other rather than complementing each other. An integrated system is essential, and it should be sufficiently robust that, whoever within that system is the first to be contacted by the employee, the information should get through the system and relevant help be provided. Employees who have just experienced a violent incident should not be expected to have to contact more than one department.

The system must consist of two stages. The first requires a very brief report from the employee and provides immediate help from the organisation. The second, which should follow automatically from the first, requires a more extensive report so that the organisation can record a detailed account of the incident and provide longer-term help. It is important also to provide direct access to the second stage to allow reporting of incidents which did not require management assistance at the time but that employees think management should know about.

The system must be straightforward to operate, must be accessible to those needing to report and must demonstrate some advantages for people to justify the time spent on reporting. This is particularly important for less serious incidents. Serious incidents will come to light through many channels; it is the more numerous but less obvious incidents, unrecognised by management, which need to be reported routinely in order to get a true picture of violence within the working environment of the organisation.

In situations where there is a high frequency of minor incidents, such as verbal abuse or pushing, it may not be feasible, in terms of time, for staff to report *all* incidents in detail. Other strategies are required. It might be appropriate periodically to have a 'reporting week', for example, when employees are requested to report all such incidents. High levels of reporting may be maintained over a limited period and thus give a truer picture of the violence faced by employees on a day-to-day basis. Alternatively, staff could keep an incident diary, consisting of a simple sheet for each day which details possible types of incident. Staff simply tick off any incidents that occur that day. This strategy loses detail, but should give a more accurate idea of the number of problems staff have to face.

The reporting instrument

The main reporting instrument is the set of questions answered by an employee at the second stage of the system and kept as a record by the organisation. It is likely to be held as a report form on paper, but may be held as a computer file or in some other medium. The requirements for a reporting instrument may include that it elicits all the hard factual information necessary, that it prompts further descriptive information about how the incident occurred as well as the outcome, and that it allows staff to make comments or requests to management. Additionally, it must be easily understood and not too long or cumbersome.

The reporting instrument will represent a balance between the amount of information required for useful analysis and the time available for employees to spend on reporting. If it is too long employees will not bother to report less serious incidents. It is rarely possible to include the sophisticated measures that might be used in a one-off questionnaire. Simplicity is vital, particularly if there is the possibility that information may sometimes have to be collected over the telephone.

Although the minimum amount of information that needs to be recorded is now determined by the Reporting of Injuries, Diseases and Dangerous Occurrences Regulations 1995, in practice the questions need to be tailored not only to the industry in which they are to be used but perhaps also to particular working groups. Combined forms for recording both violent incidents and accidents are unlikely to be satisfactory as the main reporting instrument, being either so general that they elicit only superficial information or difficult to fill in because many of the questions do not apply to the particular situation.

The layout of the form must be clear and uncluttered and the questions should follow in a logical sequence, probably grouped into a number of distinct sections. Questions should be unambiguous, easily understood and straightforward to answer. Care needs to be taken to allow enough space for descriptive answers; too small a space will encourage too brief a description. Piloting of the report form is essential to pinpoint any problems in this area.

The reporting instrument should include a mixture of open and closed questions. Closed questions are required for very specific details such as time, location, number of assailants, injury, damage, whether the police attended, etc. Tick boxes can be used to indicate a choice of answers. Open questions are needed to get less predictable details, for example to ask for a description of the incident. This may be helped by prompts such as 'What were the circumstances leading up to the incident?'; 'What was the employee doing at the time?'; 'What happened during the incident?'; 'What brought the incident to an end?' These encourage a description of how the incident progressed, in terms of what the initial problem was, how matters escalated, what triggered any violent action, how the situation was resolved, what the consequences were, etc. Further open questions should be used to encourage employees to make comments about the incident, to indicate management action they would like to have seen and to suggest ways of preventing further incidents.

Distribution, completion and collection

People reporting violent incidents have undergone traumatic experiences of varying severity and may well be emotionally upset. Having to recount details of the incident may add to their distress. It is important, therefore, that there are people available to assist them in completing the form who are aware of, and sensitive to, their needs.

Whether the reporting instrument is on paper or is on a computer system will depend on the organisational structure and the technology available. Where staff routinely work with terminals and where information can be held securely and confidentially, it may be less time consuming to report directly on to a computer-based system. The danger is, however, that this can be very impersonal and may restrict the provision of emotional support that may be necessary during completion of the form. An example of a computer-based accident reporting system, the Bath System, is described by the Health Services Advisory Committee (1986).

Methods of distribution and completion will depend on the geographical spread of employees and the types of job they do, as well as on existing management structures and responsibilities. In general, it is preferable to appoint one or more 'facilitators' in a company or division to be responsible for the distribution, completion and collection of the incident report forms. Whether facilitators are security, health and safety or personnel staff, or are independent of other departments, will depend on the existing structure and the culture of the organisation. Facilitators must be in a position to engender the trust of employees and be able to establish a ready means of contact. They need to have their own telephones on which to receive confidential calls and, preferably, to be able to visit the people reporting incidents to help them in completing the report form.

Facilitators require training in what the reporting system aims to achieve and how it works, in interviewing and recording techniques and in the awareness of post-trauma reactions and disorders. They also require information about obtaining further psychological help, although counselling and referral should not be part of the facilitators' role unless they are suitably qualified or undergo extensive training.

Analysis of data

The choice of methods of analysis will depend on the amount of data that is expected to be generated and the computer facilities available. Unless the number of incidents expected is very small, computer analysis is likely to be considerably more efficient than manual analysis. Many statistical and database packages are available which could be used and much will depend on the systems already in use by the organisation or any independent analysts. It is essential to ensure that all data are held securely and confidentially.

Design of the database and the coding system must be sufficiently flexible to allow for changes over time, for new information to be added and for different analyses to be carried out as further information requirements evolve. Some different types of analysis have already been discussed. Provision should also be made for rapid interrogation of the database in response to specific queries.

Dissemination of findings

The system needs to provide information to the organisation on both a proactive and a reactive basis. It requires methods of regular reporting to higher and line management, security and health and safety staff, facilitators, trainers, union representatives and employees in general. It also requires mechanisms for dealing quickly with specific issues raised by management.

Written reports of findings are indispensable as they are easily available for repeated consultation and can contain a large amount of detailed information. However, presentations may be more effective in conveying particularly important information. Presentation of statistical results must be straightforward and eye-catching while retaining scrupulous accuracy;

complex statistics will confuse most people. Bar charts and pie charts are more effective for conveying numerical data than are tables of figures. It is essential that written reports include an accessible summary of the main points; few people will have the time or inclination to read right through a long document.

The frequency of summary reports needs to be determined initially so as to keep management up to date with the progress of the system itself and then its early findings. Quarterly reports are perhaps the most appropriate at this stage. As the system becomes established main reports will probably become more widely spaced, possibly six-monthly or even annually, but with special, short reports highlighting particular findings or trends as these are revealed by the data or answer particular questions of interest to organisation personnel. Different versions of reports might be considered, each emphasising issues of interest to particular groups, such as trainers, line managers, security or health and safety personnel.

Facilitators require reports on how the system is functioning, particular problems or features to note and the use that is being made of the findings and the system as a whole. They should be encouraged and thanked for their part in sustaining the system and should be consulted for their views about the system and how it might be improved.

Important and relevant findings of the monitoring should be communicated to those employees who are directly involved in serving the public and are most likely to be affected by the problem of violence. Effective means of dissemination include initial and on-going training, trade papers, in-house newsletters and computer-based bulletin boards.

Arrangements should be made for organisation staff to get answers to specific queries about violent incidents while maintaining confidentiality. Analysts should be available to give a rapid response from the database or to carry out literature searches or mini research projects to obtain relevant information. A record of the queries should be kept to assist with evaluation of the monitoring system.

Links into training

Provision has to be made for findings from the reporting system to be incorporated into training schemes for staff at all levels. Detailed reports, including summaries of the most important points and implications of findings, should be made available to trainers so that they have up-to-date information to pass on to staff in support of the course objectives. Conversely, training courses should be used to encourage staff to report incidents.

Evaluation

After the system has been in operation and incident reports are coming in regularly, the efficacy of the system can be assessed. Included in the assessment should be the examination of the type of information obtained (Does it match that required?); the quantity of information obtained (Is it consistent with the amount expected from initial research?); the quality of information obtained (Is it accurate? Is it detailed enough?); the distribution and use of findings throughout the organisation (Are reports getting to the right people? Are they being read? Is the information being used? How is it being used?).

Assessment of the system needs to be repeated on a regular basis to take account of inevitable changes within any organisation. Changes in organisational structure may result in new divisions being created or departments disappearing, with responsibility for reporting becoming ignored. Changes in personnel may result in loss of knowledge about, or commitment to, the scheme. It is vital for those operating the system to be in close contact with management at all levels, so as to keep abreast of organisational changes, and to note the numbers and the quality of reports coming from each division of the organisation, so as to spot any reporting problems.

Modification

A reporting system should never be thought of as static but must evolve as organisations and circumstances change. However, while revision of the system is desirable to keep it up to date and responsive to the changing needs, it is counterproductive to alter things too often and cause confusion. Each alteration should be accompanied by an explanation and possibly further training for facilitators.

Once the system is operational and data is analysed, any weaknesses requiring modification of the report form should come to light. Further amendment is likely to be necessary over time as new information is required, as practice changes because of the introduction of new laws, government schemes or organisational initiatives, and as social behaviour changes, for example the more widespread use of drugs.

Experience of the system in operation may throw up procedures which are unsatisfactory, or pinpoint practices that one facilitator has used that have proved to be particularly effective. Similarly, methods of analysis may require modification. As the number of incidents reported increases, the original coding scheme derived from the initial research and the pilot scheme should be reviewed to see whether it describes the reported data adequately or whether it causes too great a loss of information. For instance, events leading up to an incident might originally have been coded into a small number of categories, but as more incidents are reported some do not fall into any of those categories and new ones need to be created. Further, the whole method of coding may require overhaul if better methods are suggested. Analysis methods should be continually reviewed to glean as much useful information as possible to feed back to employees and management.

Conclusion

A violent incident reporting system is a means of sharing information about an important problem throughout an organisation on an on-going basis; it indicates to employees that the problem is recognised by higher management and it provides a method of communication from 'front line workers' to higher management. Further, it can reveal common elements in violence which need to be identified in order to design effective intervention strategies. It provides information for each of the three levels of intervention which can be used to mitigate the effects of violence (Cox and Leather, 1994; Cox and Cox, 1993). By identifying the types of situation which most commonly precede violence, it suggests preventative strategies; by identifying actions taken by employees during the incident in attempting to end it or to reduce the severity of the outcome, and assessing the outcome of those actions, it suggests reactive strategies; and by obtaining information about the effects of violence, both physical and psychological, and by eliciting suggestions for actions from those directly involved, it suggests rehabilitative strategies.

With respect to risk assessment in light of the Management of Health and Safety at Work Regulations (Health and Safety Executive, 1992), reporting systems are invaluable in providing evidence about types of risk and characteristics of situations where the risk is greatest, in other words they are useful qualitatively. In quantitative terms, there is some measure of physical harm, but estimates of the extent of under-reporting and of psychological harm need to be gained from supplementary studies such as periodic surveys or diary studies. Risk analysis must not be based on the reporting of incidents alone; rather, it should use reporting to indicate areas of concern where further investigation is required.

References

Beale, D., Cox, T. and Leather, P. (1996) 'Work-related violence – is national reporting good enough?' *Work and Stress*, 10, 99–103.

Beale, D., Cox, T., Clarke, D., Lawrence, C. and Leather, P. (1998) 'Temporal architecture of violent incidents', *Journal of Occupational Health Psychology*, 3(1), 65–82.

Beale, D., Dickson, R., Leather, P. and Cox, T. (1992) *Ansells Managed House Incident Reports: An Analysis*, Report prepared for Ansells Limited. Nottingham: Centre for Organizational Health and Development, Department of Psychology, University of Nottingham.

Beale, D., Lawrence, C., Leather, P. and Cox, T. (1995) *Keeping Public Houses Peaceful Incident Report Forms: An Interim Analysis to December 1994*, Report TW22/95 prepared for Allied Domecq Retailing Limited. Nottingham: Centre for Organizational Health and Development, Department of Psychology, University of Nottingham.

Bulatao, E. R. and VandenBos, G. R. (1996) 'Workplace violence: its scope and the issues', in G. R. VandenBos and E. Q. Bulatao (eds) *Violence on the Job*, pp. 1–24, Washington, DC: American Psychological Association.

Choy, T. and de Bosset, F. (1992) 'Post-traumatic stress disorder: an overview', *Canadian Journal of Psychiatry*, 37, 578–583.

Cox, T. and Cox, S. (1993) *Psychosocial and Organizational Hazards at Work: Control and Monitoring.* European Occupational Health Series No. 5. Copenhagen: WHO Regional Office for Europe.

Cox, T. and Leather, P. (1994) 'The prevention of violence at work: application of a cognitive behavioural theory', in C. L. Cooper and I. T. Robertson (eds) *International Review of Industrial and Organizational Psychology*, Vol. 9, pp. 213–245, Chichester: Wiley and Sons.

Department of Health and Social Security (1988) *Violence to Staff. Report of the DHSS Advisory Committee on Violence to Staff*, London: HMSO.

Dickson, R., Leather, P., Beale, D. and Cox, T. (1994) *Working in Licensed Houses: a Study of the Licensee's Job*, Report TW20/94 prepared for Allied Domecq Retailing. Nottingham: Centre for Organizational Health and Development, Department of Psychology, University of Nottingham.

Education Services Advisory Committee (1990) *Violence to Staff in the Education Sector*, Health and Safety Commission. Sudbury, Suffolk: HSE Books.

Health and Safety Executive (1991) *Violence to Staff*, Sudbury, Suffolk: HSE Books.

—— (1992) *The Management of Health and Safety Regulations*, Sudbury, Suffolk: HSE Books.

—— (1993a) *Prevention of Violence to Staff in Banks and Building Societies*, Sudbury, Suffolk: HSE Books.

—— (1993b) *The Costs of Accidents at Work*, Health and Safety Series, HS(G)96, Sudbury, Suffolk: HSE Books..

—— (1995) *Preventing Violence to Retail Staff*, Sudbury, Suffolk: HSE Books.

Health Services Advisory Committee (1986) *Guidance on the Recording of Accidents and Incidents in the Health Services*, Health and Safety Commission. Sudbury, Suffolk: HSE Books.

—— (1987) *Violence to Staff in the Health Services*, Health and Safety Commission. HSE Books, Sudbury, Suffolk.

—— (1997) *Violence and Aggression to Staff in Health Services: Guidance on Assessment and Management*, Health and Safety Commission. HSE Books, Sudbury, Suffolk.

Hillas, S., Cox, T. and Higgins, G. (1988) *Results of the Main Questionnaire Survey*, Report TW5/88 prepared for Allied Breweries Limited. Nottingham: Centre for Organizational Health and Development, Department of Psychology, University of Nottingham.

Leather, P., Lawrence, C., Beale, D. and Maxwell, P. (1996) *Keeping Pubs Peaceful: A Trainer's Guide*, Sutton Coldfield: Maxwell and Cox Associates with Centre for Organizational Health and Development, Department of Psychology, University of Nottingham.

Painter, K. (1987) 'It's part of the job', *Employee Relations*, 9(5), 30–40.

Poyner, B. and Warne, C. (1988) *Violence to Staff: A Basis for Assessment and Prevention*, Health and Safety Executive. London: HMSO.

Reporting of Injuries, Diseases and Dangerous Occurrences Regulations 1985, Statutory Instrument 1985 No. 2023, London: HMSO.

Reporting of Injuries, Diseases and Dangerous Occurrences Regulations 1995, Statutory Instrument 1995 No. 3163, London: HMSO.

Scott, M. J. and Stradling, S. G. (1994) 'Post-traumatic stress disorder without the trauma', *British Journal of Clinical Psychology*, 33, 71–74.

Van der Schaaf, T. W., Lucas, D. A. and Hale, A. R. (1991) *Near Miss Reporting as a Safety Tool*, Oxford: Butterworth-Heinemann.

6 Organisational and environmental measures for reducing and managing work-related violence

Diane Beale, Claire Lawrence, Chris Smewing and Tom Cox

Introduction

This chapter deals predominantly with the management of work processes and the working environment to reduce the likelihood and impact of violence within the workplace, particularly that which arises from personal interactions. Such management forms an essential part of an integrated organisational approach to workplace violence and assumes that rigorous monitoring and risk assessment are undertaken (see Chapter 1). These analyses should reveal aspects of the work which place employees or others at particular risk from violent attack and can be used as a basis for developing safe procedures. Each workplace will have its own peculiar risks and management issues. It is not the aim of this chapter to cover all possible scenarios or violence-management strategies. Consideration must be given, however, to the possibility that *any* employee might be at risk from violence either inside or outside the workplace whilst carrying out their work duties. The instigators of violence could be customers (or clients), workers or outsiders, as indeed could the victims. All combinations need to be considered, although each organisation will be more prone to some types of incident than others.

The terms conflict and violence, used throughout this chapter, are distinct from each other in important ways. Conflict is not necessarily a dysfunctional interaction. Disagreement may reveal inefficient work strategies or personal difficulties for staff or customers which may be resolved by adapting the work environment and work procedures. Violence occurs when conflict situations escalate into manifest hostility or physical exhibitions of aggression, such as verbal abuse, threat or physical attack on people or property.

Reducing the risk from violence requires both preventative and reactive strategies (Cox and Leather, 1994). Cox and Cox (1993), using a health and safety framework, regard the risk from a hazard to be a function of exposure to the hazardous situation and the magnitude of the harm caused. If we apply this to violence, bearing in mind that most people have the potential to act violently given the wrong combination of circumstances, the hazard can be regarded as any individual, the hazardous situation as interpersonal conflict and the harm as including physical and psychological injury, property damage and financial cost. Thus the risk from violence can be regarded as a function of four factors:

- the frequency of conflict situations
- the duration of conflict situations
- the likelihood of the individuals involved acting in a violent manner, and
- the magnitude of the harm caused.

Preventative strategies for reducing the risk attempt to reduce both the frequency with which conflict situations occur and the likelihood of the individuals concerned reacting violently, which can be considered as a combination of the individuals' general tendency to act in a violent manner and their experiences immediately prior to, or particularly relevant to, the conflict situation. Reactive strategies attempt to resolve the conflict as quickly and satisfactorily as possible and to reduce the magnitude of harm should violence occur.

In order to devise appropriate strategies, it is necessary both to have an understanding of the factors that cause people to behave aggressively and to examine how conflict situations can arise, and escalate, in the context of normal work processes, the particular work environment and the experiences and behaviours of the people in the workplace. These factors do not operate independently of each other but are inextricably and interactively linked. The management of violence within any workplace must take account of these relationships, recognising that a series of adverse experiences can have a cumulative effect on an individual's state of mind. This assumption under-lies the model used throughout this chapter and shown in Figure 6.1.

The model acknowledges the significance of factors leading up to the conflict situation, management of that situation and the consequences of the incident. It also highlights individuals' experiences outside the workplace as well as within it. This model takes, as its starting point, the personal characteristics and experiences of the individual entering the worksite. It then proceeds to examine the interactions between the individual, the physical environment and the people within it. It focuses particularly on the social and physical antecedents of conflict. Finally, it examines possible outcomes and consequences of conflict. Each stage of the model will be considered in turn, drawing on a psychosocial model of what causes people to become aggressive or violent (Cox and Leather, 1994) to suggest particular features that organisations should take into account in order to reduce the risks. Finally, more extensive checklists of points for consideration at each stage of the model are given at the end of the chapter.

The individual

The individual in this model can be an employee, a customer or anyone who enters the site. When people come into the workplace, they bring with them

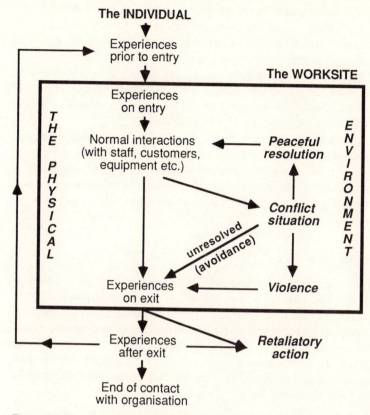

Figure 6.1 Experiences of the individual using the worksite

their own agendas, motivations and intentions resulting from their own prior experiences and personal characteristics. When designing the workplace and work procedures, it is important to consider the types of individuals likely to enter the site or use the service, particularly if they have special needs or requirements or may be accompanied by, for example, small children or carers. Further, it is appropriate to consider how to deal effectively with people who don't fit the normal customer profile. It is necessary, also, to look at the selection and deployment of staff to minimise the presence on site of people who might cause or escalate conflict.

Experiences prior to entry

Experiences immediately prior to arrival at the worksite, or particularly relevant to the organisation, may be especially influential in shaping the individual's emotional state. Some of these experiences can be anticipated from the function of the workplace itself, e.g. accident, trauma or sudden illness (accident and emergency units); legal disputes, divorce, criminal incidents (courts); financial problems (social security offices, banks, building societies); tiring journeys (airports, motorway service stations). Others may be expected from the siting of the premises, e.g. near a football stadium or a hospital. Many of the prior experiences brought to the workplace will be beyond the control of the organisation but it is important that employees are aware of these issues and are sensitive to them. However, there can be control over such things as the expectations generated by advertising or publicity, advance information provided, particularly about getting to the site, and prior telephone contact with the organisation.

It is also necessary to be aware of the possibility of individuals entering the work site being affected by drugs or alcohol. This may be a frequent occurrence, as in a public house, a drug rehabilitation centre or hospital. It is essential for staff to be aware of the possible signs of drunkenness and drug use, and for clear procedures to be drawn up regarding the management of such individuals.

Experiences on entry

Individuals arriving at the site may be affected by the ease or difficulty in locating the site and parking vehicles, ease of access, directional informational and security procedures on entry. Frustration experienced at this stage may result in negative feelings towards the organisation and people associated with it, particularly if the frustrating incidents are seen as the organisation's fault. Information such as opening hours, directions to main areas, toilets etc., should be available at all entrances either on clear, conspicuous signs or from reception staff.

Entry restrictions

Policies for any entry restriction should be stated clearly and applied consistently. Normally, entry control is better carried out at the entrance to the establishment rather than inside it. It is generally easier to keep people out than to remove them once they have gained entry.

Staff carrying out entry control should also be aware of how important gaining entry may be to some individuals. If being refused entry to a nightclub results in individuals being humiliated in the eyes of their friends, then aggressive or hostile reactions are more likely. Staff members responsible for turning people away must be socially skilled and trained in negotiation techniques. It is essential that reasons for the refusal of entry are given in a calm but firm manner and that the person refusing entry is not perceived to be arbitrary in their decision. Back-up should always be available if problems arise.

Reception

Reception staff are often in a vulnerable position as they are usually the public's first encounter with the organisation; if they are unable to deal adequately with the range of demands put upon them, they may become the target for hostility. They must have sufficient knowledge of the organisation to answer common queries and be trained in social skills and conflict resolution.

It is important that the provision of information in reception areas is as full as possible, and reasons for delays or events which are likely to irritate or frustrate people are clearly conveyed. In order to provide such full and up-to-date information, the organisation needs to ensure that an efficient communication system is in place to link relevant departments and company personnel to the reception area.

The reception area should be designed to reduce the likelihood of personal attack if conflict arises and should have an 'escape route' in case of assault. The installation of CCTVs may also deter potential assailants and provide a record of any assault. The installation of panic buttons or personal alarms requires consistent procedures, staff familiarisation and an effective back-up system. Although there is a commonly held concern that the noise of alarms may aggravate an already violent person, experience has shown that they are often effective and can boost the confidence of the user (Health Services Advisory Committee, 1987). Any concerns from staff should be addressed, however, and if possible, staff should be involved in decisions about the type of alarm system implemented.

Queuing

Queuing for service can be stressful, particularly if people have no idea how long they will have to wait, if they are under time pressure, if there is no obvious queuing procedure or if they feel anxious about the task in hand. Much of the irritation experienced is the result of uncertainty, lack of knowledge, frustration, worry and high arousal. The situation may be exacerbated by a belief that aggression may be used instrumentally to regain control (Cox and Leather, 1994).

In structured settings, service points could be fed from a single queue to remove the frustration of queue lines seeming to move at different speeds. Similarly, ticketing systems may remove some of the irritation, as customers are able to move away from the service point knowing that their place in the queue is secure. Adequate numbers of staff must be provided in relation to the numbers of people queuing, and, if possible, staff should be trained in social skills and calming techniques and be encouraged to support each other, particularly at peak times or when faced with difficult cases.

If it is impractical to implement a formal queuing system, it is important that individuals have some idea about when, or if, they are likely to be dealt with. In public houses, for example, a member of bar staff may simply inform individuals of the order of service by acknowledging them as they arrive to be served. Individuals then know that they have been seen and are part of a queue. This procedure clearly requires vigilance from staff, and training and strategic work redesign may be required.

Impact of the physical environment

The general quality of the physical environment sets people's expectations of appropriate behaviour (Graham, La Rocque, Yetman, Ross and Giustra, 1980; Felson, Baccaglini and Gmelch, 1986). Specifically, incidents of aggression have been linked with environments which are shabby or ill-maintained (White, Kasl, Zahner and Will, 1987). It is important, therefore, for management to realise the importance of achieving a workplace environment which is pleasant and well kept to create an impression that ordered standards of behaviour are upheld.

It is important to identify and modify specific aspects of the physical environment which may act as stressors and increase the likelihood of aggressive behaviour. Such factors include high temperatures, inappropriate lighting, irritating or distracting noise, poor air quality (including smoky atmospheres) and crowding. Management of these factors should take into account the tasks undertaken within the particular environment and the views of staff and other users. For example, dim lighting may contribute to a relaxed atmosphere within a public house but it would create a problem for people required to complete detailed forms. Such physical factors might need to vary within the same work area dependent on time of day, user group or activity.

It is also important to take account of the role that the physical environment plays in contributing *directly* to conflict. Privacy, competition and equipment breakdown should all be considered when designing a workplace, or public area within the work site.

Privacy

Privacy is a priority where financial or personal matters are discussed. Lack of privacy may result not only in information being withheld, but also in hostility being directed towards the staff member present. The provision of private areas, however, can present problems in that any aggressive behaviour is out of public view. The safety of staff must be ensured. Particularly where there are separate interview rooms, support systems, escape routes and the means of summoning assistance should be established for use in the event of aggression from customers.

Competition for space

There is significant evidence to suggest a link between aggression and competition (e.g. Schuster, 1984). It is sensible, therefore, that workplaces should be designed to minimise the competition for space between individuals. Tables or chairs placed in doorways or corridors, for example, can cause irritation and hostility if individuals have to move frequently to allow others to pass. Insufficient space for people to use equipment, to access frequently used storage areas, or simply to wait for service unimpeded can also cause frustration. Competent planning designs out such problems and removes such physical flash points.

Interactions with staff, customers and equipment

Interactions with equipment

The frustration experienced when individuals do not get the results they expect from equipment can lead to irritation, anger and aggressive behaviour. Every effort should be made, therefore, to ensure that all equipment on the premises is in good working order, or that notice is given clearly when the equipment is faulty. Clear instructions should be displayed for how to use the equipment and what to do if problems are encountered. Such instructions are known to reduce violence towards the equipment itself (Moser and Levy-Leboyer, 1985); the more control people feel they have, the less likely they are to behave aggressively (Geen, 1990).

Interactions between individuals

It is important that clear rules for appropriate behaviour are implicitly or explicitly communicated. When the standards or rules for behaviour are clear, consistent and well established, the likelihood of peaceful dispute management is increased as the possibilities for misunderstanding are reduced (Gibbs, 1986; Leather and Lawrence, 1995). The behaviour of all members of staff helps to create an atmosphere where aggression is either condoned or condemned.

Generally, interactions between individuals within the workplace run smoothly; occasionally, however, there may be a clash of interest, disagreement or misunderstanding. When conflict occurs there are three main outcomes: conflict avoidance, conflict resolution or conflict escalation, possibly resulting in violence.

Conflict avoidance

When faced with conflict, one option is to avoid the problem. Sometimes people simply 'drop the argument' because it is too much effort or too time consuming to resolve it. The difficulty with this approach is that it takes control of the problem out of the hands of the organisation. Although disputes appear to be resolved, often issues are simply 'buried' and are likely to erupt at another time. As a result, there may be repercussions relating to the unresolved conflict. The individual may not return to the organisation, perhaps resulting in the loss of a valued member of staff or an important customer. Alternatively, as described later, the individual may return to the organisation with the express intention to 'settle the score', putting staff and customers at prolonged risk.

Furthermore, whilst conflict situations may be difficult to manage, they may also provide useful knowledge about work processes and staff/customer relations. Such knowledge may be fed back into the system and serve to assist future conflict reduction. Ignoring the situation deprives the organisation of valuable information.

Peaceful resolution

When conflict occurs between customers, care must be taken by staff that any intervention does not exacerbate the situation. Consequently, it is essential that the attitude of staff is calm and conciliatory. At all times, the member of staff must be seen to be a representative of the organisation and not simply another customer, as such misunderstanding may lead to further hostility. Similar rules apply when the dispute is between customer and staff. Organisational procedures for dealing with complaints and related issues must be in place and known by all staff. Staff who are likely to encounter disputes should be trained in conflict-resolution techniques and 'non-confrontational' interpersonal skills. A calm approach is essential if the member of staff is not to be drawn into escalating interaction, where the likelihood of aggression increases (Forgas, 1985; Cox and Leather, 1994; Leather and Lawrence, 1995).

If possible, individuals involved in conflict should be encouraged to deal with the situation somewhere more private, to reduce both the opportunity for individuals to 'act to the audience' and the likelihood of other people joining in. If the conflict has arisen as a result of private issues between customers, then moving the debate to a more private location allows personal matters to remain private between the antagonists. If an individual feels humiliated, particularly in public, the likelihood of aggression is increased (Felson and Tedeschi, 1993).

If the conflict arises from organisational issues, it may be appropriate for a suitably trained member of staff to intervene and attempt to reconcile the parties. It is essential that the member of staff approaches the situation with confidence, whilst at all times being aware of the effect she or he may have on the intensity and nature of the conflict. Staff should use a relaxed and open body posture and a non-threatening, calming manner; they should avoid invading 'personal space' and keep a comfortable distance from the individual, if possible (see Chapter 3). Any objects, such as glasses or heavy ashtrays, which could be used as weapons to inflict harm on others should be removed from the area, perhaps by other members of staff, if this can be achieved without alerting the antagonists.

Evidence suggests that empathy can have an ameliorating effect on aggression (Wicklund, 1975; Carver, 1975). Staff must communicate to the individuals that they are being listened to and understood and that any problems they encounter will be treated seriously. Staff must avoid 'taking sides' at this stage, as this may serve to intensify the conflict. Peaceful means of resolving the problem should be offered to the individuals to highlight a non-aggressive culture within the workplace (Moser and Levy-Leboyer, 1985). This assumes that appropriate procedures are already established, and comprehensively communicated to staff during training.

Conflict and violence between employees

Conflict between members of staff is frequently the product of longstanding disputes, the origins of which may be obscure. Managers need to be aware of conflict or personal antipathies between staff members, to seek to resolve disputes at an early stage and to deal with any ensuing hostility and resentment. Disputes should be dealt with away from the public view, wherever possible, to avoid onlookers forming negative attitudes towards the organisation and the individuals.

It is important that managers treat their staff with respect and consideration. Formal grievance procedures for staff must be seen to be accessible, confidential and fair. Satisfactory resolution is especially important where individuals have to continue working together following the incident. Conflict may affect productivity and have a divisive effect on the staff group as a whole, if sides are taken and underlying resentments expressed; additionally, there may be a negative knock-on effect on customer groups.

The reduction of harm when violence occurs

Occasionally, despite efforts to the contrary, violence erupts. Minimising the impact then becomes the imperative. Sometimes, even when violence has already begun, conflict-resolution strategies may still be an option, although great care must be taken to ensure that the intervention does not escalate the intensity of the violence. However, in some circumstances, this approach is clearly inappropriate and damage-limitation strategies must be initiated by removing potential weapons, if possible, and moving onlookers away from the immediate vicinity for their own safety and to prevent them becoming involved.

Emergency action plans, rapid response back-up and support procedures should be in place to assist in the calming of assailants or their safe removal from the worksite. Procedures for contacting the police and other emergency services should be clear and well known to all staff. Telephones and other equipment should be regularly checked to ensure that they are in good working order, that they are accessible in realistic situations and that emergency responses are as quick and effective as possible.

In some cases, physical restraint may be necessary and the use of 'minimum reasonable force' is acceptable in controlling violent situations. However, this is a difficult term to define and great care must be taken with this approach (see Chapter 2). Staff must know their own limitations and wait for the police if at all possible. Physical restraint should only be considered a feasible option if the persons using this strategy have the necessary ability to accomplish it safely and effectively. They should clearly state their intentions and give reasons for restraint or ejection, so that members of staff or the organisation are not seen as acting arbitrarily or malevolently (Ohbuchi, 1982; DeRidder, 1985). Assailants should be removed from the scene or isolated following restraint.

After the incident victims, onlookers, first aiders and rescuers, and perhaps the aggressor, will need care and support to minimise both physical and psychological harm. Line managers and other staff should be made aware of the possible short- and long-term effects of violent incidents and the types of support that are appropriate. There should be properly monitored procedures for post-incident care of individuals, including debriefing by trained staff and access to specialist counselling if necessary. Appropriately trained personnel should be available to help staff deal with the press, the police and any court appearances. Damage needs to be repaired and normal working resumed as quickly as is both possible and appropriate.

Experiences on exit

It is important that staff ensure, as far as is possible, that people have fulfilled their objectives in visiting the site, are satisfied with the outcome and have agreed and understood any further action before they leave.

Exit routes should be clearly labelled, particularly if the ways out are different from the ways into the building. Not being able to get out of an unfamiliar place may be frustrating, even frightening, leading to increased arousal and a greater susceptibility to act aggressively. This may be exaggerated if the person is in a hurry or has left the work site feeling annoyed or dissatisfied with the events which took place within it (see Berkowitz, 1989).

Closing times should be prominently displayed; warning of closure should be given in good time for people to prepare to leave and be followed by reminders, if necessary. Requests to leave should be firm but polite, and explanations given to avoid misunderstanding and potential conflict.

Experiences within the workplace, particularly closing procedures, can have a significant impact on the mood of the individual as they leave the premises. If a dispute has occurred, there are four possible outcomes:

1   both parties can be satisfied with the outcome ('win–win')
2   one party may have been victorious at the expense of the other ('win–lose')
3   both parties may still feel as though the conflict has not been sufficiently resolved
4   both parties' discontentment may have been intensified ('lose–lose').

Clearly, the whole organisation needs to appreciate the benefits of achieving a satisfactory 'win–win' outcome and to encourage the skills required to achieve it, rather than implicitly rewarding 'win–lose' outcomes. It is obviously preferable that individuals leave the work site with self-esteem intact and with a positive view of the organisation.

If, however, individuals leave feeling as though they have been humiliated, they may feel resentful towards the organisation as a whole, particularly if the 'victor' were a member of staff, and the likelihood of retaliatory behaviour is increased. Similarly, if both parties remain dissatisfied, retaliation against the organisation, or those associated with it, becomes more likely (Chapter 3 offers a more detailed explanation of this process). It is crucial that staff ensure that individuals who have been involved in conflict leave the work site feeling satisfied that they have been understood, and that any grievances have been taken seriously.

Experiences after exit

Negative attitudes towards an organisation or individual can be increased or moderated by what happens after leaving the workplace. Such negative attitudes contribute to the 'experiences prior to entry' of an individual when a further visit is made to the premises and increase the likelihood of conflict occurring and the individual reacting in a violent manner.

If promised action is not forthcoming or differs from that agreed, for example if cheques, documents or appointments are not received, phone calls, visits or deliveries are not made, then frustration or annoyance will be initiated or increased. This is particularly so if the expected action is important to the individual or such oversights happen repeatedly. Staff need to be aware of the problems that failure to fulfil undertakings can create, and should monitor promised action. Apology, explanation and possibly alternative arrangements should be made to ameliorate the effects of unavoidable delays or alteration in action.

Retaliatory action

If individuals have not been satisfied on exit, or expected action does not happen, a sense of injustice or anger can build up and retaliation can result. This may occur immediately on leaving the building, individuals may return later, perhaps bringing other people or weapons, or the action may be delayed by days, even months or years. Retaliatory action could range in severity from non-cooperation, letters of complaint and withdrawal of business, through the spreading of adverse publicity to physical attack on the premises, on members of staff or on their families. Around a quarter of the incidents of public house violence reported by Allied Domecq Retailing licensees (Beale, Cox, Clarke, Lawrence and Leather, 1998) either arose as repercussions from previous incidents or themselves led to further action such as attacks on the outside of the building while leaving the site, or assailants returning later to attack staff or customers. Retaliatory action may be directed against any individuals connected with the organisation, not only those who were directly involved in the initial conflict. The US Postal Service, for example, has undergone a spate of incidents in which employees have shot and killed several co-workers, as well as themselves, after losing their jobs or being rejected for promotion (DeAngelis, 1993; Baxter and Margavio, 1996).

It is vital that complaints procedures are well publicised, that staff notify managers if people have left the premises dissatisfied or angry and that staff are prepared to expect retaliatory action and maintain vigilance, particularly when the individuals involved are known to have a past history of violence or psychiatric disturbance or are members of gangs or troublesome families.

Working away from the workplace

The above model assumes that the employing organisation has some control over the work environment. However, there are numerous instances where employees are required to visit people away from the workplace, and they can often be placed in a vulnerable position. The abduction of Suzie Lamplugh, an estate agent, focused a growing concern, in the UK, about the safety of house visits in general.

Because the employing organisation can provide less direct protection to employees working away from the office, even greater emphasis must be given to ensuring that these employees have the necessary knowledge, skills and ability to deal with possible difficulties. Training in areas such as inter-personal skills and conflict resolution becomes more important in these circumstances. Additionally, a number of practical steps can be taken to reduce the threat of assault (Health Services Advisory Committee, 1987). These concern both preparation prior to the visit, and conduct of the visit itself.

Employees visiting someone for the first time should familiarise them-selves with any available information about the area and the person to be visited in order to prepare for likely problems and determine how to conduct the visit. Employees who make home visits should leave details of where they are going, their likely timetable and how they can be contacted, including their home telephone number. Employees may be particularly vulnerable while travelling to and from the meeting, especially if unaccom-panied, on foot and/or at night. The use of taxis might be appropriate, as might visiting in pairs, provided this does not exacerbate a potentially threatening situation. Alternatives would be to have colleagues nearby who are easily contactable, and to have mobile phones. Employees also need to be careful not to enter locations from which exit may be difficult. These steps are particularly relevant for employees who make visits at night.

As to the visit itself, many of the points outlined above, with regard to the workplace, apply when working elsewhere. In particular, the visiting employee must be able to deal with queries or know where to find out the necessary information. On completion of the visit, it is important that the employee carries out any tasks which have been agreed and records details of the meeting for other employees who might visit. These steps lessen the likelihood of conflict in the future.

Conclusion

Many of the analyses and measures implemented to reduce the likelihood and impact of violence also ensure business efficiency, customer satisfaction and employee welfare. Complaints and misunderstanding cost valuable time and energy as well as increasing the likelihood of violence occurring. Such analyses should be carried out in the earliest planning stages for new organisations and be reviewed and repeated at regular intervals, not just when a problem becomes obvious. Underlying problems may be masked because an individual member of staff has become skilled at dealing with them and may only erupt when that staff member is no longer able to cope or leaves the organisation. This type of scenario emphasises the need for the whole organisation to be involved in violence-reduction strategies and to establish a consolidated approach to violence at work. Overemphasis on any one component of this strategy, at the expense of others, can result in inconsistencies in work practices and a lack of back-up measures. Generally, several strategies should be employed to ensure that no single method is relied upon and put under strain (see Cox and Leather, 1994).

As a fundamental principle, it is essential that staff have the necessary resources to carry out their jobs properly, thus avoiding grounds for customer dissatisfaction and potential conflict. It is important that, in all procedures, staff are supported by back-up from senior management and that the physical layout and work practices are designed and maintained to aid staff in their attempts to sustain a violence-free environment.

Checklists of questions

The following checklists give examples of the types of questions that should be considered in attempting to reduce the risk from violence in an organisation. They are by no means exhaustive. Each organisation needs to look at its own operations and consult both staff and customers for suggestions in order to produce checklists tailored to their own needs. Many of the measures suggested are simply good business practice which enhances customer satisfaction and staff well-being. However, the fact that they may also reduce the risk of violence occurring gives these measures added importance.

Individuals

- Do the people who use the site have particular characteristics, e.g. age, special needs, disability, language problems, cultural demands, psychiatric disorders, etc., that require special consideration?
- Are we flexible enough to deal with people who don't fit the normal client/customer profile?
- Do we cater for accompanying individuals as well as the primary customers, e.g. parents, carers, hospital visitors, small children?
- Can we/should we select who uses the site?
- Have any staff been selected for their aggression or toughness that might cause or escalate conflict, e.g. some sportsmen, security staff, some managers?
- Are there people on the staff whose manner or refusal to listen could frustrate and engender violence in others?

Experiences prior to entry

- Have many customers had particular recent experiences, e.g. trauma, illness, tiring journeys, court cases, divorce, bereavement, financial or housing problems, football matches, that could affect their emotional state?
- Is there a likelihood that individuals might have taken drugs or alcohol?
- Does our advertising or publicity produce unrealistic expectations?
- Has our correspondence been clear and polite, sufficiently informative and accurate?
- Are telephone procedures efficient; are staff well informed and polite when giving information, making appointments or dealing with problems on the telephone?
- Do we provide good information about getting to the site?
- Is public transport sufficient or do we need to provide special transport?
- Can appointments and working hours be flexible enough to suit individual needs? Might staff or customers arrive rushed and flustered, or become anxious if they are unable to get away on time?

Experiences on entry

- Are parking arrangements adequate?
- Is there easy access to the site, even out of hours or at weekends when some areas are closed, e.g. in hospitals, and also for those with mobility problems?

- Is access to *all* areas well signposted?
- Are reception and door staff polite and well informed?
- Are security procedures well explained and understood and not degrading?
- When entry is refused is it handled sensitively and fairly?
- Is access too easy for people who have no business on the site?

Physical environment

- Are the heating, lighting, noise levels and air quality suitable for the activities undertaken in every area of the site?
- Is the site kept suitably clean and tidy?
- Is there sufficient space for the numbers of people expected, even at the busiest times?
- Are facilities, such as seating, toilets, entertainment and refreshment areas, sufficient for the number of people expected to use them, easily accessed even when crowded, well signposted and sensibly positioned in relation to each other, i.e. not too far away, but not encroaching on each other?
- Are areas for confidential business sufficiently private?
- Are there facilities to cater for any accompanying small children?

Interactions with equipment

- Is equipment easy to use with straightforward instructions?
- Is help easily obtained if there are problems?
- Is all equipment well maintained and reliable?
- If equipment breaks down are there back-up procedures and rapid repair?
- Is there sufficient equipment, is it easily accessed and sensibly positioned in relation to other facilities?

Interactions with other people

Customer–staff interactions

- Are *all* staff trained to be polite and helpful, not just obvious 'front line' staff?
- Do staff always acknowledge others quickly, even if they are not yet ready to deal with them?
- Are staff on time for appointments?
- Are unavoidable delays explained and estimated waiting times given?

- Are staff trained to be aware that what is familiar and routine to them may be strange and of extreme importance to the customer?
- Are staff *all* given up-to-date information or do they know how to find out information quickly?
- Do staff have the necessary resources to carry out the tasks expected of them?
- Are there adequate arrangements for checking monetary transactions without delay if disputed?

Staff–staff interactions

- Do *all* staff, including senior management, treat others with respect and consideration?
- Are staff given encouragement rather than criticism?
- Are staff expected to work unreasonably long hours; do they get sufficient breaks?
- Are front line staff consulted about difficulties or possible changes in procedure?
- Are organisational changes, e.g. departmental reorganisations, changes of site, redundancies, promotion (or lack of it) explained satisfactorily?
- Are staff interpersonal antipathies noted and dealt with sensitively, quickly and fairly?

Customer–customer interaction

- Are customers who are likely to be in conflict kept apart, e.g. rival sports teams or fans, opposing sides in court cases?
- Are queuing procedures fair, unambiguous and well explained and are they adhered to?
- Does crowding or the physical layout cause too many accidents or misunderstandings?

Experiences on exit

- Has any future action been determined, e.g. next appointment, next step to be taken by staff or customers, and has it been agreed and understood?
- Have any conflicts been resolved to the satisfaction of all concerned?
- Are exits accessible and easy to find?
- Are closing times clearly posted? Is adequate warning of closing given? Can these warnings be seen or heard in all areas of the site?

• Are closing procedures carried out fairly, politely and firmly?

Experiences after exit

• Has promised action been undertaken in the estimated time and in the agreed manner, e.g. cheques, letters or appointment times sent, other people contacted.
• Is consistent information given to all parties, e.g. to pupils and parents, or could conflicting information cause annoyance?
• Could conflicting information be obtained from other agencies, is there sufficient co-ordination?

Conflict situations

• Are complaints procedures (for both staff and customers) straightforward and understood?
• Are staff trained to treat complaints seriously and efficiently?
• Are staff trained in calming and conflict-resolution skills?
• Are senior staff readily available to deal with serious complaints or conflict situations?
• Are staff encouraged to report problems or will reporting be counted against them and reflect on their professional competence?
• Are there facilities to deal with problems out of public view but where staff are not made vulnerable?

Violent incidents

During the incident

• Are there emergency procedures that all staff know?
• Have the procedures been tested in a variety of realistic situations?
• Are there efficient and accessible means of summoning assistance, e.g. personal attack alarms, accessible telephones?
• Do these unambiguously indicate where the incident is occurring?
• Is emergency equipment regularly maintained and tested; does it work in all circumstances, e.g. when someone else is using another telephone?
• Is there an escape route or access to a secure area?
• Are security staff trained to use minimum physical intervention?

Following the incident

- Are there trained first aiders readily available? Is first aid equipment regularly checked?
- Can emergency services reach the location easily?
- Can damage be repaired and normal working resumed as soon as is possible and appropriate?
- Are staff prepared to cope with any follow-on action, e.g. assailants returning, threatening phone calls, etc.?
- Are line managers and other staff aware of the possible short- and long-term effects of violent incidents on victims, onlookers, first aiders and rescuers, and the types of support they may need?
- Are there properly monitored procedures for post-incident care of individuals, including debriefing by trained staff and access to specialist counselling if necessary?
- Are there personnel trained to help staff deal with the press, the police and court appearances?

References

Baxter, V. and Margavio, A. (1996) 'Assaultive violence in the US Post-Office', *Work and Occupations*, 23, 277–296.

Beale, D., Cox, T., Clarke, D., Lawrence, C. and Leather, P. (1998) 'Temporal architecture of violent incidents', *Journal of Occupational Health Psychology*, 3(1), 65–82.

Berkowitz, I. (1989) 'Frustration aggression hypothesis: examination and reformulation', *Psychological Bulletin*, 106, 59–73.

Carver, C. S. (1975) 'Physical aggression as a function of objective self-awareness and attitudes towards punishment', *Journal of Experimental Social Psychology*, 11, 510–519.

Cox, T. and Cox, S. (1993) *Psychosocial and Organizational Hazards at Work: Control and Monitoring*, European Occupational Health Series No. 5, Copenhagen: WHO Regional Office for Europe.

Cox. T. and Leather, P. J. (1994) 'The prevention of violence at work: A cognitive behavioural approach', in C. L. Cooper and I. T. Robertson (eds) *International Review of Industrial and Organizational Psychology*, Vol. 9, Chichester: Wiley and Sons.

DeAngelis, T. (1993) 'Psychologists aid victims of violence in post office', *American Psychological Association Monitor*, 24(10), 1 and 44–45.

DeRidder, R. (1985) 'Normative considerations in the labeling of harmful behavior as aggressive', *Journal of Social Psychology*, 125, 659–666.

Felson, R. B. and Tedeschi, J. T. (1993) *Aggression and Violence*, Washington DC: American Psychological Association.

Felson, R. B., Baccaglini, W. and Gmelch, G. (1986) 'Bar-room brawl: aggression and violence in Irish and American bars', in A. Campbell and J. J. Gibbs (eds) *Violent Transactions*, Oxford: Blackwell.

Forgas, J. P. (1985) *Interpersonal Behaviour: The Psychology of Social Interaction,* Oxford: Pergamon.

Geen, R. G. (1990) *Human Aggression,* Milton Keynes: Open University.

Gibbs, J. J. (1986) 'Alcohol consumption, cognition and context: examining tavern violence', in A. Campbell and J. J. Gibbs (eds) *Violent Transactions,* Oxford: Blackwell.

Graham, K., La Rocque, L., Yetman, R., Ross, T.J. and Giustra, Y. (1980) 'Aggression and bar-room environments', *Journal of Studies on Alcohol,* 41, 277–292.

Health Services Advisory Committee (1987) *Violence to Staff in the Health Services,* Health and Safety Commission. Sudbury, Suffolk: HSE Books.

Leather, P. J. and Lawrence, C. (1995) 'Perceiving pub violence: the symbolic influence of social and environmental factors', *British Journal of Social Psychology,* 34, 395–407.

Moser, G. and Levy-Leboyer, C. (1985) 'Inadequate environment and situation control: is a malfunctioning phone always an occasion for aggression?' *Environment and Behavior,* 17, 520–533.

Ohbuchi, K. (1982) 'On the cognitive interaction mediating reactions to attack patterns', *Social Psychology Quarterly,* 45, 213–218.

Schuster, I. (1984) 'Female aggression and resource scarcity: a cross-cultural perspective', *Aggressive Behaviour,* 10, 171.

White, M., Kasl, S. V., Zahner, G. E. P. and Will, J. C. (1987) 'Perceived crime in the neighbourhood and mental health of women and children', *Environment and Behavior,* 19, 588–613.

Wicklund, R. A. (1975) 'Objective self-awareness', in L. Berkowitz (ed.) *Advances in Experimental Social Psychology,* Vol. 8, New York: Academic Press.

Part II

Tackling work-related violence

Practical applications

7 Introducing trauma care into an organisation

From theory into practice

Noreen Tehrani

Introduction

The Post Office, in common with other employers, has a responsibility to provide a safe working environment for its workers and, as the UK's largest employer, has been looking for appropriate organisational responses both to reduce the incidence of trauma and to minimise the psychological damage caused to employees. The chosen strategy has been the development of a core trauma care programme which can be adapted to meet the specific needs of the different Post Office businesses. Each business accommodates the needs of the programme by modifying existing policies on the selection and training of staff, security, risk assessment and police liaison, and introducing post-trauma care, monitoring and evaluation.

This chapter deals with some of the issues facing the Post Office businesses in setting up the trauma care programme. It also outlines a number of problems which had to be overcome before the programme was acceptable to both the organisation and the workforce. Some early evidence of the effectiveness of trauma care on reducing sickness absence is also presented.

Background

The effect of traumatic shock on individuals exposed to life-threatening or severely distressing events has not always been acknowledged. However, the recognition that large numbers of American servicemen and women returning from Vietnam had severe psychological and psychiatric disorders, brought about by their experiences of war, led to a formal recognition of the effects of trauma on individuals. The American Psychiatric Association's Diagnostic and Statistical Manual [DSM-III] (APA, 1980), which provides a listing and diagnostic criteria for psychological and psychiatric illness, introduced the term post-traumatic stress disorder (PTSD) to describe the features of the post-traumatic aetiology and symptoms. The latest version of the American Psychiatric Association's Diagnostic and Statistical Manual [DSM-IV] (APA, 1994) builds on DSM-III; it is used as a clinical assessment tool for PTSD and is recognised by psychologists, psychiatrists and courts throughout the world.

In Britain, the term 'nervous shock' has been used by the legal profession to describe the non-physical effects of trauma, and as early as 1890 damages had been awarded for nervous shock despite a lack of physical injury (Bell *v.* Great Northern Railway, 1890). Lord Wilberforce expressed his criticism of the term 'nervous shock' in the case of McLoughlin *v.* O'Brian (1982). Mrs McLoughlin had been awarded damages for the shock she suffered when she witnessed the injuries suffered by her husband and children. In his summing up, Lord Wilberforce said 'English law and common understanding have moved some distance since the recognition was given to this symptom as a basis of liability'.

Reactions to trauma

The immediate responses of individuals to traumatic events are similar to, albeit generally more pronounced than, the normal responses of individuals to any stressful event. The first response is often one of disbelief; statements like 'I could not believe it was happening' and 'I thought it was a joke', for example, are common initial reactions reported by Post Office employees involved in armed raids. As soon as the reality of the event is understood, reactions change, with the individual's cognitive, emotional, physical and behavioural functioning being affected (Mitchell and Everly, 1993). During the traumatic event the individual may experience perceptual distortions of time and space, be unable to think or make decisions, become very upset or cool and withdrawn, or behave in an unusual or bizarre way. Trauma may also result in physiological reactions such as loss of bowel or bladder control, sweating or uncontrollable shaking. Immediate, short-term and long-term reactions to trauma are described in some detail in Chapter 4.

The long-term effects of trauma can be observed in individuals who have developed PTSD with the three groups of distressing symptoms which have been described in DSM-IV. The first group of symptoms involves re-experiencing the traumatic event in dreams or flashbacks, or by acting out the event. The second group includes avoiding thoughts, feelings or activities associated with the events. Finally, the third group involves increased arousal causing problems in going to sleep, outbursts of anger, hypervigilance and exaggerated startle response. In addition to the DSM-IV criteria, Davidson, Swartz and Kronenberger (1990) found that PTSD patients suffered the associated problems of high levels of alcohol and other substance abuse, anxiety, depression and relationship difficulties.

Disaster planning

When a traumatic incident reaches the proportions of a disaster there is a need for the community to join forces with the organisation to provide support for the victims and others involved directly or indirectly in the incident. Tierney (1989) describes four types of emergency and longer term responses to disasters. Type 1 responses involve the emergency services such as the police, ambulance service and fire-fighters who perform their normal role and tasks in the disaster as in any emergency situation. Type 2 responses involve emergency service support, which includes such groups as the Red Cross, WRVS and other agencies. These groups provide support which augments those provided by the emergency services and others involved in the incident. Type 3 responses involve local government, health authorities and specialist voluntary groups such as Victim Support and CRUSE, who provide for the longer term needs in terms of counselling and support for the victims of the incident. Finally, Type 4 responses involve people who have been personally affected by the traumatic event and who form themselves into self-help groups to provide immediate and longer term assistance. Hodgkinson and Stewart (1991), in an investigation of disasters in the UK, found a general lack of preparedness by the health, social services and voluntary organisations to mount the essential long-term psychological and social support required by victims of disasters.

Natural disasters, such as floods, forest fires and earthquakes, are regarded as 'acts of God' and provide little opportunity for the victims to seek financial compensation. However, where a disaster involves organisational negligence, as is sometimes the case with air crashes, oil rig fires, chemical plant explosions, etc., organisations have a legal responsibility to provide reasonable support and compensation for the victims.

Small-scale traumatic incidents

Although disasters are the traumatic events most widely reported in the media, the total number of people involved is relatively small in comparison to the thousands traumatised each year in small-scale incidents. Such incidents include assaults, robberies, road traffic and other accidents, rape, violent death or injury, and serious verbal threats or abuse. For the individuals concerned, involvement in a small-scale event can be just as traumatic as involvement in a large-scale disaster. The determining factor for post-traumatic stress is not the size of the incident, but the perception of the level of danger or horror experienced by the victim (Cramer, Burgess and Pattison, 1992).

Organisations' responses to trauma at work

Employers have duties under both common law and statute law. These duties include the need to take reasonable care for the health and safety of the workforce (Goldman, 1994). In common law it has been established that there is no such thing as a perfectly safe environment (Thomas *v.* General Motors-Holden Ltd, 1988). The issue which courts consider when making their judgements on employer liability is the balance between the cost of reducing or eliminating a trauma hazard, and the risk of a traumatic event occurring. The law does not expect organisations to eliminate risks but rather to take reasonable action to reduce foreseeable risks.

The Health and Safety at Work (HSW) Act (1974) assigns the duty of every employer to ensure, so far as is reasonably practicable, the health, safety and welfare at work of all its employees. The Management of Health and Safety Regulations (Health and Safety Executive [HSE], 1992) build on the HSW Act to require that all employers:

1   make a sufficient assessment of the risks to the health and safety of employees (Regulation 3) and
2   give due consideration to employees' capabilities and levels of training, knowledge and experience to undertake tasks (Regulation 11).

The key responsibilities for handling trauma are set out in guidelines (HSE, 1993). These responsibilities include introducing risk management and auditing procedures, developing education and training programmes, providing post-incident support systems and employing public relations strategies. Although safe working practices and environments are a high priority for organisations, it is clear that there are some jobs where dangers cannot be eliminated. In roles where there is a risk of trauma, reasonable care must be taken by employers to protect staff from the possibility and effects of trauma. It is important that organisations undertake an assessment of the nature of the work itself (Poyner and Warne, 1988).

Risk management and auditing

The risk of being assaulted at work appears to be rising. The Banking, Insurance and Finance Union (1992) reported that assaults on staff were increasing, with the number of bank robberies in London doubling in one year. The 1992 British Crime Survey found that violence at work had risen by 110% over a ten-year period (Mayhew, Aye Maung and Mirrlees-Black, 1993). Some jobs inevitably involve a higher incidence of violence than others. Harkness (1997) showed that the greatest risks were faced by employees who (1) handled money, (2) carried out inspection or enforcement duties, (3) worked with drunk or potentially violent people, (4) worked alone or at night.

The Incomes Data Services (IDS, 1990), in a review of violence against staff, found a wider range of employees who were 'at risk', including those whose roles involved (1) giving a service, (2) caring, (3) education, (4) money transactions, (5) delivering/collecting, (6) controlling and inspecting. The review suggested that any employee with a role which includes dealing with the public in a face-to-face interaction is vulnerable to violent assault which can range in seriousness from murder, hostage taking, hijack and hold-ups, resulting in physical injury, to verbal threats and abuse.

Unfortunately, accurate information on the prevalence of violence in the workplace is lacking. This is partly due to the tendency for traumatised employees to fail to report their incident. Warshaw and Messite (1996) suggested a number of reasons for this tendency to under-report which included a lack of agreement on what constituted a traumatic event, a cultural acceptance of the violence related to certain jobs as being 'normal', the lack of a reporting system in the organisation, and a fear of being blamed or suffering a reprisal for making a report. This widespread under-reporting of violence demands that organisations do not rely solely on incident reports to quantify the risk from violence, but must carry out a detailed risk assessment involving multiple sources of information.

The United States Postal Service (1992) undertook such a risk assessment in its organisation, identifying a number of traumatic hazards which affected postal workers and drivers. These included armed robbery, assault, rape, violence, threats of violence, motor vehicle accidents, terrorism, fire, natural disasters, homicide and suicide.

The Post Office in Britain has also undertaken trauma risk assessments within its businesses (Tehrani, 1995). The assessment process involved gathering information from managers and employees, and inspecting incident reports and sickness absence data. This assessment has enabled risk profiles to be developed for each business. Overall the risk data have indicated that there are three main categories of incident in the Post Office; these are:

- attacks involving robbery or attempted robbery
- attacks which are an expression of anger or frustration at an authority figure
- attacks of a random or sexual nature where the attacker appears to have no particular motive other than personal gratification.

The range of traumatic incidents recorded within the Post Office businesses include being:

- held hostage
- hi-jacked
- kidnapped
- robbed
- physically assaulted
- witness to a traumatic event
- threatened with violence
- involved in a road traffic accident
- attacked by a dog
- verbally abused.

Many of the attacks reported in the Post Office involve the use of weapons such as firearms, knives and blunt objects. These weapons are generally used to threaten or intimidate, but, in a few cases, they are used to harm the employee. Table 7.1 provides an assessment of the risks associated with four of the Post Office businesses.

The Post Office has been involved in efforts to reduce the effects of trauma on its workforce for a number of years (Allison and Reynolds, 1989). Although an employee in the Post Office is no more likely to suffer a traumatic event than an employee in other comparable organisations, the

Table 7.1 Degree of risk from traumatic occurrences for Post Office employees

	Business			
	Royal Mail	*Counters*	*CASHCO*	*SSL*
Category of attack				
Robbery	**	***	***	—
Anti-authority	*	**	—	***
Sexual	*	—	—	*
Random	**	—	—	***
Nature of attack				
Family/colleague taken hostage	—	*	*	—
Hijack of vehicle	***	—	***	*
Kidnap (held against will)	**	***	**	*
Physical attack	**	**	**	**
Dog attack	***	—	—	***
Witness to traumatic event	*	***	***	—
Road traffic accident	**	—	**	—
Threat of violence	***	***	***	***
Verbal abuse	*	***	—	***
Tied up/blindfolded	**	***	**	—
Use of weapons				
Firearms	**	***	***	*
Noxious substances, e.g. CS gas	**	*	***	—
Knives or other sharp objects	***	*	*	*
Blunt objects, e.g. bats, fists	***	***	*	***
Effect of trauma on others				
Managers/colleagues	**	***	**	**
Family	**	***	***	**

Notes:
*** High risk;
** Medium risk;
* Low risk;
— No significant risk

sheer size of the workforce (180,000 employees) determines that the absolute number of trauma victims is quite high.

The Post Office trauma care programme

Much has been written about the aftercare of victims of trauma (Alexander, 1990; Duckworth, 1991; Dyregrov, 1989; Fraser, 1991; Turner, Thompson and Rosser, 1989). However, very little has been reported on any organisational or clinical evaluation of the effectiveness of the intervention. This situation must cause concern in the light of work undertaken by Benjamin, Shieber, Levine and Halmosh (1988) which has shown that some trauma intervention increased, rather than reduced, the traumatic disorder experienced by the victim. The Post Office was keen to ensure that it appropriately monitored and evaluated its trauma care programme from both organisational and clinical perspectives.

There is a recognition in the Post Office that the policies and procedures used to deliver a trauma care programme (HSE, 1993) need to be accommodated and assimilated within the existing business policies and procedures. Due to the different organisational needs of each of the Post Office businesses, individual trauma care programmes have been designed around a basic core programme adapted to meet the unique requirements of Royal Mail, CASHCO, Post Office Counters and Subscriptions Services Limited (SSL). Each programme is designed to provide a 'reasonable response', which is recorded and audited in order to meet the requirements of the health and safety legislation.

In 1992 CASHCO, the Post Office's cash carrying business, approached the Occupational Health Service to develop a trauma care programme for its security van crews. At that time there was little information available on organisational trauma programmes, although McCloy (1992) discussed the need for effective management of trauma in organisations. McCloy developed a three-stage model involving immediate action, short-term management and long-term management of the outcomes of trauma. HSE guidelines on the prevention of violence to staff in banks and building societies (HSE, 1993) and to retail staff (HSE, 1995) have been useful in providing the framework for the Post Office trauma care programme. Systematic approaches similar to those suggested by the HSE have been adopted by a number of organisations (see Flannery and Penk, 1996; Harrington, 1996; IDS, 1994; Richards, 1994; Warshaw and Messite, 1996). The main differences in the various trauma care programmes are (1) the person trained to conduct the initial debrief (i.e. peer, manager or specialist debriefer) and (2) the model or models of debriefing and counselling employed in support of the traumatised employee.

The programme designed for CASHCO had to take account of that business's involvement in the transportation of high-value goods including cash. The carrying of valuables has resulted in the CASHCO crews suffering a higher than average number of armed raids compared with staff in other parts of the Post Office. CASHCO crews belong to a culture where security is paramount. There is an expectation that crew members will conform to, and carry out, all the security systems and procedures. This conformity of behaviour requires a significant training and monitoring programme from CASHCO. This approach has been found to protect the crew members and reduce the loss of property. It works because of the level of trust and team-working which has built up between the crew members and the managers in each of the CASHCO depots. The concept of the two crew members being a team is a highly valued part of the culture, and 'looking out' for your partner is one of the most important ways of avoiding becoming the victim of a crime.

The trauma care programme for CASHCO has taken account of the fact that there are normally two crew members involved in any incident. The requirement to debrief two people at the same time resulted in the development of the CASHCO manager debrief undertaken with two victims together. Another feature of the CASHCO trauma care programme is the need to handle breaches of security appropriately. This has involved the introduction of a clear statement in all the educational and promotional material which says that all personal information will be kept confidential; however, any criminal activities and breaches of procedure will be addressed through normal organisational procedures.

Subscription Services Limited (SSL), having heard of the CASHCO trauma care programme, wanted a similar programme for its Television Enquiry Officers. SSL is involved in administering the collection and recording of television licence fees from the viewing public. The enquiry officer's role is to visit the homes of those people for whom no record of a licence is recorded on the SSL database. Where there is no acceptable explanation for the absence of a licence, the enquiry officer will make arrangements for the householder to be prosecuted. Regardless of whether the householder has a television licence or not, the enquiry officer is never a welcome figure on the door-step. As a result of this negative perception, enquiry officers suffer a relatively high level of verbal and physical abuse. Enquiry officers normally work on their own and away from their base, which is their own home, and therefore are required to be self-sufficient and resilient. The trauma care programme had to take account of the fact that the traumatised enquiry officer would be away from immediate support and often in a hostile environment. The need to provide immediate support resulted in the introduction of open telephone lines to the enquiry officers' managers. The manager takes on the responsibility of handling the immediate needs of the enquiry officer over the telephone and arranges a manager debrief within two days.

Much of the violence experienced by enquiry officers is at a constant but relatively low level (e.g. verbal abuse, threats, physical pushing or jostling). To cater for this, SSL decided to introduce a special diffusing session at each of the monthly team meetings with management. These sessions help enquiry officers to share their experiences and to use their team to identify ways of dealing with the stresses and traumas of the job.

Royal Mail commissioned an audit of the Post Office's current trauma care arrangements to ensure that the programme it adopted met its needs and represented best practice. Maxwell and Cox Associates were appointed to audit the provisions of the post-incident support services in the Post Office and to recommend a single system of delivery for support (Cox, Smewing and Beale, 1993). The recommendations of the audit were examined by a project team, made up from the Post Office's Occupational Health and Employee Support Services, and a formalised core trauma care programme was developed (Table 7.2). This process encompassed six stages of response which have built on the experience gained in developing the trauma care programmes for CASHCO and SSL, and the models of debriefing developed for those programmes (Tehrani and Westlake, 1994). The trauma care approach was accepted by Royal Mail for introduction to its postal workers in 1994–5 and by Post Office Counters in 1996. The Post Office now has a core trauma care programme which is common to all of its businesses. However, it allows adaptations in the first three steps of the programme to interface with the individual organisational and operational needs of each of the businesses.

Post Office stages of response to trauma in the workplace

Stage −1: Pre-incident information and training

It has been shown (HSE, 1993) that, if an individual undertakes a process of mental preparation for the possibility of a traumatic event, this will lessen the impact of a real incident should it occur. Training in how to handle predictable traumatic incidents enables employees to build up important coping skills which help to protect them from traumatic stress reactions. The Post Office's trauma care programme involves training both managers and employees regarding the effects of trauma on the individual. Another important aspect of the training is clarification of the role of managers in the post-trauma period. Managers are responsible for ensuring that the

Table 7.2 Post Office stages of response for victims of trauma

	Stages of response
Stage −1	Pre-incident information and training
Stage 1	Crisis management (first 24 hours)
Stage 2	Manager debrief (24–48 hours)
Stage 3	Critical incident debrief (3–7 days)
Stage 4	Trauma counselling/psychiatric care (2–4 weeks)
Stage 5	Follow-up (3, 6 and 12 months)

appropriate levels and types of support are made available to the workforce following a traumatic event.

The training is supported by a trauma care video which uses the experiences of real victims of trauma to demonstrate (1) the physical, psychological and social effects of trauma, and (2) how the employee can develop simple coping mechanisms to reduce the likelihood of long-term post-traumatic disorders. The video also highlights the support which is available from managers, the business, the Occupational Health Service and the Employee Support Service. A range of information leaflets is also available, dealing with (1) the organisation's policies and procedures relating to trauma care, (2) guidance notes on where to get help, (3) advice on dealing with the effects of trauma, and (4) information on what to do if asked to help the police with their enquiries, and on what will happen when making a court appearance.

Stage 1: Crisis management (first 24 hours)

In the first hours after an incident the main focus of support for the individual is on managing the crisis. The line manager's role is to handle this process and to ensure that the immediate physical and psychological needs of trauma victims are met. The manager also gives the victims information about the trauma care programme, the normal symptoms of trauma and any other support which may be available. Although there are operational and business needs which must be met following a traumatic event, the Post Office's aim is to put the needs of its traumatised employees first.

Stage 2: Manager debrief (24–48 hours)

During Stage 2 of the trauma care programme the emphasis changes from managing a crisis to providing essential psychological first aid for victims. Most trauma care interventions use managers or peers to deliver the early stages of trauma care (McCloy, 1992; Mitchell and Everly, 1993). There are two main reasons for this approach. The first is that peers have a better understanding of the nature and context of the trauma and the likely impact on the victim. The second reason is one of logistics, in that manager or peer debriefers are normally able to reach the victims of trauma more quickly than the specialist trauma debriefers. The Post Office has trained around five hundred operational managers in debriefing skills. Only fully trained and competent managers are allowed to undertake manager debriefs.

The manager debrief provides the traumatised employee with an opportunity to re-experience the traumatic event in a safe and controlled environment. This re-experience helps the victim to begin the process of coming to terms with what has happened to them and to start the recovery process. The debrief also gives the manager debriefer an opportunity to assess whether the employee has any requirements for further debriefing. The manager debrief is made up of four stages:

1   *Introduction.* This is an essential opening phase of the debrief in which the manager clearly defines the process and boundaries of the debrief. In view of the nature of the manager–employee relationship, there is a need to deal with failure to comply with organisational policy. The manager debrief is voluntary and, where employees are unwilling to be debriefed by their manager, the option of being debriefed by an Employee Support Adviser or Occupational Health Nurse is offered.

2   *Telling the story.* The second stage of the manager debrief is telling the story. This is done in a slow systematic way with the story beginning before the event and ending at the present. The manager debriefer sticks to the *facts* of the incidents; thoughts and feelings are acknowledged but are not explored in this debrief.

3   *Information.* The manager then moves on to providing information to the trauma victim. This information is designed to help the employee to return to normal life and to help to prevent the occurrence of secondary problems such as alcoholism or phobias.

4   *Close.* In the closing phase the manager checks that the employee is safe to go home and will try to ensure that there is someone at home to stay with them. Where necessary, the manager will arrange for the employee to be taken home and that a colleague is made available to stay with them. The manager will also arrange to contact the employee again and, where further help is needed, will organise an appointment for a critical incident debrief.

Stage 3: Critical incident debrief (3–7 days)

Following the manager debrief, employees may require a deeper level of debriefing. In this case, the manager will refer the employee for a critical incident debrief to be carried out by a trained and competent Occupational Health Nurse or Employee Support Adviser. The critical incident debrief used by the Post Office has been designed for use with individual employees (Tehrani and Westlake, 1994), unlike the models of Mitchell and Everly (1993), Raphael (1986) and Dyregrov (1989), where debriefing is undertaken with groups of victims. The critical incident debrief is undertaken in a single session with a follow-up session. Employees who are not showing clear signs of recovery following a critical incident debrief and follow-up session are referred to a Post Office Occupational Health Physician who will assess the victim's clinical condition and advise on further action.

The main difference between the critical incident debrief and the manager debrief is that in the critical incident debrief the story is told three times, concentrating firstly on the facts, then on the thoughts associated with those facts and finally on the feelings experienced.

Stage 4: Trauma counselling/psychiatric care (2–4 weeks)

Where an employee is not recovering from the effects of a traumatic event, the Occupational Health Physician makes a clinical decision on the needs of the employee. This may involve consulting with the employee's general practitioner. Where the problem is seen as psychological, the employee may be referred to a trauma counsellor from the external counselling network which is retained by the Post Office. If the employee requires referral to a psychiatrist or other medical specialist, this is arranged via the employee's general practitioner.

Stage 5: Follow-up (3, 6 and 12 months)

All employees who have experienced a traumatic incident are followed up at 3, 6 and 12 months after the incident. This is to ensure that the employee is continuing to progress and has not suffered any delayed trauma reactions. The follow-up also provides evaluation data on the success of the trauma care programme as an intervention for supporting victims of trauma.

Audit and evaluation

The Post Office has a number of mechanisms for auditing the quality of the service provided. First, it measures the service against agreed service standard levels. Service standard agreements, which are set up with each business, set out the speed, quality and nature of the services which are to be provided. The service standard approach is part of the total quality working adopted in the Post Office. Second, Occupational Health and Employee Support Services undertake internal audits of case handling and clinical standards to ensure that the performance and competency of the practitioners are monitored, and opportunities for service improvement are identified. All critical incident debriefers are supervised by experienced counselling supervisors who are responsible to the organisation for ensuring that the debriefers are working within their level of competency.

The programme evaluation is based on a number of indicators. First, each employee is offered a post-incident questionnaire which gathers both qualitative and quantitative data for analysis. This questionnaire obtains the employee's perception of the quality of the support they have received and its effectiveness in helping them recover from the incident. It also includes an adapted Post Traumatic Stress Scale (Impact of Events Scale: Horowitz, Wilner and Alvarez, 1979). Second, the level of sickness absence and medical retirements for employees who have experienced traumatic events are monitored by the Post Office businesses. These are compared with the levels which were the norm prior to the introduction of the trauma care programme.

Initial introduction difficulties

Within the Post Office there has been strong support for the trauma care programme from both employees and managers. Not surprisingly, there were some initial teething problems which had to be overcome before the programme was totally accepted. First, the existing Post Office culture had tended to be 'macho'; this caused many traumatised individuals to deny their experiences of fear or anxiety. The macho culture prevented an open expression of feelings and resulted in traumatised employees trying to 'put on a brave face' and suffer in silence. Major parts of the Post Office senior managers' contribution to introducing the trauma care programmes were (1) the open acknowledgement of the effects of trauma on individuals and (2) a recognition that the organisation has a role to play in providing support for victims of trauma. The organisational acceptance of the role of managers and colleagues in helping employees recover from traumatic experiences has provided the essential change in climate which has made talking about feelings in a safe environment acceptable. The introduction of manager debriefing training provided an opportunity for managers not only to learn about debriefing but also to raise a wide range of operational problems. Undertakings were given by senior managers in each of the businesses that any operational issues which impacted on the effectiveness of the trauma care programme would be addressed. The rapid response and effectiveness of this problem-resolution process was made possible by the priority and importance given to the programme by the senior management teams.

Many of the debriefer managers were concerned that the caring approach required to undertake debriefing would conflict with their need to manage more difficult employee situations, such as disciplinary meetings. This anticipated problem of a conflict of the management role with a caring role did not occur. Many managers found that they were able to understand that debriefing requires the skills both of caring and of control and the debriefing course had been designed to address the issue of handling difficult situations in a firm but caring manner. Reports from manager trainees revealed that the skills they had learnt on the training course not only enabled them to undertake manager debriefs but also helped them to manage other difficult situations, such as performance reviews and disciplinary meetings. Initially some managers thought that staff would not choose to be debriefed by their line manager. This has not been shown to be the case; most employees prefer to be debriefed by someone who understands them and the situation, rather than to be debriefed by a stranger.

In the beginning, it was thought that a single trauma care programme would be appropriate throughout the Post Office. However, it soon became clear that each of the businesses needed to have the programme adapted and adjusted to its own specific requirements. Table 7.3 gives details of some of the differences between the four programmes. The commitment of each business's workforce was essential to the effectiveness of the programme. This ownership was helped by the fact that each of the businesses developed its own support material, video and training programme based on the core trauma care programme.

Table 7.3 Trauma care programmes tailored for different Post Office businesses

| | Post Office business | | | |
	Royal Mail	Counters	CASHCO	SSL
Stage −1	Presentations to managers; trauma care policy leaflets, video; articles in in-house magazine.	Presentations to managers; trauma care policy leaflets, video; employee briefings.	Health declaration; pre-employment questionnaire; personality profiling; presentations to all employees on hostage and trauma care programmes; booklets, leaflets; door chains and spy holes; update presentations.	Health declaration; pre-employment questionnaire; personality profiling; presentations to all employees; trauma care video; peer support groups; policy booklets, leaflets.
Stage 1	Helpline support; first aid; public relations policy; security procedures; communications procedures.	Crisis management; first aid; manager diffusing; public relations policy; security procedures; helpline support.	Crisis management; first aid; police co-operation with trauma policy; public relations policy; security procedures; communication procedures.	Emergency contact procedures; public relations process; legal policy/support; police liaison; communications procedures.
Stage 2	Designated manager debrief (individual); traumatic stress leaflets; letter for GP; consultative support for debriefers.	Manager debrief (individual); traumatic stress leaflet; letter for GP; consultative support for debriefers.	Manager debrief (two crew members); traumatic stress leaflet; letter for GP; peer support; consultative support for debriefers.	Manager debrief; traumatic stress leaflet; letter for GP; peer support at team meetings; consultative support for debriefers.
Stages 3 to 5	Psychological debrief; trauma counselling; employee satisfaction questionnaire; sickness absence monitoring; post-incident follow-up.	As Royal Mail.	As Royal Mail.	As Royal Mail.

Early results

CASHCO

CASHCO, the first business to adopt the trauma care programme, obtained financial and personal data on the operation of the programme from the CASHCO personnel databases. These contain staff records, including the number of days of sickness absence recorded for employees following a traumatic event. Inspection of the employee records for three years prior to the commencement of the programme showed that individuals involved in traumatic incidents took, on average, eight days sick leave. During the three years following the introduction of the trauma care programme, the average number of post-incident sickness absence days had fallen to four days, making an average saving of four days per affected employee.

The total cost of the manager debriefing training for CASHCO was £88,300, made up as follows: training courses, £40,000; two videos, £41,300 and the provision of personal security devices for the homes of the operations staff, £7,000.

The average level of savings, over the three years following the introduction of the programme, was £103,000 per annum. The savings were made up of £37,000 from the reduced level of sickness absence following incidents; £56,000 from the reduction in the number of employees needing to be medically retired as unfit for work; and an estimated £10,000 in non-measurable costs such as the cost of temporary staff to cover for the sickness absence of traumatised staff, overtime payments for existing staff to cover the duties of absent colleagues, and recruitment costs for new staff to replace staff who are medically retired or resign following a traumatic incident. The data show that, even as early as the first year, the programme more than paid for itself. The second and third years provided an overall saving of over £200,000. CASHCO anticipate a need to arrange one manager training course per year to train newly appointed managers. In addition, some of the existing manager debriefers have undertaken refresher training courses, at a cost of £10,000 per annum.

Subscription Services Limited (SSL)

SSL evaluated its trauma care programme by comparing the number of stress-related sickness absence days for the year before the introduction of the trauma care programme with that for one year following the completion of the manager debrief training. SSL found that there was a reduction of 32% in stress-related sickness absence and medical retirements. This reduction translated into a saving of £115,000 each year after deduction of the cost of the trauma care programme.

In 1996, SSL decided that there was a need to augment the trauma care programme with a second programme designed to deal with stress and burnout. This new programme involves educating managers in common stress reactions and coping methods and trains them to deal with a wide range of job and personal problems which may impact on the well-being of their staff. Although not part of the trauma care programme, the new Employee Well-being Programme is hoped to provide additional support for the enquiry officers.

The future

The Post Office trauma care programme cannot be considered complete or perfect and is being continually revised and improved. The objective for the next few years is to evaluate the programme on the basis of both the psychological assessments of the victims of trauma and the organisational benefits. Further work has still to be done to evaluate the project on the effectiveness of the trauma care interventions, but some of the tools of the evaluation are already in place. In order to satisfy business needs, organisational measurements have been established so as to assess the value of the change in organisational effectiveness brought about by the programme.

References

Alexander, D. A. (1990) 'Psychological intervention for victims and helpers after disasters', *British Journal of General Practice*, 40, 345–348.

Allison, T. and Reynolds, P. (1989) 'Criminal assault at work: effects, responses and alternative organisational strategies', *Counselling, Journal of the British Association of Counselling*, 67, 15–23.

American Psychiatric Association (1980) *Diagnostic and Statistical Manual: DSM-III*, Washington DC: American Psychological Association.

—— (1994) *Diagnostic and Statistical Manual of Mental Disorders: DSM-IV*, Revised 4th Edition, Washington DC: American Psychological Association.

Banking, Insurance and Finance Union (1992) *The Hidden Cost*, Raynes Park, London: BIFU.

Bell *v.* Great Northern Railway Co. (Ireland) (1890) 26 LR Ir 428.

Benjamin, M. D., Shieber, A., Levine, K. and Halmosh, A. F. (1988) 'The iatrogenic contribution in post-traumatic stress disorders', *Journal of Occupational Health and Safety*, 4(1), 68–73.

Cox, T., Smewing, C. and Beale, D. (1993) *The Post Office: An Audit of Post Trauma Support Services*, Sutton Coldfield: Maxwell and Cox Associates (internal Post Office report).

Cramer, M., Burgess, P. and Pattison, P. (1992) 'Reaction to trauma: a cognitive processing model', *Journal of Abnormal Psychology*, 101, 452–459.

Davidson, J., Swartz, M. and Kronenberger, W. J. (1990) 'A diagnostic and family study of post-traumatic stress disorder', *American Journal of Psychiatry*, 142, 90–93.

Duckworth, D. H. (1991) 'Managing psychological trauma in the police service: from the Bradford fire to the Hillsborough crush disaster', *Journal of Social and Occupational Medicine*, 41, 171–173.

Dyregrov, A. (1989) 'Caring for helpers in disaster situations: psychological debriefing', *Disaster Management*, 2, 25–30.

Flannery, R. B. and Penk, W. E. (1996) 'Program evaluation of an intervention approach for staff assaulted by patients: preliminary inquiry', *Journal of Traumatic Stress*, 9, 317–324.

Fraser, D. E. (1991) 'Occupational health management of police officers involved in the Piper Alpha disaster', *Journal of Social and Occupational Medicine*, 41, 174–175.

Goldman, L. (1994) 'Violence in the workplace', *Occupational Health*, 146, 166–167.

Harkness, L. (1997) 'Part of the job? A study of violence at work', *Occupational Health Review*, Jan/Feb, 25–27.

Harrington, G. (1996) 'In the line of fire', *People Management*, 2(22), 36–38.

Health and Safety Executive (1992) *Management of Health and Safety Regulations*, Sudbury, Suffolk: HSE Books.

—— (1993) *Prevention of Violence to Staff in Banks and Building Societies*, Sudbury, Suffolk: HSE Books.

—— (1995) *Preventing Violence to Retail Staff*, Sudbury, Suffolk: HSE Books.

Hodgkinson, P. E. and Stewart, M. (1991) *Coping with Catastrophe: A Handbook of Disaster Management*, New York and London: Routledge.

Horowitz, M. J., Wilner, N. and Alvarez, W. (1979) 'Impact of Events Scale: a measure of subjective distress', *Psychosomatic Medicine*, 41, 209–218.

Incomes Data Service (IDS) (1990) *Violence Against Staff.* Study 458, London: Incomes Data Services Ltd.

—— (1994) *Violence Against Staff.* Study 557, London: Incomes Data Services Ltd.

Mayhew, P., Aye Maung, N. and Mirrlees-Black, C. (1993) *The 1992 British Crime Survey.* Home Office Research Study 132, London: Home Office Research and Statistics Department.

McCloy, E. (1992) 'Management of post-incident trauma: a fire service perspective', *Occupational Medicine*, 42, 163–166.

McLoughlin *v.* O'Brian (1982) 2 All ER 298.

Mitchell, J. T. and Everly, G. S. (1993) *Critical Incident Stress Debriefing: An Operations Manual for the Prevention of Traumatic Stress among Emergency Service and Disaster Workers*, Ellicot City, USA: Chevron Publishing Corporation.

Poyner, B. and Warne, C. (1988) *Preventing Violence to Staff*, Health and Safety Executive, London: HMSO.

Raphael, B. (1986) *When Disaster Strikes: A Handbook for Caring Professionals*, London: Unwin Hyman.

Richards, D. (1994) 'Traumatic stress at work: A public health model', *British Journal of Guidance and Counselling*, 22, 51–64.

Tehrani, N. (1995) 'An integrated response to trauma in three Post Office businesses', *Work and Stress*, 9, 380–393.

Tehrani, N. and Westlake, R. (1994) 'Debriefing individuals affected by trauma', *Counselling Psychology Quarterly*, 7, 251–259.

Thomas *v.* General Motors-Holdens Ltd (1988) 49 SASR 11.

Tierney, K. J. (1989) 'The social and community contexts of disaster', in R. Gist and L. Lubin (eds) *Psychosocial Aspects of Disaster*, New York: Wiley.

Turner, S. W., Thompson, J. A. and Rosser, R. M. (1989) 'The Kings Cross Fire: planning a 'phase two' psychosocial response', *Disaster Management*, 2, 31–36.

United States Postal Service (1992) *The Red Book: A Guide for Effective Response to Critical Incidents and Trauma Recovery*, New York: United States Postal Service.

Warshaw, L. J. and Messite, J. (1996) 'Workplace violence: Preventative and interventive strategies', *Journal of Occupational and Environmental Medicine*, 38, 993–1,006.

8 Violence in public houses
An integrated organisational approach

Claire Lawrence, Diane Beale, Phil Leather and Rosie Dickson

Violence as a hazard for public house staff

While the majority of licensed premises experience little violence on a regular basis, the violence that can occur in and around public houses and bars is a well-recognised problem. One-sixth (16%) of incidents of violence reported in the 1992 British Crime Survey occurred in pubs and clubs (Mayhew, Aye Maung and Mirrlees-Black, 1993). In the 1996 British Crime Survey (Mirlees-Black, Mayhew and Percy, 1996), one-third of assaults by strangers and one-fifth of assaults by acquaintances were reported to have occurred in or around licensed premises. Such figures have stark implications for licensees and the breweries in terms of workers' safety, health and well-being. There are few national figures available in the UK regarding injuries to pub staff, but in the US, the rate of workplace homicide for bartenders is over three times the national average for workers in general (Jenkins, 1996).

The job of licensees and pub staff involves providing a service to the public, conducting money transactions, controlling people, working late in the evening, working as part of a local community, having responsibility for cash and valuable stock. In short, the job combines not only most of the kinds of interaction with the public which are most liable to become violent but also aspects of the work environment which are recognised by the Health and Safety Executive as increasing the vulnerability of staff (Poyner and Warne, 1988).

Other factors in the pub environment also increase the risk of violence occurring. Licensees do not simply sell drinks and food; they also provide a social environment in which people spend their leisure time. Interactions between staff and members of the public are complex and varied; they may be repeated a number of times in a day as the customer remains on the premises, they may also be repeated on subsequent days. Social interaction among customers or between staff and customers can spark off an aggressive incident at any time. Indeed, as two of the authors have argued elsewhere (Leather and Lawrence, 1995), violence and aggression are crucial issues within the public house context because the pub is a location where aggressive and violent episodes can become a part of everyday life. Additionally, it is an environment where many of the events theoretically associated with aggression and violence can be found, for example the competition between customers as 'last orders' is called on a busy evening (Cox and Leather, 1994; Leather and Lawrence, 1995). Felson, Baccaglini and Gmelch (1986) suggested that bars may create opportunities for conflict because they are locations in which social control can be difficult. Certain features or characteristics of the public house, including the individuals within the environment, may influence one's interpretation of, and reaction to, conflict situations. Indeed, the atmosphere of the bar may regulate the amount and type of aggressive behaviour that can be appropriately expressed.

This 'atmosphere' can derive from the formal and informal house rules which stipulate appropriate behaviour in a given situation, for example regarding 'turn taking' and the rules of play for pool and darts. Where standards and rules are clear, consistent and well-known, disputes are likely to be managed peacefully, largely because the possibility for misunderstanding is limited (Campbell and Marsh, 1979; Gibbs, 1986). In addition, the interpersonal behavioural style of the licensee and bar staff, and the quality of the physical environment also contribute to the pub atmosphere (see Leather and Lawrence, 1995). Indeed, the atmosphere of the bar, and the rules for dispute resolution, are shaped to a great extent by the licensee and the staff. Graham, LaRocque, Yetman, Ross and Guistra (1980) found that unfriendly bar workers who avoid interaction with customers are associated with an increased likelihood of bar room aggression.

Graham *et al.* (1980) also reported a greater frequency of physical aggression in bars which were untidy and had unclean and shabby decor. According to White, Kasl, Zahner and Will (1987), such physical decay of an environment, together with signs of incivility, can imply that social order has broken down. By implication, the quality of maintenance of the physical environment of the pub, along with the friendliness of staff, may be seen by customers as indicating how orderly the public house is.

Additionally, of course, pubs provide alcohol which, Pernanen (1991) suggested, modifies both the way in which people evaluate situations and the ways in which they feel they can cope with them, in such a way as to increase the chances of them acting in an aggressive manner. Although the precise relationship between alcohol and violence is debated (British Medical Association, 1995), there is increasing evidence to suggest that alcohol often leads to hostility and violence through its effects upon interpersonal conflict (Collins, 1981; Bennett and Lehman, 1996). Explaining why drinking might lead to violence between certain individuals and groups, but not others, or on certain occasions but not others, requires 'the exploration of differences in interpretation of events', and a 'detailed situational analysis' (Gibbs, 1986). Again, analysis at the level of the total pub environment is valuable. That is, the examination of the effects of alcohol must go beyond individuals in isolation and should also consider the situation those individuals are in, and their perceptions of the prevailing social and physical environment of the pub.

Drug use in public houses is also a significant problem which has been associated with violence and aggressive behaviour (MCM Research, 1993). As there is usually easy and open access and the premises are often noisy and crowded, pubs may be seen by some as the ideal venue for illegal activities, such as drug dealing or usage. Violence can arise from the effects of specific drugs, from arguments over financial transactions or from disputes between rival dealers. Licensees are legally required to ensure that their premises are not used for drug-related activity, so are obliged to tackle any such activity they find. However, managing such potentially violent elements may place licensees in dangerous situations demanding great care and skill to avoid repercussions.

It is not surprising then, that licensees see their job as a multiskilled role and one where the potential for conflict is never far from the surface.

I don't think [people] appreciate the job we face day in and day out. We are 24 hour watchmen and we have to be very good peacemakers. Our job involves being everything from a marriage counsellor to a champion boxer. With a lot of other occupations in between.

A publican is 'king' lawmaker, judge and policeman of his own self-contained kingdom. Membership to his society is open to all.

(Hillas, Cox and Higgins, 1988)

The effects of violence may be exacerbated because the majority of licensees live on the premises, around three quarters with partners and a third with children (Dickson, Leather, Beale and Cox, 1994b). This may or may not increase the risk of violence occurring, but will certainly increase the potential for harm in terms of the involvement of the family and the home. Further, much of the work of licensees is directed towards the creation of an atmosphere in which people feel safe and comfortable, will want to stay and to return on a regular basis; violence in the pub may discourage customers and therefore affect the profitability of the business and the livelihood of the licensee. As one of Hillas, Cox and Higgins' (1988) sample of licensees put it: '[A violent incident] totally depresses the pub atmosphere and the manager, some customers will leave and will probably not return. De-motivation of all.'

Indeed, in the follow-up survey (Dickson *et al.*, 1994b), over a third of licensees (36.8%) indicated that they believed the business viability of their pub was highly at risk from the possibility of violence in the pub.

An integrated strategy for tackling public house violence

The Centre for Organizational Health and Development (COHD) has been working with Allied Domecq Retailing (ADR), the major international food and drinks retailer, since 1987, to examine and combat violence within their licensed houses (Dickson, Leather, Beale and Cox, 1994a). ADR operates around 4,500 licensed premises, spread throughout England, Wales and Scotland, and comprising a wide variety of pubs in terms of size, style, location and clientele. The overall strategy (Dickson, Cox, Leather, Beale and Farnsworth, 1993) was based on the concept of the control cycle for risk management, as described by Cox and Cox (1993). This involves acceptance of the problem, identification of hazards and the nature of harm, assessment of the risk, design of intervention strategies, implementation of those strategies, monitoring and evaluation and continuous feedback to the other stages.

Identification of the nature, the severity and the extent of the problem was achieved by extensive initial research within the London area (Hillas *et al.*, 1988). This provided three main recommendations for the longer term:

- to establish a reporting system to monitor the frequency and nature of violent incidents throughout the organisation;
- to train all licensees and higher management in methods of reducing the risk of violence occurring and in dealing with any violent, or potentially violent, situations, should they occur; and
- to increase organisational support for licensees in the aftermath of violent incidents, including the provision of access to specialist counselling where appropriate.

These recommendations have all been implemented within the 'Keeping Pubs Peaceful' scheme (KPP). The reporting system was set up with an Incident Report Centre based at Nottingham University and KPP training workshops were devised and implemented, incorporating the findings of the initial research and the reporting system. Post-incident support has been increased by ADR in various ways, including awareness training of area managers, training of post-incident debriefers and referral to specialist post-trauma counselling. Additionally there has been continuing research into the nature of violent incidents and the impact of aspects of the pub environment on people's judgements about violence. A policy document for the management of violence within licensed premises, based on official guidance and the research within ADR, has been devised and adopted.

Of vital importance is that all the measures implemented are seen as interdependent, continually feeding information back to each other and to management, as outlined in Figure 8.1. Equally important is that they are under constant review for efficacy. In ADR, monitoring and evaluation have been carried out, for example, through the reporting system, further surveys of licensees (Dickson *et al.*, 1994b) and evaluation of both the KPP training workshops (Dickson, Leather and Beale, 1994) and the trauma counselling service.

The measures taken, and their interdependence, constitute an integrated organisational approach, as discussed in Chapter 1. The ADR scheme is now considered in greater detail under each of its principal components, i.e.

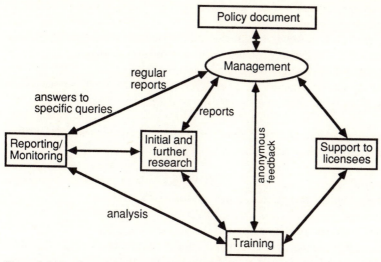

Figure 8.1 Outline of the Keeping Pubs Peaceful project

1   *Problem identification and analysis*: initial research, the incident reporting system and corroboration of findings in subsequent research;
2   *Organisational response*: the adoption of a formal organisational policy, as well as training and post-incident support;
3   *Evaluation*.

The interdependence of the measures and input from supplementary research will also be described.

Problem identification and analysis

Initial research

The Nottingham study of 1987 and 1988 (Hillas *et al.*, 1988) was designed to investigate the nature and the control of violence in managed houses. Information was gathered via questionnaires, interviews and existing incident reports, in order to investigate the effects of violent incidents upon managers and assistant managers. The effects of violence were measured in terms of:

- general effects on the managers and their families, staff and customers;
- staff turnover and intention to quit;
- effects on 'take';
- customers' patronage of the pub.

While the majority of pubs experienced little violence on a regular basis, many managers reported that violence occurred in cycles, making quantification difficult.

The results did, however, reveal that many licensees were clearly working and living under threat of violence even if it did not always materialise as actual physical assaults. The social and psychological consequences of living and working under such threat were clearly articulated by some of the licensees:

> It increases your stress, increase of alcohol and nicotine intake, fear, decrease of work performance.

> Demoralising. Causes great stress. Affects your domestic relationships and your ability to handle fatigue, amongst other things.

Customers were believed to respond to violence in a generally uniform way by taking their patronage elsewhere, albeit temporarily: 'Nobody likes drinking in a rough pub where a fight can start any minute.'

Given both the difficulties in measuring the occurrence of violence and the negative consequences when it does occur, a principal recommendation from this initial survey was the need for an on-going monitoring system to be established.

Reporting system

The KPP incident reporting system was set up in 1989 within ADR. Since 1996, it has been integrated with ADR's system for reporting injuries to people at work to the local authority. This follows the inclusion of 'an act of non-consensual physical violence done to a person at work' as an 'accident' in the Reporting of Injuries, Diseases and Dangerous Occurrences Regulations 1995 (RIDDOR 95: see Chapter 2 of this volume for more detail). However, the KPP system goes well beyond RIDDOR 95 in terms of both the type of incident that should be reported and the amount of detail that is recorded. Under RIDDOR 95, the requirement for reporting is determined entirely by the outcome of the incident in terms of injury to the worker, as discussed by Beale, Cox and Leather (1996). The KPP system, on the other hand, requires that *all* violent incidents are reported, independent of the physical outcome, thus including incidents in which there was little physical injury but which were very frightening or problematic for staff or caused damage to property. This greater scope and enhanced detail allows considerably more to be learnt about the patterns of violence throughout the licensed houses and about the nature and development of incidents. This, in turn, helps identify those specific situations and processes which training can most effectively focus upon.

When a violent incident is reported, and after the immediate problems have been dealt with, a security manager visits the pub to investigate and interview the licensee and other staff involved. Together they complete the four-page Keeping Pubs Peaceful Incident Report Form (KPP IRF). The KPP IRF includes both specific 'tick-box' questions and more open questions requiring a fairly detailed description of the incident. This combination has been found to provide the most useful information about the incident without being too time-consuming for reporting licensees. (A copy of the KPP IRF is given as Appendix 2.)

Copies of the completed form are sent to the Incident Report Centre as well as to other relevant company personnel. Analysis of the incident reports by the Centre provides valuable information for management about, for example, the people involved in incidents, what initiated incidents and how they progressed (see Figure 8.2), the outcome of incidents and any action that licensees would like to see taken. Results from the reporting system are fed back to ADR in the form of regular reports, either giving a comprehensive overview of the numbers and nature of incidents reported or concentrating on particular aspects of the incidents. Such analyses allow management to understand something of the nature of the incidents that their staff are having to face (Beale, Lawrence, Leather and Cox, 1995).

It is a legal requirement, under the Management of Health and Safety Regulations (Health and Safety Executive, 1992), for organisations to identify the risks to staff from their work environment. Data obtained from incident reporting regarding specific precursors to aggressive and violent incidents contribute towards fulfilling this requirement. Within ADR, a variety of misbehaviours on the part of customers was reported in the initial stages of half the incidents. Whilst arguments or fights between customers initiated over a quarter of incidents some more specific customer misbehaviours were: using abusive language, refusing to drink up and leave after

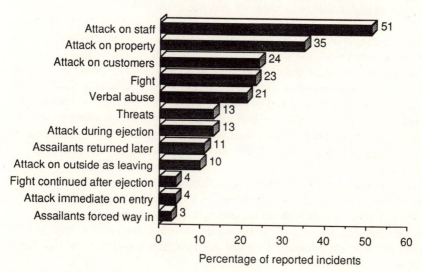

Figure 8.2 What happened in reported incidents

time or demanding service after time, exhibiting general 'rowdy' behaviour, throwing things around, annoying other customers, attempting to get behind the bar or attempting to steal from the pub premises. Other events initiating incidents were: barred customers entering the premises, arguments involving members of staff and accidents or misunderstandings. Additionally, 7.2% of incidents were thought to have occurred as repercussions from previous incidents at the premises. It is notable that pre-planned attacks, such as armed robberies or assailants coming looking for their victims, accounted for only 8.2% of reported incidents. More detailed information is given in Chapter 5.

Staff were reported to have intervened in two-fifths of reported incidents. Analysis of these incidents has indicated the high risk of staff being attacked when they intervene in incidents and of further action occurring after assailants have apparently left the premises. These findings are discussed in more detail in a later section.

Follow-up research

Following the initial research completed by Hillas *et al.* (1988), a further survey was completed in the same part of the company seven years later (Dickson *et al.*, 1994b). The primary aims of this survey were:

- to investigate the extent to which licensees felt concerned about the risk of violence in their pubs;
- to examine the effects of actual and potential violence on licensees' feelings of health and well-being, satisfaction with the job and long-term commitment to the company;
- to identify the people who provide support to licensees in managing the threat and actual occurrence of violence in the pub.

The frequencies of occurrence of different types of incident stated by the responding licensees are shown in Table 8.1. Well over a fifth of the licensees had experienced fights involving weapons at their premises; one in sixteen had experienced them at least twice a year. Almost a third of the licensees had experienced fights without weapons at least twice a year; one-ninth at least monthly. Over a third of them experienced shouting or abusive language at least once a week, one-sixth experienced it daily. Only one in sixteen reporting licensees said they never experienced any of these types of incidents.

The prevalence of violence was reflected in the measures of concern about violence. Around half the licensees scored above the mid-point of the scale provided, where high scores denoted great concern. Almost a quarter of licensees felt themselves to be highly at risk from violence and over a third felt that the business viability of their pub was highly at risk from violence.

Table 8.1 Numbers of respondents reporting different frequencies of occurrence of aggressive or violent incidents (*N* = 242)

Aggressive or violent incident	Reported frequency of occurrence						
	Daily	Weekly	Fortnightly	Monthly	2 to 6 monthly	Less than 6 monthly	Never
Shouting, abusive language	41	51	13	29	38	55	15
Pushing and shoving	4	19	15	25	47	70	53
One to one fight, no weapons	0	4	4	19	46	86	78
More than two fighting, no weapons	0	1	2	6	26	53	149
One to one fight, with weapons	0	0	0	3	12	38	181
More than two fighting, with weapons	0	0	0	2	5	31	196

Those licensees who felt very much at risk and very worried about violence experienced less job satisfaction, less loyalty to the company, and reported feeling both more 'worn out' and more 'up tight' (General Well-being Questionnaire: Cox, Thirlaway, Gotts and Cox, 1983).

Licensees were asked about the levels of support they received concerning the management of violence. Respondents reported getting most support from sources outside the company hierarchy, for example from friends and family, the police and other licensees. This type of support, however, did not affect any of their feelings of well-being, their fear of violence, or their feelings towards the company they worked for. The level of support they felt they received from the company, however, did have a great effect on these measures. In particular, high levels of support from their area manager were associated with (1) lower levels of fear of violence, (2) higher levels of job satisfaction, (3) higher levels of commitment and loyalty to the company, and (4) a more conciliatory attitude to conflict resolution. Additionally, licensees who felt they got higher levels of support from the area manager were also less up tight and less worn out (Leather, Lawrence, Beale, Cox and Dickson, 1998).

The form of entertainment and food offered in the pub were also related to the occurrence of problems in the pub. In particular, pubs which experienced a higher frequency of violent incidents were also more likely to have a pool table, a juke box, pub games and satellite television, and were less likely to serve lunch time food. The licensees of these pubs were also more likely to suspect that drugs were being taken or sold in their pubs and they felt more concerned about violence. However, pool and other games also provided a source of satisfaction to some licensees. This survey helped to focus attention on the importance of careful management of such activities.

Stress audit

A questionnaire-based stress audit, undertaken in part of ADR during 1995, served to corroborate the status of violence as a significant source of stress for licensees. This audit aimed to identify (1) important sources of work stress for pub managers, (2) characteristic ways of coping with the stress, and (3) negative effects of the stress.

Although the questionnaire made no reference to it at all, violence was reported as the fourth most frequent stressor, or problem, facing licensees. Indeed, one-third of the licensees reported violence to be a very serious problem indeed. More importantly, violence was more strongly related to a range of negative outcomes than was any other reported source of stress, including those issues that were more frequently reported as problems. The negative outcomes included reduced job satisfaction, poorer well-being and a greater intention to quit the job. Once again, the only type of support which had any real impact upon these negative consequences was that from the licensee's area manager (Leather and Lee, 1995).

Organisational response

Policy statement

It is important that an organisation's response to violence is multi-faceted and that actions are targeted at prevention and rehabilitation and are fully integrated within a uniform and common strategy. The adoption of a written policy on violence is a key aspect in achieving such integration, in marking the organisation's commitment and in setting standards by which progress can be judged. The policy is, in many ways, a statement of the organisation's values.

The ADR policy statement was briefed to the main board, line managers and licensees via a variety of existing communication channels to ensure that all staff were made aware of the document. The policy serves as a good example of what such a statement of values and intended practice ought to cover. As such, it includes a statement of:

1   the seriousness of the problem and the Company's commitment to managing it;
2   the importance of reporting and monitoring incidents of violence and committing resources to the establishing of an effective reporting system;
3   the content and delivery of whatever training is deemed appropriate to assist in the prevention of violence, or the rehabilitation of those

affected by it;

4 how line managers and other support personnel should act at the 'point of impact', that is when dealing with victims immediately after an incident has happened;

5 the availability and character of effective debriefing procedures and the mechanism by which these are to be instituted and used;

6 the availability of in-house and/or external professional services, such as counselling, should it be deemed necessary in individual cases.

In short, the policy provides both a focus for the entire programme and a framework which bonds the various elements together. Most important of all, the policy document is a clear and unambiguous statement of the Company's intention to take the problem of violence seriously and manage it in a proactive and professional way.

Training of licensees

Under the ADR policy on violence, all licensees undergo training in the handling of potentially violent situations. New licensees attend a two-hour module on violence as part of their initial training. More experienced licensees attend the two-day Keeping Pubs Peaceful training workshop (Leather, Beale, Lawrence and Maxwell, 1996).

The workshops look initially at the reasons why people might become violent, as outlined in Chapter 3, then consider methods of (1) reducing the risk of problem incidents occurring, (2) resolving conflict when problems arise and (3) managing the aftermath of any incidents that do result in violence. KPP training regards licensees as experts in their field and builds on their experience and knowledge, but it also incorporates findings from the incident reporting system, from survey research specific to ADR and from wider psychological research into violence. Goals of the training workshops are: (1) to highlight a range of possible strategies which have been found useful in reducing the likelihood of violence resulting from conflict situations, and (2) to promote change in the management of conflict away from strategies which might exacerbate violent behaviour.

Area managers, higher managers and security staff are trained alongside licensees, whenever possible, so that managers gain a wider understanding of the problems that licensees face and appreciate ways in which they can be supported. This helps to foster a learning or problem-solving culture, with respect to violence, both within the training workshop and within the company as a whole. In addition, such integrated training helps to ensure that company policies and procedures are applied consistently, and to match management and licensees' attitudes and expectations regarding violence.

A large group of company personnel, including trainers, area managers, security managers, human resources managers, as well as experienced licensees, have been trained to run the two-day workshop for other licensees.

In this way 'ownership' of the problem of violence has been incorporated more deeply into the 'organisational culture' of the company.

Post-incident support

The ADR policy document recommends that all licensees reporting a violent incident should receive visits from their area manager and regional security manager on the day of the incident, if possible. This is: (1) to talk to all staff who were involved in the incident, to listen and reassure; (2) to assist with practical problems arising from the incident, such as getting staff home, organising repairs and emergency staff cover, ensuring the security of the premises; (3) to protect the staff from the press; and (4) to assess whether a psychological debrief is likely to be required. This assessment is discussed with the human resources personnel responsible for psychological debriefing. If such a debrief is recommended, it is carried out within two weeks and includes all employees who were involved in, or who witnessed, the incident. Personnel who conduct psychological debriefs have all been trained by the occupational health adviser, a consultant psychiatrist. If specialist counselling is considered necessary, the victim is referred to an approved local counselling service or to a nominated mental health professional. All debriefing and counselling is formally recorded, but these records are strictly confidential.

Evaluation

Evaluation of the training workshops

In order to ensure that the training was achieving its goals, a direct evaluation of the workshops was undertaken in 1993. These goals had been made explicit at the outset of the development of the training and, indeed, scope for evaluation was introduced into the original design. The evaluation (Dickson, Leather and Beale, 1994) was carried out by eliciting licensees' views using a questionnaire designed to measure knowledge of, and attitudes to, the three main areas of training: (1) reducing the risk of violence, (2) resolving conflict and (3) managing the aftermath. Questionnaires were administered to licensees before and after training, and their scores were compared to a matched control group of licensees who had not taken part in the KPP training workshops but had attended a training course, of similar length and format, on an unrelated topic.

Results showed that following KPP training specifically, licensees were:

- dissuaded from simple and hasty reliance on confrontational force and were more positive towards diplomatic approaches to conflict resolution;
- awakened to the nature of the traumatic response which may follow exposure to violence, and how best to counter it; and,

• helped to realise and accept that management – and the company as a whole – were keen and available to help, as well as being effective in that help.

On the whole, the evaluation demonstrated that the training programme was effective in modifying licensees' attitudes regarding violent incidents.

Interdependence of the measures

Input to training from the reporting system

Information from the reporting system is used to update and inform the training of licensees. For example, weapons were used in more than half the reported incidents (Beale *et al.*, 1995); however, the vast majority of weapons were objects commonly found in the pub environment, such as glasses or bottles, rather than weapons intentionally brought in. This illustrates to pub staff the need to minimise the number of potential weapons, both by the choice of equipment and decor and by the prompt clearing of glasses.

Another finding regarding weapons was that, while licensees considered weapons as making an incident more serious, the reported incidents which involved weapons, and in particular those in which weapons were brought in, actually resulted in less serious injuries to staff than those which did not involve weapons. This type of finding can be used to alert staff to the fact that some of the most serious injuries were inflicted not by weapons but by head butting, punching, kicking and even biting. They need to be vigilant and cautious even when dealing with incidents where no weapon is involved and which initially do not seem particularly serious, as these may escalate to yield more serious injury.

Analysis of the incident reports by the logical pathway method (Beale, Cox, Clarke, Lawrence and Leather, 1998) revealed the most common sequence of events shown in Figure 8.3. These findings are used in KPP training to emphasise licensees' vulnerability to attack when they have to intervene in customer problems. Licensees are encouraged to consider ways to reduce the likelihood of misbehaviour by, and arguments between, their customers, methods of intervening safely and effectively when customer problems occur, and ways of minimising their own vulnerability to attack, both immediately and after the protagonists have apparently left the premises.

Around a quarter of reported incidents involved further action after assailants had apparently left the premises, and many incidents were thought to be repercussions from previous happenings in the pub. Such findings emphasise the importance of both maintaining vigilance after an incident is apparently over and ensuring that the incident is properly 'ended'. In KPP training, situations where both the licensee and the assailant or potential

The most common sequence of events was:

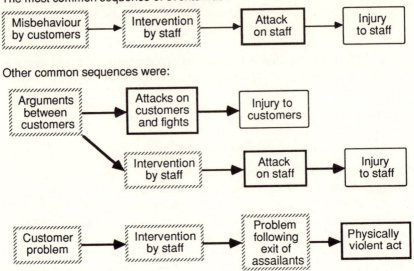

Figure 8.3 Common sequences of events in reported incidents

assailant can save face are encouraged, rather than one winning as the other loses. It is believed that in these cases, the likelihood of subsequent 'grudge' or vendetta attacks is lessened.

Input to post-incident support from the reporting system

In the KPP incident reporting system, licensees are asked to rate how serious they considered the incident to be. Seriousness ratings were seen to be determined partly by the outcome of an incident in terms of the severity of injury and the number of people injured, as would be expected. However, other circumstances were also associated with higher seriousness ratings, for example, the presence or use of a weapon, the involvement of drugs, a higher number of assailants, an attack on a member of staff, particularly if that member of staff was a woman, and the later return of the assailant.

A wide range of other factors also affected a licensee's perception of how serious an incident was, including the fear experienced during the incident, the apparent reason for the incident, the perceived intent, known previous history of violence and extent of intoxication of assailants, the potential for future repercussions or connection to previous incidents at the premises, the previous experience of violent incidents of the staff involved, the effect on licensee's family, the reaction of customers and the effect on trade. Such a variety of factors indicate that management should be aware that licensees, or other pub staff, may consider an incident to be very serious even though there was little resultant physical injury or damage. It is not appropriate for personnel who were not present at the incident to make judgements as to how frightening it was or how staff 'ought' to react.

Additionally, licensees are asked for actions they would like to see taken after the incident. Such information provides valuable insights into the needs of licensees who have experienced violence and allows management to provide appropriate support. Awareness of the issues surrounding violent incidents is now incorporated into management training and development programmes.

Input from supplementary research

From anecdotal information, it became clear that licensees believed that customers were dissuaded from returning to pubs following an incident of violence. As many assaults occurred at the point when licensees intervened during a conflict situation, research was carried out to investigate the effects of a licensee's conflict intervention style on independent observers' judgements of (1) the licensee, (2) the public house atmosphere and (3) the 'aggressor' (Leather and Lawrence, 1995). These studies aimed to discover how people judged violent events in pubs. The participants who acted as 'observers' were all aged between 18 and 25 – the age predominantly associated with high involvement in violence. All participants read a written account of a violent incident, based on actual reported incidents, in which a licensee had to deal with two men who were building up to a fight. There were two versions of the account. In one version the licensee attempted to calm the men without touching them; in a second version, he physically separated the two men. In both cases, the end result was the same: the licensee was physically assaulted by the aggressor. The setting of the incident was depicted photographically with participants being shown photographs of the same pub but with either a tidy or an untidy interior and either with or without door security, in the form of 'bouncers'. Each participant read only one version of the account and saw only one setting.

Significantly, participants regarded the licensee as less aggressive, more friendly, and less to blame for the violent outcome when he attempted a non-physical intervention, regardless of the setting. Participants who judged the licensee positively also judged the pub to be less tense, more welcoming, more friendly and less aggressive. These participants also expressed a greater likelihood that they would drink at that pub, and they estimated that violent incidents occurred at the pub less frequently.

Interestingly, the licensee was perceived more favourably when the setting was tidy regardless of his actions. Conversely, when the interior was untidy and door supervisors were present, judgements of the licensee were more negative, with 'bouncers' making the pub appear 'unfriendly', 'tense' and 'threatening'.

Importantly, participants believed that the aggressor's behaviour was more justified when the licensee physically separated the men than when he used non-physical intervention, particularly when bouncers were present and the pub was untidy.

As some degree of violence in public houses may be unavoidable, occasionally the only remaining avenues open for the licensee and staff is to limit the damage as much as possible and to manage the impressions that customers form of the pub. From this research, it is clear that it is not inevitable that individuals will judge a pub negatively when they have heard about or observed a violent incident there, but that these judgements depend crucially on the overall pub environment and the actions of the licensee. The findings are used in training to emphasise to licensees both the importance of maintaining the physical environment of the pub and the positive benefits of non-physical methods of calming problem situations. They also encourage licensees to be particularly careful of the impression that can be given by having bouncers on the door.

Conclusions

Violence at work, and within the licensed trade in particular, is an issue which can command a high profile within companies and communities. It is essential, therefore, that an analysis of the nature, prevalence and impact of violence throughout the organisation as a whole is investigated and monitored, and that appropriate action is taken on the strength of the monitoring process. Consequent interventions should always be thoroughly evaluated and updated in the light of research and any changes in the nature of violence and aggression prevalent within the organisation.

Any intervention is likely to increase awareness of the problem. Increased awareness, in turn, may increase the expectations of what is being done to tackle the problem. It is important that organisations can match the expectations of staff with appropriate action and support. A problem-solving approach tackles this using a range of interventions applied throughout the organisation and emphasising the crucial role played by higher management in this process. For an effective system of violence reduction to develop, it is essential that channels for incident reporting are confidential, are widely understood within the company and are endorsed by line managers and higher management. Similarly, it is vital that the issue of violence at work is seen as important throughout the organisation as a whole, and that strategies to reduce the effects and prevalence of violence are implemented at an organisation-wide level. The organisational culture must accept that violence is a problem to be tackled by everyone within the organisation, not just by those who are unfortunate enough to experience it.

References

Beale, D., Cox, T., Clarke, D., Lawrence, C. and Leather, P. (1998) 'Temporal architecture of violent incidents', *Journal of Occupational Health Psychology*,

3(1), 65–82.

Beale, D., Cox, T. and Leather, P. (1996) 'Work-related violence – is national reporting good enough?' *Work and Stress*, 10, 99–103.

Beale, D., Lawrence, C., Leather, P. and Cox, T. (1995) *Keeping Public Houses Peaceful Incident Report Forms: An Interim Analysis to December 1994*, Report TW22/95 prepared for Allied Domecq Retailing Limited. Nottingham: Centre for Organizational Health and Development, Department of Psychology, University of Nottingham.

Bennett, J. B. and Lehman, W. E. K. (1996) 'Alcohol, antagonism, and witnessing violence in the workplace: drinking climates and social alienation-integration', in G. R. VandenBos and E. Q. Bulatao (eds) *Violence on the Job.* pp.105–152, Washington, DC: American Psychological Association.

British Medical Association (1995) 'MPs and Portman Group clash on alcohol and crime', *UK Alcohol Alert: Incorporating Alliance News*, Series No. 12, London: Institute of Alcohol Studies.

Campbell, A. and Marsh, P. (1979) *Final Report to Whitbread Ltd*, Oxford: Contemporary Violence Research Centre, Oxford University.

Collins, J. J. (1981) *Drinking and Crime: Perspectives on the Relationships Between Alcohol Consumption and Criminal Behavior*, New York: Guilford Press.

Cox, T. and Cox, S. (1993) *Psychosocial and Organizational Hazards at Work: Control and Monitoring*, European Occupational Health Series No. 5, Copenhagen: WHO Regional Office for Europe.

Cox, T. and Leather, P. (1994) 'The prevention of violence at work: application of a cognitive behavioural theory', in C. L. Cooper and I. T. Robertson (eds) *International Review of Industrial and Organizational Psychology*, Vol. 9, pp. 213–245, Chichester: Wiley and Sons.

Cox, T., Thirlaway, M., Gotts, G. and Cox, S. (1983) 'The nature and assessment of general well-being', *Journal of Psychosomatic Research*, 27, 353–359.

Dickson, R., Cox, T., Leather, P., Beale, D. and Farnsworth, B. (1993) 'Violence at work', *Occupational Health Review*, 46, 22–24.

Dickson, R., Leather, P. and Beale D. (1994) *Keeping Pubs Peaceful Training Evaluation Executive Summary*, Report prepared for Allied Domecq Retailing Limited. Nottingham: Centre for Organizational Health and Development, Department of Psychology, University of Nottingham.

Dickson, R., Leather, P., Beale, D. and Cox, T. (1994a) 'Intervention strategies to manage workplace violence', *Occupational Health Review*, 50, 15–18.

Dickson, R., Leather, P., Beale, D. and Cox, T. (1994b) *Working in Licensed Houses: A Study of the Licensee's Job*, Report TW20/94 prepared for Allied Domecq Retailing Limited. Nottingham: Centre for Organizational Health and Development, Department of Psychology, University of Nottingham.

Felson, R. B., Baccaglini, W. and Gmelch, G. (1986) 'Bar-room brawl: aggression and violence in Irish and American bars', in A. Campbell and J. J. Gibbs (eds) *Violent Transactions*, Oxford: Blackwell.

Gibbs, J. J. (1986) 'Alcohol consumption, cognition and context: examining tavern violence', in A. Campbell and J. J. Gibbs (eds) *Violent Transactions*, Oxford: Blackwell.

Graham, K., La Rocque, L., Yetman, R., Ross, T. J. and Giustra, Y. (1980) 'Aggression and barroom environments', *Journal of Studies on Alcohol*, 41, 277–292.

Health and Safety Executive (1992) *The Management of Health and Safety Regulations*, Sudbury, Suffolk: HSE Books.

Hillas, S., Cox, T. and Higgins, G. (1988) *Results of the Main Questionnaire Survey*, Report TW5/88 prepared for Allied Breweries. Nottingham: Stress Research Group, Department of Psychology, University of Nottingham.

Jenkins, E. L. (1996) 'Workplace homicide – industries and occupations at high-risk', *Occupational Medicine – State of the Art Reviews*, 11, 219–225.

Leather, P., Beale, D., Lawrence, C. and Maxwell, P. (1996) *Keeping Pubs Peaceful Training Manual*, Nottingham: Centre for Organizational Health and Development, Department of Psychology, University of Nottingham.

Leather, P. J. and Lawrence, C. (1995) 'Perceiving pub violence: the symbolic influence of social and environmental factors', *British Journal of Social Psychology*, 34, 395–407.

Leather, P., Lawrence, C., Beale, D., Cox, T. and Dickson, R. (1998) 'Exposure to occupational violence and the buffering effects of intra-organizational support', *Work and Stress*, 12(2).

Leather, P. and Lee, L. (1995) 'Who helps? What helps? An empirical investigation of the effects of type and source of support upon occupational stress reactions', Paper presented to the *International Conference on Work and Well-Being: An Agenda for Europe*, Nottingham, December.

Mayhew, P., Aye Maung, N. and Mirrlees-Black, C. (1993) *The 1992 British Crime Survey*, Home Office Research Study 132, London: Home Office Research and Statistics Department.

MCM Research (1993) *Drugs and Pubs: A Guide for Licensees*, London: The Brewers' Society.

Mirrlees-Black, C., Mayhew, P. and Percy, A. (1996) 'The 1996 British Crime Survey', *Home Office Statistical Bulletin*, 19/96.

Pernanen, K. (1991) *Alcohol in Human Violence*, London: Guilford Press.

Poyner, B. and Warne, C. (1988) *Preventing Violence to Staff*, London: Health and Safety Executive, London: HMSO.

Reporting of Injuries, Diseases and Dangerous Occurrences Regulations 1995. Statutory Instrument 1995 No. 3163, London: HMSO.

White, M., Kasl, S. V., Zahner, G. E. P. and Will, J. C. (1987) 'Perceived crime in the neighbourhood and mental health of women and children', *Environment and Behaviour*, 19, 588–613.

Reducing violence to teachers in the workplace

Learning to make schools safe

Gerv Leyden

Introduction

Within the UK, pupil behaviour has become the subject of contentious political debate during the last decade and a half, with increasing numbers of pupils being excluded from schools for disciplinary reasons. In the 1994/5 school year 12,458 pupils were excluded, compared with just under 3,000 in 1990/1. Against this background the 1995/6 school year witnessed the shocking murder of a London headteacher in December, followed by the tragic shooting of sixteen pupils and a teacher by an intruder in Dunblane primary school, and a frenzied machete attack (again by an intruder) in a Wolverhampton infant school which left three young children and four adults seriously injured. These appalling events left behind a wake of grief for the victims, their families and friends, and fears for the future safety of pupils, teachers and parents in our schools.

The focus of this chapter is on the specific issue of occupational violence towards teachers. The aims are to examine what we know about the incidence of such violence, the nature of the relationship between the teacher and assailant, and the contribution of organisational factors to the reduction of conflict and violence. The chapter will also address the management of a seriously violent incident in school.

Schools are both teacher systems and pupil systems which interact inextricably. I will therefore draw on the contribution of both occupational and educational psychology to our understanding of violence to teachers, and in providing a framework for making our schools safer.

Violence to teachers: incidence

Several attempts have been made in the past two decades to measure the incidence of violence to teachers in the UK, mostly through teacher union surveys, but most have been hindered by low response rates and the lack of a shared definition of violence. However, they provide some vivid accounts of the assaults suffered by some teachers in carrying out their duties.

We have to look elsewhere for detailed information about the incidence, nature and context of violence to teachers. In the US, as part of a Report for Congress (National Institute of Education [NIE], 1978), 642 public junior and high schools participated in a study of teachers' perceptions of violence and vandalism. In all, 23,895 individual teachers contributed. An estimated 0.5% of the teachers reported that they had been physically assaulted during the survey month. While fewer teachers than pupils were attacked, 19% of the teacher victims required medical treatment, as opposed to 4% of the students. The risks of attack were the same for female and male teachers.

Of particular concern was the finding that an initial assault increased the risk of the teacher being further victimised. For example, while less than 4/100ths of one percent of female teachers reported the trauma of rape during the survey month, the risks escalated dramatically if the teacher had been physically assaulted in the previous two months: 'The chances of also being raped in that period shot up from less than 1 in 1,000 to almost 1 in 10 (9.5%), more than a 100 fold increase in risk' (NIE, 1978).

Multiple victimisation in the UK

A union member's account

During the last fourteen years I have been assaulted seven times, once with a knife, once with a stiletto, once with an air rifle (when I was shot in the chest), once when a pupil fed gas into my classroom when I was teaching, twice when pupils have attempted to assault me with their fists and once when an ex-pupil tried twice to run me over with a car.

National Association of Schoolmasters/
Union of Women Teachers (NAS/UWT), 1986

In the UK neither the central government nor the local education authorities (LEAs) have routinely collected figures on violence to teachers, the one exception being the former Inner London Education Authority (ILEA) which recorded a rate of 0.23 incidents per mainstream school in one school year. This rate rose to 2.48 violent incidents in each special school (Poyner and Warne, 1988). Little is known about the incidents themselves, with almost nothing being recorded about the pupil or other assailants, the staff victims or the existing relationship between them.

In the absence of a national recording system, some information about violence to teachers in England and Wales can be gleaned from the other sources. For instance the Elton Report (Department of Education and Science and the Welsh Office, 1989) enquired about teachers' experience of violence during one designated week. Of the 2,500 secondary school teachers in the sample 15% reported verbal abuse during that period, while

1.7% encountered direct 'physical aggression' when teaching. A further 1.1% of teachers described similar aggressive incidents during their general duties round the school. Follow-up interviews with individual teachers revealed a wide divergence of opinion about what constituted 'physical violence', a finding which underlines the need for a shared vocabulary and agreed definitions of violence.

Following the tragic events of the early 1990s the DfEE commissioned the Lamplugh Trust and Scarman Centre to undertake research into personal safety in schools (Gill and Hearnshaw, 1997). As with the earlier ILEA data the incidence figures related to schools rather than to teachers. Returns were received from 2,303 primary, secondary and special schools and Pupil Referral Units (PRUs) – a response rate of 60%. Disappointingly only one in four of the responding schools routinely recorded all instances of violence and the criteria employed relied on a degree of subjectivity. Any attempts to extrapolate from the findings to incidence rates for schools as a whole must, therefore, be treated with caution. Nevertheless, this report provides the most comprehensive data yet available in the UK and provides support for other findings that incidents of physical violence to teachers are relatively rare. Less 'extreme' violence, e.g. pushing and verbal abuse, is far more commonplace in the daily life of the school and a source of chronic stress to teachers (see Education Services Advisory Committee, 1990a).

Analysis of violence to teachers in schools

What do the above findings tell us about the people and interactions involved, and the context of violence in schools? Despite the absence of routine recording procedures it is possible to piece together information from a range of sources to build up a broad profile of the nature of violence to staff in schools.

Individuals and interactions

Evidence from the UK, although incomplete, is consistent with the US findings. Most violence to staff (teachers, secretaries, teaching assistants, caretakers, etc.) is committed by pupils, parents and intruders.

Pupils

The ILEA study of around 500 violent incidents found that at least 57% involved pupil assailants, 5.5% involved intruders and 4% involved parents or other members of pupils' families (Poyner and Warne, 1988). The authors pointed out that children are considered a 'risk group', in terms of becoming assailants, because of their immaturity, greater difficulty in controlling their own behaviour and susceptibility to influence by the rest of the group.

Gill and Hearnshaw (1997) provided a more detailed breakdown of pupil violence. Of participating schools 16% reported incidents of pupils spitting or pushing at teachers within the survey year, 18% recorded teachers being hit or kicked and 3% recorded teachers having been attacked with a weapon.

There is general consensus that staff were most at risk when physically restraining a pupil (usually when the latter was having a temper tantrum), intervening in a fight between pupils, excluding a disobedient pupil from the classroom, or verbally disciplining a pupil. For teachers, problems generally occurred in the classroom while for mid-day supervisors they usually occurred in the playground.

Parents and outsiders

Despite media concern over 'intruder violence', intruders were ranked fifth in the list of perpetrators (Gill and Hearnshaw, 1997). Parents were responsible for most of the assaults on staff by 'outsiders', followed by ex-pupils, pupils from other schools and excluded pupils.

Heads and deputy heads were victims in half the attacks on teachers by parents in the ILEA study (Poyner and Warne, 1988). Little information was available about the reasons for these attacks. Where information was available, the dispute often focused on a disagreement over the disciplining of a pupil. While the reporting of injury to other categories of staff was significantly lower, there were instances of assault by parents on non-teaching staff.

Additionally, we are now aware of the seriousness of incidents when armed intruders enter schools with the aim of causing serious injury and even death to pupils and staff. Yet we still know relatively little about the true incidence of intruder violence and the background of the people involved. The evidence of the most serious incidents, such as those at Wolverhampton and Dunblane, suggests that they may not be typical and were carried out by individuals at odds with themselves or the society within which they lived. The unpredictability of such attacks poses serious problems for schools in protecting pupils and staff. Furthermore, there are associated risks for all staff in challenging an intruder on school premises. This is particularly the case if alcohol or drugs are involved.

The context

Social and community factors

Both social and community factors contribute to the levels of violence in schools. The NIE (1978) study in the US found that 'the proportions of teachers reporting attacks decline markedly as we move from large cities to smaller cities, to suburbs to rural areas: A typical teacher in an urban high school stands 1 chance in 55 of being attacked within a month's time, while a teacher in a rural senior high school has one chance in 500'.

Studies of violence rates in Chicago schools also emphasise that 'socially disorganised, crime-ridden neighbourhoods produce socially disorganised, crime-ridden schools', while conceding that schools are nevertheless safer than their surrounding communities (Menacken, Weldon and Hurwitz, 1989, 1990).

School organisational factors

The debate about whether schools can overcome negative community effects has been keenly argued since the 1960s. However, there is now general consensus that schools do have an effect on pupil performance and behaviour (Ofsted, 1993). As Wayson (1985) pointed out, social and community factors are not generally under teachers' control, whereas there is much that schools can do to improve their own circumstances and ameliorate violence. The Elton Committee in particular commented on the 'positive atmospheres' that they experienced in some disadvantaged schools with good standards of work and behaviour:

> We found that we could not explain these different atmospheres by saying that the pupils came from different home backgrounds. Almost all the schools we visited were in what many teachers would describe as difficult urban areas. We had to conclude that these differences had something to do with what went on in the schools themselves.
>
> (DES/WO, 1989)

How are these positive effects to be achieved? The importance of good leadership and management is consistently emphasised in the major reports, and headteachers are identified as key figures in the creation of a safe, orderly and productive school climate (DES/WO, 1989; NIE, 1978; Ofsted, 1993). Both the NIE study and the Elton Report also found that schools with good standards of behaviour were characterised by well-defined and even-handed rule systems underpinned by clear aims for teachers and pupils.

The NIE (1978) authors found a link between pupil behaviour and the curriculum. School violence was more likely if students perceived the curriculum to be irrelevant, or if grades were seen as punitive and high grades impossible to obtain. The available evidence is consistent: safe schools are not created solely by concentrating on 'get tough' policies, perimeter fencing or visitor name badges. Any analysis of violence or assessment of risk must incorporate a review of the school as a whole.

Research on the contribution of class size to violent behaviour is often obscured in the UK by the practice of grouping together pupils with troubled and challenging behaviour within smaller teaching units. Hence it may appear from surveys that there is no increase in violence even with larger classes (e.g. DES/WO, 1989). Researchers need to remember that pupils and parents in schools with a reputation for violence also tend to vote with their feet, leading to a decline in overall pupil numbers and class sizes in such schools. In the US, the NIE (1978) study found clear evidence that teacher victimisation was increased when classes exceeded thirty pupils.

To keep a sense of perspective, serious pupil disaffection and violence is not a major problem in most UK schools, either primary or secondary:

> Standards of behaviour are satisfactory or better in almost all primary schools and good in the great majority. Standards of behaviour are satisfactory or better in most secondary schools and good in three out of four.
>
> (Ofsted, 1993)

Special schools

The Gill and Hearnshaw (1997) survey found that while risks of physical assault by pupils on teachers were virtually non-existent in Voluntary and Grant Maintained schools, they increased dramatically in PRUs and special schools. Poyner and Warne (1988) found similar enhanced risks for teachers working in LEA special schools.

School physical environment

There is a dearth of information in the UK about where violence to teachers is most likely to erupt in schools. Gill and Hearnshaw (1997) found, not surprisingly, that the majority of pupil-on-teacher assaults occurred inside the school buildings, while teachers were safer outside the school premises. The reverse was true in respect of parent or outsider attacks on teachers.

One 'high risk' area for teachers is, of course, the classroom itself. In American schools, 38% of assaults on teachers took place in the classroom, one-third of them when the teacher was not taking a class. The converse was found for pupils, who perceived the classroom to be a relatively safe setting (NIE, 1978).

In the USA, Menacken *et al.*'s 1989 analysis pinpointed heightened fears in the school car park, where only 5% of teachers felt 'very safe', and the school campus, where only 2.5% felt 'safe'. 44% of pupils felt unsafe in school and 20% also avoided the parking lot for fear of personal harm. Guetzloe (1989) found that risks of violence were highest during the crush in corridors, halls and doorways, a finding endorsed in the Elton Report (DES/WO, 1989).

The chronology of violence

We have no firm statistics in the UK about the time of day or day of the week when violent acts are most likely to occur in schools. In my own teaching days, staff-room folklore cited Friday afternoons, windy days, wet play-times and even a full moon. Do we now have any more reliable information? The NIE (1978) survey reported that violence rates to teachers and pupils were low on Mondays, rose towards midweek and returned to a low point on Friday. Curiously, the pattern for vandalism was the reverse, being higher on Mondays and Fridays. There was also a month of the year effect. Violent acts against the person peaked in February and thereafter fell month by month (with the exception of May) reaching a low in December. The pattern for vandalism was almost a mirror image. There may be different measures that schools can introduce to reduce risk at particular times of the year or term once the need and the reasons are highlighted.

Framework for change

Definitions

A consistent criticism of most studies of violence to teachers has been the lack of a shared, working definition of violence. How are we to resolve this? The ESAC (1990b) document *Violence to Staff in the Education Sector* defines violence to staff in the following terms:

> any incident in which an employee is abused, threatened or assaulted by a student, pupil or member of the public in circumstances arising out of the course of his or her employment.

This definition distinguishes between 'abuse', which includes offensive and obscene language, and 'threat', which refers directly to the victims ('I'm going to get you later!') or to their families. Both of these differ from 'assault', which involves a physical attack, with or without a weapon. Auditing systems need to be clear and specific about the nature and precise definition of the information that is being collected.

While the ESAC (1990b) definition of violence covers most situations, surprisingly it omits the possibility of occupational abuse or harassment from a line manager or professional colleague, and schools may wish to include this.

The concept of 'tolerable aggression' has been introduced by Breakwell (1989) to describe a factor that influences whether or not an incident is seen as an assault. Tolerable aggression is the acceptance that a certain amount of aggression 'goes with the territory'. 'Teachers talk about the disruption and borderline threats of physical assault...which they know they must anticipate from certain classes' (Breakwell, 1989).

A teacher's description of difficult confrontations

I've had confrontation situations in the past where there has been verbal aggression, but no physical aggression. The only physical

> aggression has been in the heat of the moment, due to a fight between two pupils, and it's not really been aimed at me, it's been aimed at the other one...but it's just that you've had to get between and separate them.
>
> (DES/WO, 1989)

Carers and educationalists are increasingly disinclined to accept such behaviour, and the norms of what is considered 'tolerable' are shifting. As Breakwell (1989) points out, this presents difficulties for recording systems and any attempts to compare incident rates over time and across cultures.

The problem-solving cycle

In the light of the available evidence, how does a school review its own needs and circumstances, and start the process of creating a safer environment? Figure 9.1 outlines a five-stage, school-based problem-solving process to guide schools.

Auditing and assessing the risk

Schools differ in their psychosocial, organisational and physical features, as well as in respect of the communities in which they are embedded. Each school, therefore, needs to establish its own risk profile as a basis for action planning.

The audit enables the school to answer the questions: Do we have a problem? If so, then how big is it? Who are the assailants and victims? What are the causes? Can we identify where and when the violence occurs? To answer these questions schools need to harness the commitment of all staff and pupils. There may also need to be community and external agency involvement. At a minimal level, a school may simply record the number of violent incidents during the term.

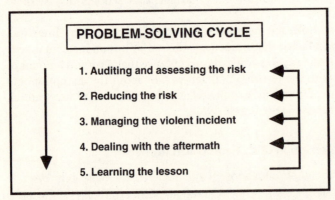

Figure 9.1 Problem-solving cycle for reducing the risk from violence

Possible questions to guide a recording system are:

1 Who was/were the victim(s)?
2 Who was/were the aggressor(s)?
3 When did the incident occur (time, day, term)?
4 Where did the incident take place?
5 What was the lesson or activity being carried out?
6 What preceded the incident?
7 What actually happened during the incident?
8 What brought the incident to an end?
9 What was the nature of any injuries?
10 Was medical attention needed/provided?
11 Who were the witnesses?
12 How was the victim's family informed?
13 Were the police informed?
14 Any other relevant information?

Further guidance can be found in 'Violence to staff: a basis for assessment and prevention' (Poyner and Warne, 1988) while Appendix 1 of *Violence to Staff in the Education Sector* (ESAC, 1990b) contains sample recording forms.

To get a true picture of the extent and nature of violence, essential as a basis for school planning and risk reduction, it is necessary to conduct a comprehensive audit, in addition to recording incidents (see Chapters 5 and 8). Such an audit identifies school-based risk factors. The National Association of Head Teachers (NAHT, 1996b) has provided an example of a risk analysis questionnaire, and the Department for Education and Employment (DfEE, 1996a) a risk assessment checklist directed specifically to the security of premises.

Staff and pupils should also be encouraged routinely to pool information about situations in which they feel unsafe, or where they recognise a gang, drug or racist problem may be simmering. Schools should also monitor evidence and symbols of a violent culture within the school, such as the distribution of racist literature or drugs at the school gates (or within the school), and graffiti or gang logos on the walls.

To determine levels of 'intruder violence' on the campus, an initial step might be to involve staff and pupils in monitoring the number of visitors on site during a given month compared with the number who have registered their presence with reception. In addition, risk assessment should also consider incidents that might happen as well as those that have happened.

Reducing the risk

There is a variety of different approaches to addressing identified risks. For instance, if problems consistently occur at lesson changeover times then building modifications might reduce circulation bottlenecks and improve sightlines for supervision (ESAC, 1990b). The Elton Report described how congestion can also be reduced by introducing 'one way systems', staggered lesson changes and avoiding the movement of pupils in 'zero time'. 'If none of the above are practicable, then the highly visible presence of senior members of staff at mass circulation points has equally proved effective' (DES/WO, 1989).

Each school is unique, and the search for solutions needs to consider psycho-organisational, training and physical factors in the search for a safer environment.

Whole-school approach

A framework for change includes not only the specific issue of violence but also the educational and managerial ethos of the school as a whole. Positive leadership by the headteacher and senior management, incorporating a consultative management style and enlisting the support of staff and pupils is the starting point for making schools safer. In the US, schools have published 'Safe School' policies, agreed by staff, pupils, parents and governors, making a clear statement of the direction they will be taking. Such an approach includes positive communication with parents so that their support can be obtained and misunderstandings avoided.

Risk reduction extends to a rejection of the language, culture and symbols in which violence is expressed. Schools can make a start by removing violent, racist or sexist graffiti and gang logos from school walls and refusing to tolerate hostile slogans or symbols on sweatshirts or school bags. Eliminating 'low level' violent conduct is the first step in reducing the risk of physical violence (and the fear of it) for pupils and staff (Curcio and First, 1993).

Staff training and support

Training and support for staff need to address the risky situations identified in the audit, such as the use of physical restraint, dealing with a fight between pupils or ejecting a pupil from the classroom. Conflict is inevitable and it is important to recognise that staff can be trained in non-violent conflict resolution techniques. The school and LEA clearly have the major responsibility for training in personal safety and for the health and safety of staff. (For examples of training in conflict resolution, see Higgins and Priest, 1994.)

Staff who work in highly fraught situations may require extra, specialised support. For example, potential risks inherent in isolated teaching blocks or in playground supervision by non-teaching staff can be reduced by the introduction of mobile phones or two-way audio systems between the area and office. Lessons can also be monitored, at least for sound. While some staff may be resistant to this, it is worth serious consideration where there is concern for staff safety.

Schools should adopt a routine and well-maintained 'logout–login' system for staff involved in home visiting and should consider the advisability of providing a personal alarm or mobile phone where there are grounds for concern about a particular visit. When in doubt, the school should enable staff to double-up or operate a 'buddy system' on such visits. (See also DfEE, 1996b; NAHT, 1996a, 1996b.)

Colleges, schools and the LEA need to provide support and training in personal safety and classroom management for all potentially vulnerable staff (DfEE, 1996b), particularly newly qualified staff, and those who have recently been the victim of an assault.

Teachers and pupils from minority groups may face additional problems. The school's response needs to embody its commitment to a multiracial community and rejection of racism. Gillborn (1993) described how community tension during the Gulf War resulted in vandalised mosques and inter-school raids on a predominantly 'white' school. The school involved senior teachers, key representatives of the black community and the police in talking to each year group and successfully resolved the conflict.

Violence and the curriculum: a course of study for all pupils

Violence is itself a legitimate and important study topic for pupils. It draws on a range of related curriculum areas, such as the humanities, media studies, personal and social education (PSE), biology and statistics. Suderman, Jaffe and Hastings (1994) have developed a school-based study programme for students and staff on understanding, managing and reducing violence.

Support for all pupils

Most pupils turn to subject teachers or pastoral staff for personal support at some time during their school life. The Working Group on School Security (DfEE, 1996b) underlined the value of this role, and called for a greater emphasis on training for teachers in pastoral care as part of a violence-reduction programme. The pastoral system contributes to making schools safer by meeting pupils' personal needs, and is particularly effective when supported by 'fair' rule systems and school procedures aimed at improving behaviour and relationships (Galvin, Mercer and Costa, 1990).

Support for pupils with special educational needs and challenging behaviour

There is undoubtedly concern today about behaviour problems among children in schools – particularly in secondary schools. Beyond this statement however, little consensus can be found on the topic.

(Wedell, 1977)

Wedell's comment could have been written today. However, since the passing of the 1981 and 1993 Education Acts (Special Needs), teachers and educational psychologists have been clearer about their roles and responsibilities for identifying and meeting the needs of pupils with learning and behavioural difficulties. A violence-reduction programme includes a review of the match between the curriculum and the learner (especially for pupils with special educational needs) and of the pastoral and other arrangements for those who present troubled and challenging behaviour. The special needs 'Code of Practice' provides a common framework for teachers, parents, educational psychologists and other professionals (Department for Education, 1994) although it is not always obviously followed by schools when responding to individual pupils who present emotional and behavioural problems.

The peer group is a surprisingly neglected resource in education (Leyden, 1996). Developments such as 'Circles of Friends' enlist the peer group in creating accepting atmospheres to support and include pupils with special needs or troubled and challenging behaviour (Newton, Taylor and Wilson, 1996). Complementary approaches have involved training students as 'peace monitors', mediators or peer counsellors to prevent difficult situations from escalating. It is clear that pupils can be part of the solution!

For some pupils, their aggressive behaviour may derive from a poor understanding of social situations and a lack of personal strategies to influence events constructively, or home–school tensions. Some schools have successfully introduced social skills training groups to help such pupils develop more effective, non-violent social strategies (Frederickson and Simms, 1990).

Schools in the UK have recently recognised the problem of bullying, especially in respect of pupils with special educational needs, and the need for action to improve pupil safety through anti-bullying programmes based on careful research (Smith and Sharp, 1994). Anti-bullying, and anti-racist, strategies should always be included at the heart of a 'safe schools' policy.

Finally, in those instances where the difficulties, especially in respect of behaviour, are not solely school based, psychologist–teacher–parent consultancy approaches are producing highly encouraging results (Miller, 1996).

Disaffected pupils

Risk reduction also includes a careful review of the school's arrangements for pupils who may be seen as alienated from the educational process. Pupils are required by law to receive education up to the age of 16 years, regardless of whether they or their parents wish it. This has profound implications for teachers and other professionals working with disaffected adolescents. Following the publication of the Newsom Report (Ministry of Education, 1963), the late 1960s witnessed a period of innovative curriculum development designed to tap the motivation and engage the curiosity of reluctant learners. Widespread efforts to personalise the curriculum and make it relevant to the needs of disaffected or under-achieving pupils generated a process of enquiry in which both teacher and pupil became active learners (Stenhouse, 1975).

There has been a reaction against such 'personalised' curriculum innovations during the last decade in favour of a common National Curriculum for all pupils. Despite its many benefits, the impact of a standard National Curriculum on the teaching of less able or disaffected pupils must be recognised when evaluating pupil behaviour in school. There are very real problems for teachers in motivating older pupils in areas of high social disadvantage, where job prospects are low and unemployment is the community norm for school leavers. A 'standard' National Curriculum can only provide a relevant, broad and balanced curriculum for 'standard' pupils.

The physical environment of the school: general preventive measures

Guetzloe (1989) argued that personal safety should always be considered when modifications or new buildings are being planned. This point was reiterated by Cullen (1996) and the Working Group on School Security (DfEE, 1996b). Twenty years ago, Lee and Bishop (1975) were pointing out that good design could reduce vandalism by incorporating good sightlines for pupil supervision and facilities for playtime activities. The DES (1987) provides security guidelines for schools on design and building modifications (see also ESAC, 1990b).

The care of the physical environment contributes to a positive ethos and feeling of safety within the school. Vigilance in removing litter and carrying out repairs not only signals a welcoming atmosphere and respect for the environment, it also reduces the availability of potential weapons, such as bottles or loose paving stones. The Elton Report found that shabby, untidy classrooms, lacking posters or displays of pupils' work were associated with poorer standards of behaviour (DES/WO, 1989).

The physical environment of the school: welcoming visitors, deterring intruders

Schools have worked hard to create an open, welcoming atmosphere for pupils and visitors, and this should be preserved when building modifications are being planned. What can be done to redesign the physical environment to deal with the problem of intruder violence without rushing into a 'fortress school' mentality? There are no easy answers and, as Cullen (1996) pointed out, there is 'little if any published guidance about tackling the dangers which an unauthorised intruder could pose to the school population'.

Without deterring parents and legitimate visitors, can we gain greater control over entrances in order to make schools safer for children and their teachers? Schools should discuss with parents the most effective means of limiting access in ways that allow greater control without jeopardising home–school links.

Clear, well-signposted reception arrangements close to the main entrance with friendly staff and a comfortable seating area for visitors set the tone for welcoming and calming potentially anxious or angry visitors. The reception area should be well lit with a range of reading material (ESAC, 1990b). Schools might also consider soft background music and carpeting in reception areas.

If there is likely to be a delay, office staff should be in a position to inform visitors how long they will have to wait, and offer drinks if the waiting period is likely to be lengthy. For 'difficult' interviews, the room chosen should have a relaxed, calming atmosphere, with the minimum of objects that might have potential as weapons. Ciscell (1990) offers colourful advice on room layout when preparing for a potentially hostile meeting: 'Parents should be treated like an 800lb gorilla. Where do they sit? Wherever they want!'

Good reception arrangements can defuse a volatile situation, alert staff to the need for a rapid response to contain a critical incident, or deny access to an unauthorised visitor. Many schools now routinely ask visitors to 'sign in' and to wear an identity badge while they remain on the premises. However, asking visitors to wear a badge is of little use unless decisions are taken about how staff and pupils respond to 'unbadged' visitors.

These arrangements can be supported by the introduction of perimeter fencing and the closure of some 'traditional', unofficial entrances (e.g. kitchens, playgrounds and fire exits). Self-closing and self-locking devices provide additional control for unsupervised doors but must not improve personal safety at the expense of increased fire risks.

New technology such as entry phones, closed-circuit television, intruder alarms and security lighting can serve both as a deterrent and as a means to identify visitors and monitor movements around the campus. Cameras can also provide valuable video evidence in the event of an incident. However, technology alone is at best a palliative, and at worst a means of distancing staff from their pastoral and community influences within the school. Technology may also offer a false sense of security and decrease staff vigilance, for example, when swipe cards are introduced to gain access to premises: a swipe card only identifies the card and not the holder. New technology therefore needs to be seen in the context of the 'safe school' philosophy in which it offers additional information, improved control of premises and better communications.

Managing the violent episode

Pre-incident planning

Situations in which armed, emotionally unstable intruders commit violent assaults on staff or pupils are mercifully rare. But as we have seen, they can happen: 'Violence can occur in the best run schools' (DES/WO, 1989).

The Dunblane Enquiry

It is unrealistic to expect that the risk of a violent intruder gaining access can be eliminated. All that can be done is to take whatever measures are reasonably practical.

(The Cullen Report: Cullen, 1996)

As has been argued throughout this chapter, the active involvement of all staff in pre-incident planning contributes to the safety of the whole community by increasing awareness, commitment and vigilance. The eight core elements of pre-incident contingency planning are:

1 Involving all staff at the initial planning phase.
2 Determining roles and responsibilities.
3 Devising 'back-up' and signalling systems.
4 Practising de-escalation – the guiding principle.
5 Managing the incident – the safety principle.
6 Dealing with intruder violence.
7 Providing support for the victim (immediate and long-term).
8 Informing others (staff, pupils, parents, media).

Each step should be the named responsibility of a specific member of staff, with the headteacher and senior management taking the major roles and responsibilities. The contingency arrangements need to cover the absence of any named staff member.

Managing the incident

The guiding principle for managing incidents is that action should be taken quickly to defuse any potentially critical situation, and calm the assailant(s) as a basis for establishing some initial contact. Attempts to confront and dominate inflammatory encounters are less effective and more dangerous to staff than de-escalating the situation and stepping back from the flashpoint. In a crowded setting, some degree of de-escalation and control can be introduced by dispersing other pupils and isolating the assailant(s) in a particular part of the school to avoid the incident spreading. Potential aggressors should be kept apart.

Wherever possible, the aim is to 'buy time' to allow a cooling down period, and initiate some negotiations to resolve the immediate or perceived source of the conflict. 'Buying time' depends upon back-up systems so that the time bought allows the arrival of more help, including (when necessary) the police. The procedures for summoning assistance, for example via the school bell or a card system (Gill and Hearnshaw, 1997), and providing back-up should be well known and practised by relevant staff. Curcio and

First (1993) advocate a specially trained 'first response team' for schools with a serious problem.

Regarding situations where the assailant or potential aggressor is not a member of the school community, the Elton Report (DES/WO, 1989) summarises police powers to remove intruders suspected of committing an offence. (See also DfEE, 1996b, and NAHT, 1996a for relevant summaries of current law.) Contacting the police sends an unambiguous signal to staff and pupils about the school's commitment to a 'safe school' policy.

Intruder violence

On the 5th of July 1993 at about 2.50pm, a young man aged 17 entered a Birmingham secondary school for girls, apparently following an argument with his girl friend, a pupil at the school. The man was armed with a machete, a meat cleaver and a firearm which later proved to be an air pistol...

The young man proceeded to cause considerable damage, smashing classroom equipment, including computer monitors, and then threatened the girls, at one stage asking, 'Who wants to die first?'

(Mallon and Best, 1995)

Whether the assailant is a pupil, a parent or an intruder, great caution should be used in making any physical challenge or intervention. Techniques of physical restraint require careful training in their safe and justifiable use, and should only be used to prevent serious, immediate injury to another person or the person him/herself, or the dangerous handling of property (Trendall, 1993). Schools and LEAs should agree policies about legitimate responses for staff in respect of self-defence and the defence of others, and secretarial and caretaking staff should be included in personal safety training. As Hewitt and Arnett (1996) conclude:

> The principles of using overpowering physical force only when there is a direct and immediate threat of injury seems right, liberal and reasonable. It would appear that we are still able to intervene quickly in serious physical disputes; grab someone who is about to step out into the road; hold a child who is about to put his or her head through a window pane.

In the event of personal injury to pupils or teachers, the named member of staff should organise prompt medical assistance, and make sure the victims have personal support from friends or colleagues until such time as their families can be contacted.

Dealing with the aftermath

Informing the school and community

Rumour and misinformation can inflame a relatively minor in-school incident into a neighbourhood crisis. Senior management need to provide the LEA, staff and pupils with an early account of what has happened and the steps taken to control it. This briefing should include parents and governors, with contingency plans for a press release and communication with local press, radio and television. (For a more detailed account see Curcio and First, 1993; Yule and Gold, 1993.)

Dealing with those directly involved

Clinical experience and research studies have identified the distressing psychological consequences, including post-traumatic stress disorder (PTSD), experienced by many victims of violence (see Chapter 4). How can this be minimised? A sympathetic and understanding response by senior management and all colleagues, as well as family and friends, is essential. An understanding of the personal and emotional reactions to violence should be provided for all staff as part of the general awareness training, remembering that witnesses and all members of the school community are likely to experience strongly emotional reactions.

All victims of assault should be offered immediate and follow-up support from the school and LEA. This should cover medical needs, time off work to recover, and sensitive understanding of their emotional well-being.

Teachers who have suffered personal injury or damage to property should be offered support and advice from the school, LEA or professional union in deciding what steps to take. The graphic evidence provided by the union case studies and the NIE (1978) survey indicates that an initial assault may increase the victim's vulnerability to subsequent attack. Both the school and LEA need to offer not only sensitive personal support, including professional counselling, but also a practical understanding of their professional needs in preparing to return to work or in making alternative arrangements. Some LEA educational psychology services provide counselling for staff and pupils who have been assaulted (Mallon and Best, 1995).

Learning the lesson

The theme of this chapter has been the assessment and reduction of violence in schools, recognising that we are unlikely to eliminate every single incident. The final phase of the problem-solving cycle is a full reappraisal of all stages and procedures in the sequence from 'audit' to 'aftermath'. Whether or not further incidents occur, the problem-solving cycle has to be reviewed regularly as circumstances and personnel change. A violence audit should be incorporated as a routine part of the school's self-monitoring arrangements for health and safety. The safety audit provides the baseline against which subsequent anti-violence initiatives can be evaluated.

Violence in schools: whose responsibility?

While events in Dunblane, Wolverhampton and London may focus attention on some of the risks stemming from intruder violence, we still lack a reliable, comprehensive recording system as advocated in previous HSE documents. There are opportunities now to address this through the Reporting of Injuries, Diseases and Dangerous Occurrences Regulations 1995 (RIDDOR 95). (See Beale, Cox and Leather, 1996 and Chapter 5 of this volume.)

If the position is a little clearer in respect of recording and reporting, who has responsibility for ensuring the safety of those working in the school? The Cullen Report (Cullen, 1996) is in no doubt that the Health and Safety at Work (HSW) Act 1974 places the overall responsibility on the employer. A senior member of school staff should be identified for this health and safety role, which should be redefined to include safety from violence. Cullen also interprets the HSW Act remit to include the safety of pupils. A detailed risk audit is not only part of the school's responsibilities under this legislation it is also the first step in the cycle of risk assessment, risk reduction and the management of violence.

Schools clearly require additional funding for the training and building modifications necessary to create a safer environment, and central government needs to provide the financial means if schools are to meet their legal duties. A school should not be faced with a choice between losing a teacher and gaining a perimeter fence. Similarly, pupil and teacher safety will not be enhanced if classes are made bigger in order to pay for security measures.

Conclusions

Existing evidence leads us to conclude that:

- A national recording system, with agreed definitions, is urgently needed to provide reliable data on the incidence of violence to teachers.
- No two schools are alike in respect of risk factors for violence and each school needs to carry out its own safety audit. This includes special schools and PRUs.
- 'Violent incidents can occur in the best run schools' (The Elton Report, DES/WO, 1989).
- Pupils are the source of most violence to teachers.
- Risks are increased in socially disadvantaged and high crime neighbourhoods and the safety of staff and pupils in such schools requires particular attention.

- Severe, violent assaults on teachers still appear relatively infrequent, although the anticipatory fear they engender is stressful.
- Serious, life-threatening intruder violence (e.g. Wolverhampton and Dunblane) is unpredictable, rare and difficult for schools to defend against. Most other forms of intruder violence are carried out by parents and ex-students.
- Sole reliance on security devices and new technology without a 'safe schools' policy and practice may give schools a false sense of reassurance.
- Positive leadership from headteachers and senior management backed up by whole-school approaches can create a safer, more supportive learning environment for pupils and staff.
- Schools should be adequately funded to improve personal safety levels for pupils and staff.

Numerous researchers have identified the daily, cumulative exhausting stressors that most teachers experience in their work (see ESAC, 1990a). Therefore a successful approach to reducing violence in schools needs to examine the total demands on teachers in the context of increasing political and parental demands, expectations and accountability. Teachers who are working under highly stressed, unsafe circumstances are less equipped to meet the educational needs of their pupils.

Teaching in today's schools is not an easy task. But, contrary to media and political speculation, perhaps it never was.

The 'Golden Age' of education?

When I began teaching in 1950, after active service in the war and four years' training, my first two terms in a Lancashire secondary modern were a battle for survival compared with which periods in the war were like a holiday camp.

My first deputy head told me that when he started teaching in a small Lancashire textile town he, along with other young teachers, dared not go home at the end of the school day without the presence of the headmaster or he would be attacked in the street by groups of boys throwing stones and sods of earth.

(Rhodes Boyson, 1970 – former Minister of State for Education)

References

Beale, D., Cox, T. and Leather, P. (1996) 'Work-related violence – is national reporting enough?' *Work and Stress*, 10, 99–103.
Boyson, R. (1970) 'Law and order in school', *The Spectator*, 28 February, 270.

Breakwell, G. (1989) *Facing Physical Violence*, London: British Psychological Society and Routledge.

Ciscell, R. (1990) 'How to prepare for a conference with angry parents', *Middle School Journal*, 69(3), 46–47.

Cullen, W. D. (1996) *The Public Inquiry into the Shootings at Dunblane Primary School on 13 March 1996*, Report submitted to the Secretary of State for Scotland by the Hon. Lord Cullen (The Cullen Report), Edinburgh: The Scottish Office.

Curcio, J. L. and First, P. F. (1993) *Violence in the Schools: How to Proactively Prevent and Defuse It*, California: Corwin Press, Sage Publications.

Department for Education (DfE) (1994) *Code of Practice on the Identification and Assessment of Special Educational Needs*, London: HMSO.

Department for Education and Employment (DfEE) (1996a) *Improving Security in Schools*, London: HMSO.

—— (1996b) *Report of the Working Group on School Security*, London: HMSO.

Department of Education and Science (DES) (1987) *Crime Prevention in Schools: Practical Guidelines*, Building Bulletin 67, London: HMSO.

Department of Education and Science and the Welsh Office [DES/WO] (1989) *Discipline in Schools*, Report of the Committee of Enquiry chaired by Lord Elton (The Elton Report), London: HMSO.

Education Services Advisory Committee (ESAC) (1990a) *Managing Occupational Stress: a Guide for Managers and Teachers in the Schools Sector*, Health and Safety Commission, London: HMSO.

—— (1990b) *Violence to Staff in the Education Sector*, Health and Safety Commission. London: HMSO. Reissued by HSE Books, Sudbury, Suffolk, August 1996.

Frederickson, N. and Simms, J (1990) 'Teaching social skills to children: towards an integrated approach', *Educational and Child Psychology*, 7, 5–17.

Galvin, P., Mercer, S. and Costa, P. (1990) *Building a Better Behaved School*, Harlow: Longman.

Gill, M. and Hearnshaw, S. (1997) *Personal Safety and Violence in Schools*, Report commissioned by Department for Education and Employment (DfEE) (1997) Research Report No. 21, Norwich: HMSO.

Gillborn, D. (1993) 'Racial violence and bullying', in D. P. Tattum (ed.) *Understanding and Managing Bullying*, Oxford: Heinemann Press.

Guetzloe, E. (1989) 'School prevention of suicide, violence and abuse', *Education Digest*, February, 46–49.

Hewitt, D. and Arnett, A. (1996) 'Guidance on the use of physical force by staff in educational establishments', *British Journal of Special Education*, 23(3), 130–133.

Higgins, A. and Priest, S. (1994) 'Resolving conflict in schools', in P. Gray, A. Miller and J. Noakes (eds) *Challenging Behaviour in Schools*, London: Routledge.

Lee, S. and Bishop, J. (1975) *Vandalism in Schools: A Literature Survey*, Kingston on Thames: Architectural Psychology Research Unit, Kingston Polytechnic.

Leyden, G. A. (1996) ' "Cheap labour" or "neglected resource"? The role of the peer group and efficient, effective support for children with special needs', *Educational Psychology in Practice*, 11(4), 49–55.

Mallon, F. and Best, C. (1995) 'Trauma in school: a psychological service response', *Educational Psychology in Practice*, 10(9), 231–237.

Menacken, J., Weldon, W. and Hurwitz, E. (1989) 'School order and safety as community issues', *Phi Delta Kappan*, 71(2), 39–40 and 55–56.

—— (1990) 'Community influences on school crime and violence', *Urban Education*, 25, 68–80.

Miller, A. (1996) *Pupil Behaviour and Teacher Culture*, London: Cassell.

Ministry of Education (1963) *Half Our Future*, A report of the Central Advisory Council for Education (England) (The Newsom Report), London: HMSO.

National Association of Head Teachers (NAHT) (1996a) *Managing Security in Schools: General*, May, PM015, Haywards Heath,West Sussex: NAHT.

—— (1996b) *Managing Security in Schools: Buildings*, May, PM016, Haywards Heath, West Sussex: NAHT.

National Association of Schoolmasters/Union of Women Teachers (NAS/UWT) (1986) *Pupil Violence and Serious Disorder in Schools*, Birmingham: Hillscourt Education Centre.

National Institute of Education (NIE) (1978) *Violent Schools – Safe Schools*, The Safe Schools Report to Congress, Vol. 1. Washington DC: NIE.

Newton, C., Taylor, G. and Wilson, D. (1996) 'Circles of Friends. An inclusive approach to meeting emotional and behavioural needs', *Educational Psychology in Practice*, 11, 41–48.

Office for Standards in Education (Ofsted) (1993) *Achieving Good Behaviour in Schools*, London: HMSO.

Poyner, B. and Warne, C. (1988) *Preventing Violence to Staff*, Health and Safety Commission, London: HMSO.

Smith, P. K. and Sharp, S. (1994) *School Bullying: Insights and Perspectives*, London: Routledge.

Stenhouse, L. (1975) *An Introduction to Curriculum Research and Development*, London: Heinemann Educational Books.

Suderman, M., Jaffe, P. G. and Hastings, E. (1994) *A School-Based Anti-Violence Program*, London, Ontario: London Family Court Clinic.

Trendall, C. (1993) 'The road to empowerment: managing disruption and violence within a framework of caring control', in A. Miller and D. Lane (eds) *Silent Conspiracies*, Stoke on Trent: Trentham Books.

Wayson, W. W. (1985) 'The politics of violence in school: doublespeak and disruption in public confidence', *Phi Delta Kappan*, 67, 127–132.

Wedell, K. (1977) 'Introduction' to special themed issue. *Educational Review*, 29, 149–151.

Yule, W. and Gold, A. (1993) *Wise Before the Event*, London: Calouste Gulbenkian Foundation.

10 Violence in health care settings

Carol Brady and Rosie Dickson

Introduction

Violence experienced by health care workers is something of a paradox. It is newsworthy that doctors and nurses have to deal with aggression and violence at work, in hospital and in the community. However, it has long been known that both accident and emergency (A&E) units, and psychiatric services suffer high levels of aggression which are regarded by many staff as 'part of the job'.

The incidence of violence within health care has spread from the traditionally high risk areas to those of the general practitioner's (GP's) surgery and the community. In 1987, the Health Services Advisory Committee of the Health and Safety Commission reported the results of a large-scale survey of 3,000 health care staff (Health Services Advisory Committee [HSAC], 1987). 1 in 200 had suffered a major injury requiring medical attention during the previous 12 months, with over 1 in 10 suffering a minor injury which needed first aid. 1 in 21 had been threatened with a weapon, and more than 1 in 6 had been exposed to verbal threats. 30% of the major assaults reported involved a weapon.

As might be expected, high rates of the more serious incidents were found in psychiatric settings, where 1 in 4 respondents had suffered a minor injury as a result of a violent attack during the previous year. High rates of assault were also found for staff working with people with a learning disability and for staff in A&E departments. However, there were incidents across all health care settings including paediatric facilities and ambulance crews.

There is evidence that violence within health care settings has increased. Noble and Rodger (1989) reported a threefold increase over a decade. This may reflect a problem throughout society, with staff having to deal with more people prepared to employ aggression as a way of solving their difficulties. It may be that opportunities for violence to occur have increased, as more services become community based rather than hospital based. As a consequence, staff make more home visits and may spend more time in relatively isolated situations. In addition, the move to community care for people with psychiatric and learning disabilities has changed the nature of the clients seen in the community. People only come into hospital if they demonstrate that they cannot be managed within the community – in some cases by assaulting a member of staff.

The changes which have taken place over recent years within all sectors of the National Health Service (NHS), and the associated 'cost improvements' required each year, have resulted in posts being frozen rather than filled, and cover for long-term sickness and maternity leave often not being provided. Staff report anecdotal evidence that they are being forced to cope with increasing demands on decreasing resources. This has implications for the prevention of violence, and also affects the personal resources of a stressed workforce to deal with aggressive clients.

There are methodological problems in terms of analysing published research studies. Definitions of violence vary; some studies include damage to property and verbal abuse (e.g. Morrison, 1989), while others confine the definition to actual physical injury (e.g. Carmel and Hunter, 1989). Methods of data collection vary; some studies rely on officially reported incidents, while others employ confidential interviews or anonymous questionnaires. Often studies report frequency of incidents, but do not translate this into a rate of violence according to the time period and staff/patient population. Regardless of the type of measurement relied on, under-reporting is often cited as a further difficulty. Estimates as to the actual levels of incidents occurring have been as much as five times higher than those reported, for example when formal reports were compared with ward notes (Lion, Snyder and Merrill, 1981). The HSAC (1987) study estimated that as much as a third of all serious incidents occurring within the NHS were going unreported. Crowner, Peric, Stepcic and Van Oss (1994) compared incidents of violence reported during a 27-month period with videotapes of a fourteen-bedded secure psychiatric unit. A review of 3,300 hours of tape revealed 155 incidents, only 12 of which were reported.

Staff give a wide range of reasons for not reporting incidents, including difficulties with the recording system itself (Lanza, 1992; Lion *et al.*, 1981) and fear of revenge or retribution on the part of the perpetrator (Hobbs, 1991). In addition, the 'caring professions' tend to take the view that dealing with 'difficult clients' is what they are employed to do (Hobbs, 1991; Lanza, 1992; Poster and Ryan, 1989). Reporting a violent incident can be perceived by some staff as a failure in their professional ability (Hobbs, 1991; Rosenthal, Edwards, Rosenthal and Ackerman, 1992).

As organisations and unions take the issue of workplace violence more seriously, under-reporting should diminish. Tolerance of violence is decreasing with the aggression, previously accepted as being just 'part of the job', now being perceived as a shared problem for staff and employer, with the onus on the employer to provide a safe workplace (Health and Safety Executive, 1992). It is widely recognised that health care staff face particular problems in this area. A recent study carried out in British Columbia suggests that health sector workers face levels of risk similar to that of the police (Boyd, 1995).

The type of violence which staff are exposed to depends on the setting in which they work and the job that they do. The California Occupational Safety and Health Administration guidelines on violence describe three types (Cal/OSHA, 1995; see also Chapter 1 of this volume).

Type I involves planned robberies or attacks, where the assailant has no legitimate relationship to the workplace. Employees with face-to-face contact, who exchange money or goods with the public and who work alone or in small numbers have the greatest risk. Within health care, any staff who undertake home visits in high crime areas, particularly at night, or who might be perceived as carrying drugs, such as GPs, are at risk. Pharmacists are similarly at high risk. Hospital staff leaving shifts late at night can also be vulnerable to attack.

Type II comprises assault by someone in receipt of, or the subject of, a service by the victim or the organisation, or a relative or friend of such a person. This is the most prevalent form of workplace violence in a health care setting, where clients or their relatives assault the care givers.

Type III involves an assailant who has some employment relationship to the workplace, be it another employee, supervisor, or former employee. This less commonly results in serious injury than Type II but often attracts more media attention when it does.

From the HSAC (1987) study, it might be expected that staff working in psychiatric services suffer most from workplace violence. However, in a study of student nurses, Grenade and MacDonald (1995) found that while the *rate* of reported assault was indeed much higher in the psychiatric sample, the *severity* of assault was much greater in the general hospital sample.

The difficulties faced by different groups of staff in relation to workplace violence will now be considered.

Psychiatric staff

Part of the function of psychiatric settings is the control and containment of disturbed patients who may become aggressive under certain circumstances. In forensic psychiatry, the patients are in treatment as a direct result of their violent or dangerous tendencies. Staff will often be in the position of having to set boundaries on people who may be very anxious, or psychotic, and who may resist the controls put on them, perhaps by attempting to leave the unit despite being 'under section' to be compulsorily detained. Powell, Caan and Crowe (1994) looked at precursors to 1,000 violent incidents which occurred in a British psychiatric hospital over a thirteen-month period. In over 10% of cases, restrictions placed on the patient preceded the incident. In addition to dealing with the mentally disturbed, staff also have to deal with those under the influence of alcohol or non-prescribed drugs.

Poster and Ryan (1994) surveyed 557 psychiatric nursing staff and found that 76% of respondents had been assaulted at some time. Despite this, 71%

reported feeling safe at work most of the time. Recently employed staff were more confident about their workplaces not admitting unmanageable patients. Staff employed for longer were more inclined to disagree with this, and perceived their workplaces as inadequate to deal with the patients admitted. Staff expressed feelings of vulnerability, with most believing that those working with mentally ill people can expect to be assaulted at some time during their career.

Forensic psychiatry staff, who are employed to contain and treat people who present a high risk of violence, might particularly expect to face violence during their careers. A one-year study of staff injuries from in-patient violence at a large forensic state hospital found that 121 staff suffered 135 injuries, with 120 of these suffered by nursing staff (Carmel and Hunter, 1989). Nurses had an injury rate of 16 injuries per 100 staff over the year, while the rate for other medical staff was 1.9 per 100 staff, a total of 3 injuries. The majority of injuries to nursing staff (9.9 per 100 staff) were sustained while containing patient violence; the rest resulted from assaults on staff.

A study of physical violence in a British maximum security psychiatric hospital (Larkin, Murtagh and Jones, 1988) found that staff were three times as likely to be assaulted as other patients, there being 407 attacks on staff during a six-month period.

Although most assaults happen to nurses, doctors can also be victims. Gray (1989) surveyed 66 residents at a public psychiatric hospital in Los Angeles, finding an overall incidence rate of 2.8 assaults per 100 resident months at risk. The rates were highest in the child and adolescent service and lowest in adult outpatients. Incidents seldom resulted in serious injury.

Injury need not be physical however. Flannery, Hanson and Penk (1995) included verbal and non-verbal threats in their definition of violence, and found that some verbal threats produced as much psychological distress, for some staff victims, as did physical assaults.

Accident and emergency staff

A&E units are well known for problems with aggression, particularly late in the evening at weekends, when they have to deal with injuries from fights and the effects of alcohol, and there is strong evidence of a high risk of assault in emergency rooms (Mahoney, 1991). Many factors present in the A&E department make it a unique area of the hospital and leave staff more susceptible to assault. Patients, and those accompanying them, often have high stress levels and patients are likely to be in pain. They endure long waits, which may be lengthened unpredictably should more urgent cases arrive; McAneney and Shaw (1994) found long waiting times to be associated with an increased incidence of attacks on staff in a paediatric emergency department. Patients then sometimes have to undergo painful or unpleasant medical procedures. Additionally, many units have a 24-hour open door policy, drugs may be readily available and there may be opportunities to take hostages (Lavoie, Carter, Danzl and Berg, 1988). Where injuries have resulted from fights, rival gangs may be present within the unit, and patients and their friends may be under the influence of alcohol.

An independent survey of 500 A&E nurses (*Nursing Times*, 1997a) found that 90% had seen colleagues physically abused at work, and 20% of them had done so more than 20 times. 46% of the sample had been attacked themselves, 56% of these in the past year. Male nurses were more likely to be assaulted (68%) than female nurses (41%). 1 in 3 of the sample felt unsafe at work and most believed that not enough is done to protect them.

Wyatt and Watt (1995) surveyed 100 junior doctors employed in A&E departments. Of these 96 had been verbally abused, 50 had been threatened, and in 32 cases, patients had attempted to assault them; 18 doctors had been assaulted by patients on a total of 23 occasions. Only 11 of the sample had received any training in managing aggression, but 88 thought it would be useful. 32 doctors continued to feel upset and preoccupied by the aggression, but none had received counselling, and no patients had been charged with assault.

A study carried out in the USA reflects these findings. Anglin, Kyriacou and Hutson (1994) surveyed all the residents and graduates in the thirteen emergency residency programmes in California, and found that 62% of respondents worried about their own safety while working in the emergency department, and most believed that the hospitals did not provide adequate security. Lavoie *et al.*'s (1988) study of 127 emergency departments in the USA found that 32% of departments reported at least one incident of verbal threat per day, with 43% reporting that staff were attacked at least once per month; 18% reported that weapons were used to threaten staff at least once per month, and 7% of departments reported acts of violence that had resulted in death. They concluded that staff face a significant risk of fatal injury from assaults by patients or their families.

General hospital staff

Although A&E departments have been recognised as having a high risk of violence, staff working in general medical settings are also at risk. Whittington, Shuttleworth and Hill (1996) found that 21% of a sample of 396 hospital staff had been physically assaulted. 90% of these did not work in A&E, but on, for example, medical wards. Nursing staff tended to be the target more frequently than other medical staff. Younger and less experienced staff were at increased risk of assault.

Williams (1996) reported the experiences of violence of a sample of 345 registered nurses in Illinois: 57% reported personal experience of some aspect of sexual harassment, and 26% reported physical assault. About a third of those who had been sexually harassed had also been physically assaulted. Patients were the most frequent perpetrators of sexual harassment and physical assault, but over half of the sexual assaults had been committed by physicians.

Physicians themselves can be at risk of assault. LeBourdais (1995) reported on the stress experienced by physicians and their families as a result of the violence perpetrated by anti-abortion groups on doctors who carry out such procedures in North America. Four murders in Canada have been linked to these activists, and a physician was shot and badly wounded. Attacks on Boston abortion clinics have left two workers dead and five wounded, and families have been harassed by threats.

For those who have not been targets themselves, awareness of violence at work can leave them feeling vulnerable. Gillard, Dent, Aarons, SmythPigott and Nicholls (1993) reported that 45% of 1,146 preregistration house officers replying to a postal survey did not consider the protection of staff against violence to be adequate at their hospital.

General practitioners

GPs and other community-based staff encounter different types of risk to those of hospital-based staff. They tend to be isolated in practice premises where there may not be many other people and in seeing patients alone in consulting rooms. They also carry out home visits, and are on call to do so at night. The latter makes them vulnerable to OSHA Type I attack (Cal/OSHA, 1995), where the motive might be money or drugs. They are also likely to experience aggression from clients and relatives and, as with psychiatric staff, they are likely to have to continue working with those clients who have been aggressive. GPs are faced with the whole gamut of human distress, from sick children to the severely mentally ill, from battered spouses to the bereaved. They have a high turnover of patients during surgery and have only a short time with each one. This, combined with the long time which a patient may have had to wait can be a risk factor for aggression.

GPs also under-report violent incidents; they have been concerned to avoid publicising their difficulties with violence, in case they should appear as legitimate targets (Hobbs, 1994). There has been little published work as a result. The first large-scale (N = 1,093) study was by Hobbs (1991) whose retrospective survey accounted for nearly 4% of all GPs in England and Wales. Hobbs found that 62.9% of GPs had experienced abuse or violence during the previous twelve months, with 17.5% having done so at least once per month and 1% having experienced verbal abuse every day. A total of 1,664 incidents were reported; overall the annual incidence per GP was 2.42.

Most incidents involved verbal abuse or threats and happened at the surgery. However, 62.5% of the physical assaults occurred during domiciliary visits, and 66% of the injuries were received during night calls. On day visits there were 24 assaults and 8 actual injuries; there were 36 assaults and 22 actual injuries at night.

The majority of aggressors (1,166) were male (664 patients, 441 relatives) and only 5% of incidents involved the general public, the vast majority of these (90%) being described as verbal abuse only.

Those doctors who had been subject to aggression continued to feel stressed about it (Hobbs, 1994). Most of them (74%) felt intimidated on night calls; 20% of them described this as severe at times and 6% were always fearful on such calls.

14% of the respondents who had experienced aggression from patients felt that such aggression was increasing. Coping strategies for those who had suffered included striking off aggressive patients from their lists and effectively passing on the problem to someone else.

Bullying

The majority of studies reviewed above focus on the experience of aggression from patients and those connected with them, that is Type II incidents (Cal/OSHA, 1995). However, there is evidence to suggest that Type III aggression is widespread, in the form of bullying from colleagues. Preliminary results from the recent Royal College of Nursing study (Alderman, 1997) demonstrate the extent and the nature of the problem. Of 380 questionnaires analysed, 254 staff reported the experience of bullying, with 91 of these reporting sexual harassment. 33 reported racial harassment, although only 58 people were not 'white British' by ethnic origin. The most frequently cited perpetrators of bullying or harassment were managers and supervisors (195 respondents), with colleagues next (125 reports), then groups of colleagues (83 cases). A range of forms of harassment were reported including exclusion or 'freezing out', blocked promotion or training, criticism in front of others, open hostility, withholding information, excessive criticism of work, name calling, verbal abuse and threats.

Although the staff who had been bullied tended to suffer psychologically (25% required antidepressants), most did not appear to have made a complaint, due to a fear of retaliation or victimisation, a lack of faith in the complaints procedure, lack of evidence, or concerns about not being believed. Many respondents coped with the situation by leaving for another job, in some cases to a lower grade; others left nursing altogether.

Characteristics of violent situations in health care

Although health care staff are vulnerable to Type I violence (Cal/OSHA, 1995), in that they may fall victim to those wishing to rob them of money or drugs, this does not seem to be a major reason for staff to be assaulted. Indeed, Hobbs' (1991) study found that situations involving the general public were largely limited to verbal aggression. The majority of incidents occurred as a result of the interaction of a number of factors related to the environment, the staff member, the perpetrator, and the interaction between them.

The environment

Aspects of the environment which have a role to play have been addressed within Chapters 3 and 6. In considering the environment of health care, it is perhaps not surprising that violence occurs. Arrival may be problematic, as parking facilities are often limited at hospital sites. In addition, hospitals and clinics are often kept at a fairly high temperature and waiting rooms tend to be crowded. Lanza, Kayne, Hicks and Milner (1994) found an effect of overcrowding on the incidence of violence in psychiatric care, while Brooks, Mulaik, Gilead and Daniels (1994) found such overcrowding was associated with an increase in violence severe enough to warrant seclusion and/or restraint.

Long waits are common. In A&E departments, patients turn up unannounced and wait their turn. They may see others, who arrive after them but are judged as more urgent, appear to 'queue jump'. A recent *Which* survey found waiting times in excess of two hours to be common (*Nursing Times*, 1997b). In outpatient departments and GP clinics, appointment times are given, but patients are often kept waiting well beyond that time. This is common in hospital outpatients clinics where the practice is to give one appointment time to a number of patients. The frustration that being kept waiting engenders adds to the likelihood of aggression occurring.

Regimes imposed on patients are often restrictive and frustrating to them, resulting in an increased risk of aggression. Powell, Caan and Crowe (1994) found that restrictions on psychiatric patients were common antecedents to violent incidents. Lanza *et al.* (1994) assessed the influence of environmental factors on physical assault by psychiatric patients, and found an association between assault frequency, a low score on autonomy and a high score on staff control. Whittington and Wykes (1996) found that 86% of assaults by psychiatric patients on nurses were immediately preceded by the assaulted nurse having delivered an aversive stimulus to the patient in the form of a frustration of a request, an activity demand or physical contact.

Bensley, Nelson, Kaufman, Silverstein *et al.* (1995) investigated the views of both patients and staff from eight wards with high assault rates in two state psychiatric hospitals. They found that there was common ground between the two groups in that both recognised that restrictions on patients' smoking and access to the outdoors were problematic. Both groups were concerned about the use of seclusion and restraint, the ultimate restriction. Patients were also concerned about rules not being explained. Lack of information can also be problematic in other health care settings.

Particular times of the day and particular places can be more risky. Lanza *et al.* (1994) found that meal times and afternoons were associated with higher incidence of violence, which tended to occur in corridors and day rooms. Hobbs' (1991) study of GPs found that although most incidents happened in the surgery, more serious violence occurred in home visits. Night visits had a higher risk for serious assaults.

The staff member

While some studies report male nursing staff to suffer higher rates of assault (Carmel and Hunter, 1989; *Nursing Times*, 1997), others have found female staff to be more at risk (Lanza, 1996). Greater incidence of assault on either sex is likely to be related to their greater prevalence among the workforce within high-risk jobs. Both men and women are vulnerable to workplace violence.

There does seem to be an effect of experience. Less experienced staff seem more at risk. Both Carmel and Hunter (1989) and Whittington *et al.* (1996) found that recently employed staff were more likely to be assaulted than more experienced staff. Bensley *et al.* (1995) found that staff in wards with high assault rates were concerned about the staffing levels on those units. Lanza *et al.* (1994) found an inverse relationship between assault frequency and number of staff. Low staffing levels, and/or use of less experienced staff, can affect the quality of service available to patients, which may in turn lead to frustration on their part. These staff may also be less able to defuse situations as they arise, and thus prevent them culminating in a level of aggression which requires reporting. In some psychiatric settings, the lack of staff, or the presence of less experienced staff, will provide the opportunity for those who tend to use aggression as a coping strategy to take advantage of a less secure situation.

The assailant

Consumers of health care services, and those who are concerned for their well-being, experience stress due to the need which brought the patient to the setting in the first instance. Some may be there to receive good news but, until that news is delivered, these patients will be in a state of high arousal. Should their needs be frustrated in any way, for example through a particularly long wait or a problematic interaction with a nurse, then otherwise reasonable people can become aggressive. A lack of information can increase their anxiety, which, in turn, might fuel aggression and violence. This is even more likely if they are advocating on behalf of another, particularly vulnerable person, such as a child or an elderly parent. Thus violence and aggression is encountered even on paediatric wards.

There are also those who are habitually violent and who may be in the setting as a result, for example in the A&E department after a fight, or in a psychiatric facility.

Predicting violence can be difficult for staff who have no prior knowledge of the patient. In cases where information is known, or where it can be gathered from the client's presentation, factors influencing the risk of violence include:

1   Previous diagnosis of personality disorder, especially antisocial type (as in DSM-IV);

2 Age 27 or under (much increased risk); age 40 or over (decreased risk);
3 Acutely psychotic and/or violent or persecutory ideation;
4 Previous history of violence, especially if imprisoned, and seriousness of victim injury;
5 History of alcohol abuse;
6 Gender of previous assault victims (increased risk for male victims over female only victims);
7 History of violence within, for example, the family background, where violence seen as a problem solver;
8 Family and social history up to age 16:

    i   Severe maladjustment at school,
    ii Parental violence,
    iii Separation from either or both parents before age 16,
    iv Criminal arrest before age 16;

9 Previous non-compliance while on probation;
10 Number and variety of criminal offences;
11 Absence of a long-term relationship.

The first four factors have the most significance, but it is the cumulative effect that increases risk.

Patients who use violence are unlikely to do so completely unpredictably. Whittington and Wykes (1996) noted that only a minority of patients acted violently without some kind of provocation. Powell, Caan and Crowe (1994) were able to relate 92% of the 1,000 incidents they studied to characteristics of the patient, the hospital regime or interactions with others. Prior agitation or disturbance was common, as were restrictions placed on patients, or provocation from other patients. There was a 'hard core' of 21 patients who were involved in 10 or more incidents each, who also presented challenges in other ways such as arson, absconding and self-harm. Crowner *et al.* (1995) video-taped 134 assaults committed by 40 psychiatric patients, and then interviewed them to determine the reasons for the violence. Those taking part in the interviews often complained of provocation or said they employed violence as a way of stopping the objectionable behaviour of others.

The cost of workplace violence

When violence results in physical injury, the damage to staff is obvious, and the consequences may be felt immediately by the organisation in terms of time off work in recovery. Carmel and Hunter (1989) found, for example, that injuries resulting from direct assault, rather than from containment, were more likely to be head injuries, and to cause more than three weeks' absence from work. Work-related violence has a range of negative consequences beyond its physical impact, including lower job satisfaction, greater stress and increased considerations of job change (Budd, Arvey and Lawless, 1996). Health care staff are in no way immune from these effects. Williams (1996), for example, found a significant effect of both physical assault and sexual harassment on job satisfaction for registered nurses in Illinois.

Whittington *et al.* (1996) found that mental health was significantly worse amongst staff exposed to threats. The psychological impact of the experience of violence at work is outlined in Chapter 4. Health care staff are as susceptible as any others to the effects of assault, and their reactions can be made more severe because they often feel a great sense of conflict between their professional role and their own needs (Lanza, 1985). For many health care professionals an assault is an attack on their professional position and their self-belief.

Assault at work can lead staff to consider both changing jobs and leaving the profession (Alderman, 1997). Grimwood and La Valle (1993), in a study of the career paths of 791 social workers, found both widespread experience of violence and a significant relationship between feeling supported by the manager in dealing with such violence and the decision to leave. Although respondents reported receiving a lot of support from other social workers, many (41%) reported receiving no support from management. 23% of social workers who had not received support following violence had either left or had considered doing so, compared to 1 in 10 of those who had received support. Lanza (1983) found that staff who had been assaulted were often under pressure from their families to leave the job.

The fear of being physically assaulted at work can also have an impact on the recruitment of staff. Poster and Ryan (1994) found that security and the organisational response to violence have become issues about which job applicants ask at interview.

Much of the violence occurring in health care settings happens publicly and is witnessed by other staff. Those incidents which happen in private become public through rumour and the awareness that staff members may be off sick, or have left work. Lanza (1996) reports that witnesses in the health care setting often identify strongly with their colleagues and imagine that the same thing could easily happen to them. They tend to ruminate about their failure to help prevent the incident, or their apparent late intervention. Although they have not themselves been assaulted, they tend to report increased levels of fear, anxiety, vulnerability and irritability.

Strategies for intervention

Violence clearly presents a significant problem within the NHS, whether it comes from patients, staff or opportunistic offending. The question faced by managers is how it can best be dealt with. Given that, in 1996, a security conference aimed at NHS managers was cancelled due to lack of interest (Wright, 1996), it is to be hoped that the increasing level of responsibility for security issues engendered by the development of Trusts will propel management into taking action. Reducing the risks depends on the development of an integrated approach involving all areas of the organisation at all levels, from front line staff to the policy makers. Policy should determine procedures, the results of which should be monitored and reviewed, with changes made as appropriate, forming a feedback loop. This approach is the focus of this book, and issues such as monitoring are taken up in detail in other chapters. This section is limited to considering attempts which have been made to tackle the difficulties faced in health care settings.

Cox, Leather and Cox (1990) outlined three types of strategy that can be employed in the attempt to reduce the risks associated with work place violence: preventative, reactive and rehabilitative strategies.

Preventative strategies

Preventative strategies comprise control by design or employee training to remove the hazard or reduce its impact on employees or their likelihood of exposure. These strategies focus on adapting the environment to remove 'triggers' of aggression, reducing the impact of violence or changing the way that aspects of the environment are interpreted.

Control by design involves such things as increasing the level of information available to patients through, for example, signs providing waiting times, and maintaining appropriate heat, light and noise levels (Cox and Leather, 1994).

In some American hospitals, preventative measures include the deployment of private armed police forces, metal detectors and package screeners to stop weapons being brought in. This may seem extreme, but the design of the recently completed Liverpool Woman's Hospital has adopted a 'whole building' approach to security which includes closed circuit television, 24-hour security guards, 'smart' identification badges working on a proximity radar system to control access, and a retail tagging system to protect equipment. Other hospitals have their own police stations, and some have put up posters threatening legal action should any assaults take place (Naish, 1997).

Site security is important, but must have suitable procedures to back it up. Alarms are useless unless someone is available to answer them. Procedures are particularly important for community staff whose domiciliary visits are to uncontrolled sites. Sharing information about potential risk is vital, so that staff go prepared or arrange an office rather than a home visit. Preparation for any visit should include an arrangement to call the office as soon as the visit is over and a procedure to be implemented should a member of staff fail to call in. If the visit is considered to be potentially of high risk, staff should be accompanied. This raises the issue of staffing levels. Whether staff work in the community or in hospitals, the debate about safe staffing levels is relevant. Where staff are stretched, and managers are not supportive, community staff are more likely to take the risk and go alone rather than not see the client. In psychiatric hospitals, the risk has already been described. Where staff feel at risk, this issue should be debated between staff and management.

In order to prepare staff for dealing with potentially violent situations, most employers turn to training. There is evidence that this is helpful. Infantino and Musigno (1985) described the impact of a three-day course in aggression control on the incidence of patient assault and the level of injury sustained over a 24-month period. Of the 31 trained staff, only 1 suffered an assault and sustained no injury, compared to 24 out of 65 untrained staff, of whom 19 sustained injuries. 86% of the trained staff said that training made them feel more confident, more relaxed and more able to handle violent situations.

Paterson, Turnbull and Aitken (1992) evaluated a ten-day course aimed at mental health nurses, in which they assessed knowledge of theories of aggression and methods of de-escalation, disengagement, control and restraint (utilising role plays). Although there is no follow-up or control group data available, staff were significantly more knowledgeable about causes of aggression following the course, and were assessed by independent raters as being more skilled in all three role play situations. Staff also reported feeling more confident in their ability to handle aggressive incidents.

However, such long courses may be exceptional. Whittington and Wykes (1996) found that only 10% of their sample of psychiatric nurses had attended some form of violence-prevention training during their career, most of which ranged from one to three hours in total. The availability of staff for training is closely linked to the difficulty of providing a safe level of staffing within budget limits. Investment in training is often reduced when organisations are faced with stringent financial constraints, and most staff would not have the opportunity to attend a long course on managing aggression. The exception to this is those working in secure psychiatric facilities.

Reactive strategies

Reactive strategies are based on management and group reaction and problem solving to improve the organisation's ability to recognise and deal with problems as they arise.

These strategies (1) determine what staff do when faced with violence, (2) develop easy-to-use, responsive procedures, backed up by thorough training, and (3) provide continued support in using them. Procedures have to be developed on a job-related basis, backed up by policy and daily practice. For example, a home visit policy might be introduced, ratified by senior management, stating that staff should carry mobile phones, provided by the organisation, on every visit and call in immediately following the visit. It should be stated at what point office staff, who have the addresses of all visits, should intervene, and what action they should take. It may also be stated that any worker concerned about a visit should be accompanied by a colleague. Such a policy will only be followed when line managers give active support, and do not discourage the practice due to staffing implications. Colleagues also have to be supportive and encouraging rather than critical of staff who request back-up.

An innovative approach has been introduced in an Australian medical centre, in the form of a violence management team (VMT), which manages patients who exhibit violent behaviour in a general hospital (Brayley, Lange, Baggoley, Bond and Harvey, 1994). The VMT consists of a doctor, a senior nurse and four orderlies. Over about three and a half years they were called 282 times. In 45% of cases the patient had an organic mental disorder, 18% were substance misuse cases, and 15% had a personality disorder. In just under a third of cases, verbal placation was enough, but 62% of patients needed restraint, and 53% were given a sedative. They view such incidents as a clinical problem rather than the province of the police or security guards. They also note that besides managing incidents well, they are able to determine the cause of any violence and closely monitor its nature within that setting, informing future prevention programmes.

Rehabilitative strategies

Rehabilitative strategies aim to support staff members in coping with the after effects of an incident with the focus placed on helping the individual psychologically and emotionally. Such interventions need not be limited to the victim, but may be extended to witnesses. Lanza (1983) advocated the availability of counselling for all staff involved in workplace violence and Storch (1991) reported positively on the use of staff support groups. Flannery and Penk (1996) report anecdotal evidence that crisis intervention work is helpful for A&E personnel involved in critical incidents. The development of suitable services for staff is further discussed in Chapters 4 and 7.

Conclusion

Working in the health service carries with it a high risk of dealing with, or being exposed to, aggression and violence. No area is free from violence, although some seem riskier than others in terms of frequency. Staff also suffer some aggression from colleagues, which is probably under-reported even more than violence from patients. Both take their toll in terms of staff suffering psychologically and physically, and the organisation loses through absenteeism and the permanent loss of staff. A variety of strategies can be adopted to tackle the problem of violence, but these must form part of an overall organisational approach in order to be successful.

Note

Since this chapter was written several influential guidance documents concerning violence to health care workers have been published in the UK:

Health Services Advisory Committee (1997) *Violence and Aggression to Staff in Health Services: Guidance on Assessment and Management*, Health and Safety Commission, Sudbury, Suffolk: HSE Books; NHS Executive and Royal College of Nursing (1998) *Safer Working in the Community: A Guide for NHS Managers and their Staff in Reducing the Risks from Violence and Aggression*, London: Royal College of Nursing; and Royal College of Nursing (1998) *Dealing with Violence against Nursing Staff*, London: Royal College of Nursing.

References

Alderman, C. (1997) 'Bullying in the workplace: a survey', *Nursing Standard*, 11(35), 22–24.

Anglin, D., Kyriacou, D. N. and Hutson, H. R. (1994) 'Residents' perspectives on violence and personal safety in the emergency department', *Annals of Emergency Medicine*, 23(5), 1,082–1,084.

Bensley, L., Nelson, N., Kaufman, J., Silverstein, B., *et al.* (1995) 'Patient and staff views of factors influencing assaults on psychiatric hospital employees', *Issues in Mental Health Nursing*, 16(5), 433–446.

Boyd, N. (1995) 'Violence in the workplace in British Columbia: a preliminary investigation', *Canadian Journal of Criminology*, 37(4), 491–519.

Brayley, J., Lange, R., Baggoley, C., Bond, M. and Harvey, P. (1994) 'The violence management team. An approach to aggressive behaviour in a general hospital', *Medical Journal of Australia*, 161, 254–258.

Brooks, K. L., Mulaik, J. S., Gilead, M. P. and Daniels, B. S. (1994) 'Patient overcrowding in psychiatric hospital units: effects on seclusion and restraint', *Administration and Policy in Mental Health*, 22(2), 133–144.

Budd, J. W., Arvey, R. D. and Lawless, P. (1996) 'Correlates and consequences of workplace violence', *Journal of Occupational Health Psychology*, 1(2), 197–210.

California Occupational Safety and Health Administration (Cal/OSHA) (1995) *Cal/OSHA Guidelines for Workplace Security*, San Francisco, CA: State of California, Department of Industrial Relations, Division of Occupational Safety and Health.

Carmel, H. and Hunter, M. (1989) 'Staff injuries from inpatient violence', *Hospital and Community Psychiatry*, 40(1), 41–46.

Cox. T. and Leather, P. J. (1994) 'The prevention of violence at work: application of a cognitive behavioural theory', in C. L. Cooper and I. T. Robertson (eds) *International Review of Industrial and Organizational Psychology*, Vol. 9, pp 213–245, Wiley and Sons: Chichester.

Cox, T., Leather, P. and Cox, S. (1990) 'Stress, health and organisations', *Occupational Health Review*, February/March, 13–18.

Crowner, M. L., Peric, G., Stepcic, F. and Van Oss, E. (1994) 'A comparison of video cameras and official incident reports in detecting inpatient assaults', *Hospital and Community Psychiatry*, 45(11), 1,144–1,145.

Flannery, R. B., Hanson, M. A. and Penk, W. (1995) 'Patient's threats: expanded definition of assault', *General Hospital Psychiatry*, 17, 451–453.

Flannery, R. B. and Penk, W. E. (1996) 'Program evaluation of an intervention approach for staff assaulted by patients: preliminary enquiry', *Journal of Traumatic Stress*, 9, 317–324.

Gillard, J. H., Dent, T. H. S., Aarons, E. J., SmythPigott, P. J. and Nicholls, M. W. N. (1993) 'Preregistration house officers in eight English regions: survey of quality of training', *British Medical Journal*, 307, 1,180–1,184.

Gray, G. E. (1989) 'Assaults by patients against psychiatric residents at a public psychiatric hospital', *Academic Psychiatry*, 13(2), 81–86.

Grenade, G. and MacDonald, E. (1995) 'Risk of physical assault among student nurses', *Occupational Medicine*, 45, 256–258.

Grimwood, C. and La Valle, I. (1993) 'Beware of the client', *Community Care*, 12.8.93, 15.

Health and Safety Executive (1992) *The Management of Health and Safety Regulations*, London: HSE.

Health Services Advisory Committee (HSAC) (1987) *Violence to Staff in the Health Services*, London: Health and Safety Commission. HMSO.

Hobbs F. D. R. (1991) 'Violence in general practice: a survey of general practitioners' views', *British Medical Journal*, 302, 329–332.

—— (1994) 'Aggression towards general practitioners', in T. Wykes (ed.) *Violence and Health Care Professionals*, London: Chapman and Hall.

Infantino, J. A. and Musigno, S. Y. (1985) 'Assaults and injuries among staff with and without training in aggression control techniques', *Hospital and Community Psychiatry*, 36(12), 1,312–1,314.

Lanza, M. L. (1983) 'The reactions of nursing staff to physical assault by a patient', *Hospital and Community Psychiatry*, 34, 44–47.

—— (1985) 'Counseling-services for staff victims of patient assault', *Administration in Mental Health*, 12(3), 205–207.

—— (1992) 'Nurses as patient assault victims: an update, synthesis and recommendations', *Archives of Psychiatric Nursing*, 6(3), 163–171.

—— (1996) 'Violence against nurses in hospitals', in G. R. Vandenbos and E. Q. Bulatao (eds) *Violence on the Job*, Washington DC: American Psychological Association.

Lanza, M. L., Kayne, H. L., Hicks, C. and Milner, J. (1994) 'Environmental characteristics related to patient assault', *Issues in Mental Health Nursing*, 15(3), 319–335.

Larkin, E., Murtagh, S. and Jones, S. (1988) 'A preliminary study of violent incidents in a Special Hospital (Rampton)', *British Journal of Psychiatry*, 153, 226–231.

Lavoie, F. W., Carter, G. L., Danzl, D. F. and Berg, R. L. (1988) 'Emergency room violence in United States teaching hospitals', *Annals of Emergency Medicine*, 17(11), 1,227–1,233.

LeBourdais, E. (1995) 'Potential for violence causing fear among Canadian doctors who perform abortions', *Canadian Medical Association Journal*, 152, 927–932.

Lion, J. R., Snyder, W. and Merrill, G. L. (1981) 'Brief reports: understanding of assaults on staff in a state hospital', *Hospital and Community Psychiatry*, 133, 422–425.

Mahoney, B. S. (1991) 'The extent, nature and response to victimization of nurses in Pennsylvania', *Journal of Emergency Nursing*, 17, 292–293.

McAneney, C. M. and Shaw, K. N. (1994) 'Violence in the pediatric emergency department', *Annals of Emergency Medicine*, 23(6), 1,248–1,251.

Morrison, E. F. (1989) 'Theoretical Modeling to predict violence in hospitalized psychiatric patients', *Research in Nursing and Health*, 12, 31–40.

Naish, J. (1997) 'Under siege', *Nursing Times*, 93(15), 36–38.

Noble, P. and Rodger, S. (1989) 'Violence by psychiatric inpatients', *British Journal of Psychiatry*, 155, 384–390.

Nursing Times (1997a) 'A&E staff threatened by rising violence', *Nursing Times*, 93(19), 5.

Nursing Times (1997b) 'Nurses "part of A&E reception"', *Nursing Times*, 93(19), 6.

Paterson, B., Turnbull, J. and Aitken, I. (1992) 'An evaluation of a training course in the short term management of violence', *Nurse Education Today*, 12, 368–375.

Poster, E. C. and Ryan, J. A. (1989) 'Nurses' attitudes toward physical assaults by patients', *Archives of Psychiatric Nursing*, 3(6), 315–322.

—— (1994) 'A multiregional study of nurses' beliefs and attitudes about work safety and patient assault', *Hospital and Community Psychiatry*, 45(11), 1,104–1,108.

Powell, G., Caan, W. and Crowe, M. (1994) 'What events precede violent incidents in psychiatric hospitals?' *British Journal of Psychiatry*, 165(1), 107–112.

Rosenthal, T. L., Edwards, N. B., Rosenthal, R. H. and Ackerman, B. J. (1992) 'Hospital violence: site, severity and nurses' preventative training', *Issues in Mental Health Nursing*, 13, 349–356.

Storch, D. D. (1991) 'Starting an in-hospital support group for employee victims of violence in the psychiatric hospital', *Psychiatric Hospital*, 22(1), 5–9.

Whittington, R., Shuttleworth, S. and Hill, L. (1996) 'Violence to staff in a general hospital setting', *Journal of Advanced Nursing*, 24, 326–333.

Whittington, R. and Wykes, T. (1996) 'Aversive stimulation by staff and violence by psychiatric patients', *British Journal of Clinical Psychology*, 35(1), 11–20.

Williams, M. F. (1996) 'Violence and sexual harassment: impact on registered nurses in the workplace', *AAOHN Journal*, 44, 73–77.

Wright, C. (1996) 'Soft target', *Nursing Times*, 92(29), 16–17.

Wyatt, J. P. and Watt, M. (1995) 'Violence towards junior doctors in accident and emergency departments', *Journal of Accident and Emergency Medicine*, 12, 40–42.

11 Managing work-related violence

The way forward

Phil Leather, Claire Lawrence, Diane Beale, Tom Cox and Carol Brady

In 1996, the World Health Organization (WHO) declared violence to be a leading worldwide public health problem (WHO, 1996). Four priority objectives were identified in the plan of action adopted by the WHO to combat violence, whether in the home, on the street, in the classroom, or in the workplace (WHO, 1997). These were:

1 To describe the problem;
2 To understand the problem;
3 To identify and evaluate possible interventions;
4 To disseminate knowledge and implement effective action.

This book has attempted to meet each of these four objectives with respect to work-related violence. Specifically, it has sought (1) to provide an accurate assessment of the nature, size and scope of the problem of work-related violence; (2) to provide a sound analysis of its origin and escalation; (3) to outline and illustrate some of the important means of intervention to which this analysis gives rise and (4) to provide a means of disseminating research-based theoretical knowledge to the user community.

A principal theme emphasised throughout this book has been the view that any assessment and management of work-related violence must be informed by a reliable and valid knowledge base. However well intentioned, action and intervention built upon unsound knowledge or poor theory are unlikely to be effective. For this reason Part I has provided an overview of the knowledge base available to inform attempts to manage and control work-related violence. This knowledge base comprises:

- an accurate definition and identification of the problem (Chapter 1);
- the legal framework within which individual and organisational responses to violence must be framed (Chapter 2);
- the social and psychological dynamics which underpin the origin and escalation of many violent incidents (Chapter 3);
- the nature and range of reactions which might be expected in those who are exposed to work-related violence (Chapter 4);

- the design and implementation of effective incident reporting systems (Chapter 5);
- the scope of possible interventions (Chapter 6).

There are, however, many myths and popular misconceptions surrounding work-related violence. One such misconception concerns the origin and causes of violence. Put simply, there are many popular explanations of violence which emphasise a single causal variable, for example that violence is solely a matter of instinct, alcohol consumption or individual maladjustment and deviance. However popular, such single-factor explanations do not stand up to rigorous scientific scrutiny (Siann, 1985). The reality is that violence and aggression, whether perpetrated in the workplace or elsewhere, typically result from the interplay of a diverse range of biological, individual, cognitive, social, situational and environmental factors (Neuman and Baron, 1997).

Recognising this broader causation, work-related violence must be construed not simply as an individual, episodic problem but as one which is rooted in wider interpersonal, social, organisational, cultural and political processes (Chappell and Di Martino, 1997). As the contributors to this book have emphasised, action and intervention to reduce the amount and impact of work-related violence must therefore embrace structural and organisational factors as well as interpersonal and individual factors. Such structural variables include work and organisation design, as well as the physical design of the workplace itself. At the organisational level, the parts played by organisational policy, culture and climate must all be considered. At the individual level are factors such as interpersonal dynamics, social skills training, anger management and conflict-resolution skills, and post-incident counselling.

A second popular misperception of work-related violence has been the view that it is only a problem for certain obvious occupations concerned with public order and security such as the police and prison service. This view has encouraged an attitude on the part of many other organisations that violence is not an important issue for them to consider. This narrow-mindedness is fuelled by a further misperception, that it is only the extreme forms of physically aggressive behaviour which need to be addressed, for example homicide, wounding and severe physical assault.

A new profile of work-related violence is beginning to emerge, however, which gives equal emphasis to the damage that is caused by so-called minor acts of violence, including verbal assault, threat and intimidation (Leather, Beale, Lawrence and Dickson, 1997). This profile is captured in the definition of violent incidents, accepted by the European Commission, DG-V and examined in Chapter 1, which is:

> Incidents where persons are abused, threatened or assaulted in circumstances related to their work, involving an explicit or implicit challenge to their safety, well-being or health.
>
> (Wynne, Clarkin, Cox and Griffiths, 1997)

Adopting this European Union definition means that all forms of work-related violence must be taken seriously, not just the more extreme manifestations. This involves an acceptance that all forms of work-related violence are capable of inflicting damage both to the individual and to the organisation (Leather *et al.*, 1997). Moreover, when it is construed in these broader terms, then work-related violence is a problem for all organisations and not just for those traditionally thought to be at risk.

How then can an organisation respond to and manage work-related violence in all its forms? This book has emphasised a common approach to the management of all physical and psychosocial hazards in the workplace which is equally applicable to the management of work-related violence. This approach advocates the use of a problem-solving framework, or control cycle (see Chapters 1, 6 and 9), coupled with the need to integrate action and intervention at all levels: the individual, the work-group or team, and the organisation as a whole. In addition, action and intervention must embrace three respective time-points: before, during and after violence occurs. It is this integration of action across both time and organisational level which embodies the integrated organisational approach to the management of work-related violence advocated throughout this book.

The control cycle provides the strategy by which fundamental knowledge can be translated into effective guidance and action. Such action can take a variety of forms, many of which have been considered or illustrated in this book. These include organisational policy and procedures (Chapters 1, 6 and 8), training design and implementation (Chapters 6 and 8), workplace design, custom and practice (Chapters 6, 9 and 10), and the utilisation of professional help (Chapters 4 and 7). Whatever is attempted by way of an organisation's response to work-related violence, it must be rigorously evaluated. The results of such evaluation serve as invaluable feedback for the refinement and improvement of the control and management strategy.

It is necessary to apply this kind of integrated and proactive approach to the management of work-related violence so that the emphasis is as much upon eliminating the causes of violence as upon alleviating its consequences. Indeed, this requirement is encapsulated in recent health and safety legislation in a number of European countries. In The Netherlands, for example, the 1980 Working Environment Act was amended in 1996 to include provisions aimed at preventing both psychological and physical aggression and violence at work. Similarly, in 1993, the Swedish National Board of Occupational Safety and Health brought in ordinances under the 1977 Work Environment Act to cover the explicitly recognised issues of 'violence and menaces in the working environment' and 'victimization at work'.

There are, of course, other means for the prevention and control of work-related violence which have not been fully considered in this book. The social interactionist model of aggression offered by Lawrence and Leather in Chapter 3, for example, suggests several ways in which individual differences might conceivably contribute to the development and escalation of violence.

Put simply, this model places considerable emphasis upon cognitive (interpretive) factors and emotional responses (feelings) in both the origin and management of violence. Specifically, in any social interaction people are more likely to act aggressively when they perceive the other person's actions as intentionally malevolent and nasty, thereby legitimating retaliation, or when the exchange generates excessively negative moods and emotions.

It follows, therefore, that the identification of individuals prone to (1) attributing others' actions to hostile intentions (Dodge, Petit, McClaskey and Brown, 1986; Sancilio, Plumert and Hartup, 1989), (2) experiencing a generally negative mood or affect (Watson and Clark, 1984), or (3) responding aggressively to mild rebuke, provocation or frustration (Glass, 1977; Strube, 1989), could prove valuable in two ways. First, it might reduce levels of worker-on-worker violence, that is Type III in the scheme proposed by the California Occupational Safety and Health Administration (Cal/OSHA) (1995) discussed in Chapter 1. Second, it might reduce any inflaming effect of an employee's attitude or behavioural style in the handling of potentially difficult relationships between staff and customers or clients (Cal/OSHA Type II violence).

There are, however, a number of serious limitations to the likely effectiveness of any selection-based identification procedures. First, there remain serious legal issues to be considered, such as whether the information generated might violate employment opportunity laws or an applicant's privacy rights (Felsenthal, 1995). In short, the fear of being sued might be the biggest obstacle for individuals and organisations alike in providing the kind of information that would be required for any screening device to be effective.

Moreover, even if all the necessary information were made readily available, the complex interplay of factors which gives rise to violence and aggression, as discussed above and in Chapter 3, is likely to mean that the predictive validity of such pre-employment measures would remain low. As Neuman and Baron (1997) emphasise, individual predispositions or inclinations do not lead inevitably to aggression. Rather, they play a part interactively with the situational and environmental conditions known to be the antecedents of aggression. Put simply, the complex social and environmental dynamics which typically underpin work-related violence are likely to outweigh the input of any single individual difference factor.

It is the view of the contributors to this book that work-related violence can only be successfully managed when the full complexity of its origins and development are both recognised and utilised to inform assessment and intervention. However, good theory alone is not enough. We must have, in addition, a strategy or heuristic for linking theory with practice. In this book, the control cycle has been emphasised as the most appropriate strategy.

The problem of work-related violence will not simply go away. Legislation, social values and organisational necessity all demand that it is addressed in a reliable, responsible and effective way. Against this context,

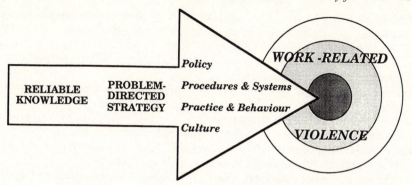

Figure 11.1 Targeting work-related violence: the integration of knowledge and
strategy

this book has argued that two things are prerequisite for the effective
management and control of work-related violence (see Figure 11.1).

First, fundamental knowledge of its nature, origins and dynamics is
needed. From this knowledge, a working model can be derived to inform
principles of management and control. Second, a strategy or heuristic is
required to translate the knowledge provided by the working model into
policy, procedures and other forms of guidance. It is this combination of
fundamental knowledge and an effective integrated strategy for implementation which provides the only sound basis for a valid and responsible
approach to the management and control of work-related violence.

References

California Occupational Safety and Health Administration (Cal/OSHA) (1995)
  Cal/OSHA Guidelines for Workplace Security, San Francisco, CA: State of Cali-
  fornia Department of Industrial Relations, Division of Occupational Safety and
  Health.
Chappell, D. and Di Martino, V. (1997) *Violence at Work*. Draft Report to the Inter-
  national Labour Organization. Geneva: International Labour Office.
Dodge, K. A., Petit, G. S., McClaskey, C. L. and Brown, M. M. (1986) 'Social
  competence in children', *Monographs of the Society for Research in Child Develop-
  ment*, 51, 1–85.
Felsenthal, E. (1995) 'Potentially violent employees present bosses with a Catch-22',
  Wall Street Journal, 5.4.95, pp. B1, B5.
Glass, D. C. (1977) *Behaviour Patterns, Stress and Coronary Disease*, Hillsdale, NJ:
  Lawrence Erlbaum.
Leather, P., Beale, D, Lawrence, C. and Dickson, R. (1997) 'Effects of exposure to
  occupational violence and the mediating impact of fear'. *Work and Stress*, 11(4),
  329–340.
Neuman, J. H. and Baron, R. A. (1997) 'Aggression in the workplace', in R. A.
  Giacalone and J. Greenberg (eds) *Antisocial Behaviour in Organizations*, London:
  Sage.

Sancilio, M. F. M., Plumert, J. M. and Hartup, W. W. (1989) 'Friendship and aggressiveness as determinants of conflict outcomes in middle childhood', *Developmental Psychology*, 25, 812–819.

Siann, G. (1985) *Accounting for Human Aggression: Perspectives on Aggression and Violence*, Boston: Allen and Unwin.

Strube, M. J. (1989) 'Evidence for the Type A behaviour: a taxonomic analysis', *Journal of Personality and Social Psychology*, 56, 972–987.

Watson, D. and Clark, L. A. (1984) 'Negative affectivity: the disposition to experience aversive emotional states', *Psychological Bulletin*, 96, 465–490.

World Health Organization (1996) *Prevention of Violence: Public Health Priority*. WHO World Health Assembly, Resolution 49.25 of 25 May 1996.

—— (1997) Document EB/99/INF. Doc/3 of 7 January 1997. World Health Organization Executive Board.

Wynne, R., Clarkin, N., Cox, T. and Griffiths, A. (1997) *Guidance on the Prevention of Violence at Work*, Luxembourg: European Commission, DG-V.

Appendix 1

NATIONAL AND INTERNATIONAL GUIDANCE DOCUMENTS ON VIOLENCE AT WORK

United Kingdom

Department of Health and Social Security (1988) *Violence to Staff. Report of the DHSS Advisory Committee on Violence to Staff*, London: HMSO.

Education Services Advisory Committee (1997) *Violence in the Education Sector*, Sudbury, Suffolk: HSE Books.

Health and Safety Executive (1992) *The Management of Health and Safety Regulations*, London: HSE.

—— (1993) *Prevention of Violence to Staff in Banks and Building Societies*, Sudbury, Suffolk: HSE Books.

——(1993) *The Costs of Accidents at Work*, Health and Safety Series, HS(G)96. Sudbury, Suffolk: HSE Books.

—— (1995) *Preventing Violence to Retail Staff*, Sudbury, Suffolk: HSE Books.

—— (1995) *A Guide to the Reporting of Injuries, Diseases and Dangerous Occurrences Regulations 1995*, L73. Sudbury, Suffolk: HSE Books.

—— (1996) *RIDDOR: Everyone's Guide to RIDDOR 95*, HSE 31. Sudbury, Suffolk: HSE Books.

—— (1996) *Violence to Workers in Broadcasting*, HSE Information Sheet, Entertainment Sheet No. 2.

—— (1996) *Violence to Staff at Work: a Guide for Employers*, IND(G)69L (Rev). Sudbury, Suffolk: HSE Books.

Health Services Advisory Committee (1987) *Violence to Staff in the Health Services*, Health and Safety Commission. Sudbury, Suffolk: HSE Books.

—— (1997) *Violence and Aggression to Staff in Health Services: Guidance on Assessment and Management*, Health and Safety Commission. Sudbury, Suffolk: HSE Books.

NHS Executive and the Royal College of Nursing (1998) *Safer Working for in the Community: A Guide for NHS Managers and their Staff in Reducing the Risks from Violence and Aggression*, London: Royal College of Nursing.

Poyner, B. and Warne, C. (1988) *Preventing Violence to Staff*. Health and Safety Executive, London: HMSO.

Reporting of Injuries, Diseases and Dangerous Occurrences Regulations 1995, (RIDDOR 95) Statutory Instrument 1995 No. 3163. London: HMSO.

Royal College of Nursing (1998) *Dealing with Violence Against Nursing Staff*, London: Royal College of Nursing.

Ireland

Health and Safety Authority. *Violence at Work*, Dublin: HSA.
—— *Violence at Work in the Health Services Sector*, Dublin: HSA.

Europe

Wynne, R., Clarkin, N., Cox, T. and Griffiths, A. (1997) *Guidance on the Prevention of Violence at Work*, Luxembourg: European Commission, DG-V.
International Council of Nurses (1994) *Draft Guidelines on Coping with Violence in the Workplace*, Geneva: International Council of Nurses.

United States

California Occupational Safety and Health Administration (Cal/OSHA) (1995) *Cal/OSHA Guidelines for Workplace Security*, San Francisco, CA: State of California Department of Industrial Relations, Division of Occupational Safety and Health.
California Occupational Safety and Health Administration (Cal/OSHA) (1995) *Model Injury and Illness Prevention Program for Workplace Security*, San Francisco, CA: State of California Department of Industrial Relations, Division of Occupational Safety and Health.
Occupational Safety and Health Administration (1996) *Guidelines for Preventing Workplace Violence for Health Care and Social Service Workers*, OSHA 3148–1996. Washington, DC: US Department of Labor, Occupational Safety and Health Administration.
Occupational Safety and Health Administration (1996) *Guidelines for Workplace Violence Prevention Programs for Night Retail Establishments*, Draft. Washington, DC: US Department of Labor, Occupational Safety and Health Administration.
Occupational Safety and Health Administration (1996) *Protecting Community Workers against Violence*, Fact sheet No. OSHA 96–53. Washington, DC: US Department of Labor, Occupational Safety and Health Administration.

On the Internet

Documents

Assault Prevention Information Network. Safety Precautions.
   http://www.einet.net/galaxy/Community/Safety/Assault-Prevention/apin/SafetyPoffice.html
Defense Personnel Security Research Center (PERSEREC) Combating Workplace Violence.
   http://www.amdahl.com/ext/iacp/pslc1.toc.html
Federal Protective Service. Security Guidelines for Government Employees.

http://www.gsa.gov/pbs/fps/office.htm
Long Island Coalition for Workplace Violence Awareness and Prevention (1996). Workplace Violence Awareness and Prevention: an Information and Instructional Package for Use by Employers and Employees.
  http://www.osha-slc.gov/workplaceviolence/wrkplaceViolence.intro.html
National Criminal Justice Reference Service. Threat Assessment: An Approach to Prevent Targeted Violence.
  http://www.ncjrs.org/txtfiles/threat.txt
Occupational Safety and Health Administration, U.S. Department of Labor. Publications (text given).
  http://www.osha.gov/oshpubs/

Useful sites (with links to others)

Assault Prevention Information Network.
  http://www.einet.net/galaxy/Community/Safety/Assault-
  Prevention/apin/WorkSD.html
Health and Safety Authority (Ireland). Publications list.
  http://www.hsa.ie/osh/pubs.htm
Health and Safety Executive (U.K.). Fortnightly List of Publications.
  http://www.open.gov.uk/hse/flist.htm
National Institute for Occupational Safety and Health (U.S.). Other WWW Sites: Violence (occupational).
  http://www.cdc.gov/niosh.violence.html

Appendix 2
Keeping Pubs Peaceful Incident Report
Form (KPP IRF)

KEEPING PUBS PEACEFUL
INCIDENT REPORT FORM

Ref. no.

Trading company

House name & address

Pub category   Name of licensee

Date   Day of week   Time

Opening hours on day of incident (please be specific)

EMPLOYEE involved in the incident

Name

Address

Any other details

Sex:	**Age:**
Female [ ]	under 21 [ ]
Male [ ]	21-25 [ ]
	26-30 [ ]
	31-40 [ ]
	over 40 [ ]

Job title:

MAIN ASSAILANT (Use Page 3 for further assailants)

Name

Address

Is he/she local?   No [ ]   Yes [ ]

Is he/she   Regular customer [ ]   Non-regular [ ]   Staff [ ]   Ex-staff [ ]?

Had he/she been barred *prior* to the incident?   No [ ]   Yes [ ]

Any other details

Sex:	**Estimated age:**
Female [ ]	under 21 [ ]
Male [ ]	21-25 [ ]
	26-30 [ ]
	31-40 [ ]
	over 40 [ ]

Number of assailants: _____

Where did the incident take place?   Outside [ ]   Lounge bar [ ]   Public bar [ ]

   Restaurant [ ]   Entrance [ ]   Pool room [ ]   Toilet [ ]   Other room [ ] (please specify)

Was the house crowded at the time of the incident?   No [ ]   Yes [ ]

DESCRIPTION OF THE INCIDENT

What were the circumstances leading up to the incident?

What was the employee doing at the time?

What happened in the incident?

What brought the incident to an end?

Were the police called to the incident?   No [ ] Yes [ ]

What action did they take?

Did the assailant have or use any weapon?   No [ ] Yes [ ] If so, what?

Gun [ ]   Knife [ ]   Baseball bat/club [ ]   Gas/spray [ ]   Brick/concrete [ ]   Glass [ ]

Furniture, chair etc. [ ]   Pool cue/ball [ ]   Ash tray [ ]   Food/drink [ ]   Bottle [ ]

Other (please specify) [ ]

Was the weapon: intentionally brought in [ ]   obtained from pub premises [ ] ?

Was the employee injured?

No injury	[ ]
Upset, no physical injury	[ ]
Injury not requiring medical attention	[ ]
Injury requiring medical attention	[ ]
Injury requiring short hospitalisation	[ ]
Injury requiring long hospitalisation (+24 hours)	[ ]
Permanent disability	[ ]
Death	[ ]

Part(s) of the body injured: Face [ ]   Head/neck [ ]   Arms/hands [ ]   Trunk [ ]   Legs/feet [ ]

Please give details

Did he/she have to take time off work?   No [ ] Yes [ ]   How much time?...............(days)

Were any **other** employees or customers involved?   No [ ] Yes [ ]
Please state who:

Were they injured?   No injury   [ ]

                                   Upset, no physical injury   [ ]

                                   Injury not requiring medical attention   [ ]

                                   Injury requiring medical attention   [ ]

                                   Injury requiring short hospitalisation   [ ]

                                   Injury requiring long hospitalisation (24 hours+)   [ ]

                                   Permanent disability   [ ]

                                   Death   [ ]

Part(s) of the body injured: Face [ ] Head/neck [ ] Arms/hands [ ] Trunk [ ] Legs/feet [ ]

    Please give details

Did they have to take time off work?   No [ ] Yes [ ]   How much time?...............(days)

How many people were injured in total?   _____

    Employees : Men ____ Women ____   **Customers :** Men ____ Women ____

Was property damaged or stolen?   No [ ] Yes [ ]   If so, what?

Was clothing damaged?   No [ ] Yes [ ]   If so, whose and what?

ADDITIONAL ASSAILANTS

ASSAILANT 2   **Sex:**   **Estimated age:**
Name   Female [ ]   under 21 [ ]
                                                     Male [ ]   21-25 [ ]
Address   26-30 [ ]
                                                                           31-40 [ ]
Is he/she local? No [ ] Yes [ ]   over 40 [ ]

Is he/she a   Regular customer [ ] Non-regular [ ] Staff [ ] Ex-staff [ ]?

Had he/she been barred *prior* to the incident?   No [ ] Yes [ ]

ASSAILANT 3   **Sex:**   **Estimated age:**
Name   Female [ ]   under 21 [ ]
                                                     Male [ ]   21-25 [ ]
Address   26-30 [ ]
                                                                           31-40 [ ]
Is he/she local? No [ ] Yes [ ]   over 40 [ ]

Is he/she a   Regular customer [ ] Non-regular [ ] Staff [ ] Ex-staff [ ]?

Had he/she been barred *prior* to the incident?   No [ ] Yes [ ]

How serious do you rate this incident to have been? ___

(Please give a number from 0 to 10, where 0 is 'trivial' and 10 is 'the most serious you could ever imagine'.)

Please state the reasons for this score or give further comment:

Do you have any reason to believe the incident was linked to drug activity or drug problems?
No [ ]   Yes [ ]

If 'Yes': What are these reasons?

Were the assailants drunk?   No [ ]   Yes [ ]

What action would you like/have liked your Area Manager/Trading Company to take?

Have you any other suggestions to prevent re-occurrence?

TO BE COMPLETED BY THE TRADING COMPANY

What action was/will be taken by the Area Manager/Trading Company?

Author index

Subject index